eccentric
SEATTLE

To My Wife, Jodi,
without whose encouragement and understanding
I might be just another writer *thinking* about
composing books, but not actually *doing* it.

eccentric
SEATTLE

*Pillars and Pariahs Who Made the City
Not Such a Boring Place After All*

J. Kingston Pierce

Washington State University Press
Pullman, Washington

WASHINGTON STATE
UNIVERSITY

Washington State University Press
PO Box 645910
Pullman, Washington 99164-5910
Phone: 800-354-7360
Fax: 509-335-8568
E-mail: wsupress@wsu.edu
Web site: wsupress.wsu.edu

Library of Congress Cataloging-in-Publication Data

Pierce, J. Kingston, 1957-
 Eccentric Seattle : pillars and pariahs who made the city not such a boring place
after all / J. Kingston Pierce.
  p. cm.
 Includes bibliographical references.
 ISBN 0-87422-269-9 (Paperback : alk. paper)
  1. Seattle (Wash.)—Biography—Anecdotes. 2. Eccentrics and
eccentricities—Washington (State)—Seattle—Biography—Anecdotes.
3. Seattle (Wash.)—History—Anecdotes. I. Title.

F899.S453A27 2003
979.7'772'0099—dc21   2003012583

WSU PRESS
Fine Quality Books from the Pacific Northwest
YEARS

TABLE OF CONTENTS

Maps:

ACKNOWLEDGMENTS

As the contents of this book represent work completed over almost two decades, the roster of people to whom I owe debts of gratitude is probably longer than I can remember now. Surely, I've forgotten about the assistance provided to me by an intern here, a tightly focused historical researcher there. But I cannot fail to mention three editors who endorsed my explorations into the past, even when the topics I was pursuing seemed initially to be obscure or unpromising: Knute "Skip" Berger, of *Eastsideweek* and later *Seattle Weekly*, who never failed to trust that I could follow a lead to something extraordinary; David Brewster, also of *Seattle Weekly*, whose own interest in our city's heritage inflamed mine; and Giselle Smith, of *Seattle Magazine*, who essentially let me loose to unearth and report stories large, small, and salacious. Their faith in my efforts led me to write most of the essays in *Eccentric Seattle*.

Also due appreciation are many descendents of the characters I profile in these pages, who shared their memories and often their delicately preserved historical records with me. Due special credit in this category are Ruby Calkins, whose memories of her big-dreaming father, C.C. Calkins, were an unexpected gold mine; Doris Beecher and her late husband, Henry Ward Beecher—the grandson of artist Harriet Foster Beecher—who invited me into their home to see sketchbooks left behind by this *other* renowned ancestor; and Elizabeth Linden, whose recollections of her father-in-law, Camlin Hotel co-developer Adolph Linden, were extensive and blessedly detailed. Laurance B. Rand, the great-grandson and biographer of publisher/visionary Leigh S.J. Hunt, was no less generous with the research he'd completed for his book *High Stakes: The Life and Times of Leigh S.J. Hunt*.

For encouraging me to dig into the rambunctious excitement of the Klondike gold rush, I must thank David Nicandri, editor of *Columbia* (the quarterly magazine of the Washington State Historical Society), as well as my grandfather, Ewart E. Sprinkling, who frequently recited Robert Service poetry to me when I was a boy and would've made one hell of a

Klondiker had he been born a little earlier. My architect father, Alexander Bolton Pierce II, can be credited with having interested me from a very early age in buildings and their designers—an interest that is expressed in several stories here. My old Portland colleague Dick Pintarich, who originally inspired my popular history-writing avocation, introduced me to the dramatic story of outlaw Harry Tracy and was my co-author on one of the chapters in this volume, "God's Own Sinner," about perverted preacher Edmond Creffield. Another fine friend, Stephanie Irving, proved to be a valuable and often courageous companion in researching several of these yarns, while Charles Smyth lent me an attentive ear whenever I needed to talk out the frustrating nuances of my historical inquiries.

A round of applause should be given to the Humanities Department staff of the Seattle Public Library, for their willingness to help me track down the most overlooked and dustiest arcana, as well as to the archivists at Seattle's Museum of History and Industry and the Mercer Island Historical Society. Equally deserving of commendation are Walt Crowley and the other editors responsible for HistoryLink.org, an unparalleled online source of information about the growth of Seattle and surrounding King County. For her persistency in vetting my work on a variety of the stories included here, I want to acknowledge Ellen L. Boyer, who also served as my crack research associate on *America's Historic Trails with Tom Bodett*. And this book would not now be in your hands were it not for Glen Lindeman and Jean Taylor of Washington State University Press, who kept me on task with the project, and Amy Rennert, my agent and ceaseless supporter.

Finally, as the writing process can often be a lonely one, I would be remiss were I not to thank Tex, our late but beloved cat, who was my loyal companion through so many years of being hunkered over a hot computer.

INTRODUCTION

G IVEN SEATTLE'S REPUTATION for sogginess, it's only appropriate that the first white settlers landed in this locality amid a torrential rainstorm on November 13, 1851. Led by Midwesterners Arthur and David Denny, Carson Boren, and William Bell, the two dozen adults and children had spent monotonous months in a wagon train traveling west over the well-rutted Oregon Trail, enduring malarial fevers and skunk assaults on their food caches. They'd originally planned to take up residence in Oregon's fertile Willamette Valley. But along the way they had been convinced to try the Puget Sound region instead, because so many pioneers already were staking claims along the Willamette.

After arriving in Portland, David Denny and another stalwart member of the company, John Low, had separated from their fellow travelers in mid September and tromped due north with their cattle, hoping to scout out a suitable townsite on Puget Sound. In Olympia, which was then little more than an aggregation of one-story frame cabins and Native American huts, they picked up another would-be city builder, Leander Terry, and finally reached present-day West Seattle at the end of September 1851. Soon, they commenced erecting a log cabin at what the Duwamish Indians knew as *sbuh-kwah-buks*—today's scenic Alki Point. But they hadn't yet gotten around to putting a roof on the shanty before the balance of their party debarked from the schooner *Exact* in the early morning hours of November 13.

The women, especially, were unimpressed by this place it had taken them seven months to reach. "I remember it rained awful hard that day—and the starch got took out of our bonnets and the wind blew," wrote Mrs. Robert Fay, the wife of the *Exact*'s captain, who'd come along for the ride. "When the women got into the rowboat to go ashore they were crying every one of 'em…and the last glimpse I had of them was the women standing under the trees with their wet sun bonnets all lopping down over their faces and their aprons to their eyes."

An ill omened beginning, to be sure—with worse to come. Although they'd optimistically dubbed their colony "New York *Alki*," translated from the northwest coast Chinook trading jargon as "New York By-and-By," it didn't take long for these young pioneers (only two of whom had celebrated their 30th birthdays) to realize that their new home wasn't likely to become a hinterlands Gotham. Yes, it offered breathtaking panoramas of the Sound and the jagged-spined Olympic Mountains to the west, and its beaches surely would be pleasant to walk along—*when and if* the sun ever showed itself. But the locale's shallow, wind-scoured harbor and high bluff tree line made it a less than ideal anchorage for ships hoping to take on the area's single marketable resource—timber, which was much in demand down the West Coast at burgeoning San Francisco.

Before four months had passed, the settlers decided to abandon the original site and haul their worldly possessions east across deep Elliott Bay to a hilly, copiously forested tract on the far side, which the Duwamish called *Duwamps*. Not long after, a habitually unsuccessful merchant and physician from Ohio, David "Doc" Swinton Maynard, arrived from Olympia and—determined to make his new interests on the Sound pay off—encouraged his fellow founding fathers to survey the downtown blocks that one day would comprise their seaport city.

Also partly due to Maynard's efforts, a laconic Ohioan named Henry Yesler (who'd proposed erecting a steam-powered sawmill at Alki) was convinced that the shores of Elliott Bay would be a better location. Maynard, Carson Boren, and Arthur Denny enticed Yesler by agreeing to give him not only 320 acres of woodland above the town, but also a ribbon of property linking it to the waterfront, down which oxen could drag felled evergreens for milling. That strip, layered at one time with small, greased logs, was known for years as Mill Street before being renamed Yesler Way. Early on, however, it earned the sobriquet by which it become renowned—"Skid Road," which years later was mangled into "Skid *Row*," an early 20th-century insult applied to neighborhoods that had fallen on hard times.

Henry L. Yesler, 1870. *UW Libraries, UW 223252*

The settlers slowly grew confident of their hamlet's durability. Confident enough, in fact, that they decided it deserved a more euphonious moniker than Duwamps. As history records it, Doc Maynard encouraged his neighbors to designate the place in honor of an elderly leader of the Duwamish and Suquamish natives, whom the gregarious sawbones had befriended shortly after coming to the Puget Sound country. (Maynard apparently didn't know—or didn't care—that local natives were terribly superstitious of having their names spoken after death.) But the white men and women couldn't easily wrap their tongues around the chief's name, Sealth, so they altered it slightly to "Seattle."

Thus the city was born. It would prove to be a fast-growing but troubled child, which didn't always play well with others.

On January 25, 1856, as many as 300 armed Indians, led by Yakimas and Nisquallys, descended upon the community. They were irate over unsatisfactory treaty negotiations with the U.S. government and took it out on white squatters on both sides of the Cascades. The few Seattleites were chased into a log blockhouse at the foot of Cherry Street, and it took cannon fire from the U.S. warship *Decatur*—which had shown up fortuitously to defend the pioneers—to drive the warriors back into the woods. This attack was followed by a few more months of sporadic fighting nearby (and another couple of years of clashes across eastern Washington Territory). Maybe a dozen whites and scores of Indians lost their lives in events associated with the "Battle of Seattle." But that confrontation also broke the fragile bonds between settlers here and their indigenous neighbors, and sent Elliott Bay's incipient society into a decade-long slump.

Still, from early on, Seattleites were convinced that their village one day would be something special—the "Queen City of the Sound," as optimistic boosters called it. That conviction led to the establishment of Washington's Territorial University (later the University of Washington) and calls for the territorial capital to be situated at Seattle—a plum that eventually went to Olympia. Smug confidence in the town endured even through the many years it was overshadowed not just by Portland, but also by its south Sound rival, Tacoma, which in 1873 won the Northern Pacific transcontinental railway connection that Seattle had craved and thus seemed to legitimize its nickname, the "City of Destiny."

Many observers thought the Great Fire of 1889, reducing Seattle's downtown (today's Pioneer Square historic district) to malodorous ruins of blackened, isolated brick chimneys, would spell the city's end at last. Rather, it marked a fresh start. Washington became the 42nd state in the Union just five months later, and within the next decade, Seattle was linked by steel rails to the rest of the nation. The city also began the Herculean task of leveling its hilly core to ease real-estate development, and—after being clobbered by a nationwide 1893 financial panic that drove land values down and unemployment figures up—Seattle found great prosperity as the jumping-off point for tens of thousands of men hoping to strike it rich in northwest Canada's gold fields.

World wars, an epidemic, Prohibition, earthquakes, a riot here and there, even a volcano—none of these things succeeded in shutting down Seattle. It went from *terra incognita* (a place to which at least one San Francisco captain sailed in the mid 19th century looking for icebergs to be used in cooling Barbary Coast drinks) to being a media darling—a burg made regrettably homogenous by shorthand plaudits such as "livable" and "world city." In the early 21st century, however, Seattle lost some of the luster it enjoyed during the 1990s technology boom when new residents flooded in and bellied up to the nearest *latte* stand. And the decision in 2000 by the Boeing Company—once the area's largest employer—to relocate its headquarters to Chicago (leaving only the commercial airplane division behind) was a shock to the city's system. Yet Seattle has endured serious problems before with grace, if not also with a muted chorus of "I told you so."

Like San Francisco, New York, and Chicago, Seattle has been home to big dreamers and equally big schemers. They found here the opportunity to make their names, or make their points, or make their millions, whether by changing the look of the city (as architect Elmer Fisher and landscaper John C. Olmsted did), running profitable but criminal enterprises (like madam extraordinaire Lou Graham or bootlegger Roy

Olmstead), or endeavoring to reweave Seattle's social and political fabric (the goal of Mayor Bertha Landes and reformer Anna Louise Strong). Regardless of the popular impression held even by longtime residents that Seattle grew up a bit duller and more civilized than other U.S. metropolises, the local history is far from boring.

This is, after all, the town that in the 1860s tried to solve its shortage of marriageable women by importing "pure young ladies of high intelligence and moral character" from New England. It also was near here that one of the Pacific Northwest's largest Ku Klux Klan rallies was held, and where an early version of the anti-Communist "witch hunts" (later to be led nationally by U.S. Senator Joseph McCarthy in the early 1950s) was exploited for political gain. Seattle was where President Warren G. Harding made his last speech; where serial killer Ted Bundy sought his first victims; and where Pulitzer poet Theodore Roethke found himself in the middle of a nervous breakdown. For better or worse, it was here as well that that ubiquitous symbol of sanguinity, the Happy Face, allegedly began its jaundiced career.

These tales and more are collected in *Eccentric Seattle.* Rather than examine the heritage of the Pacific Northwest's largest city in exhaustive detail, I have focused on a cast of ambitious or ne'er-do-wellish characters through whom some of the most intriguing aspects of Seattle's evolution can be examined. I learned long ago that history isn't merely about dates, places, and statistics; what gives it life are the people who charted its course, whether they were empire builders or avaricious businessmen, eristic newspaper editors or erratic preachers, artists or murderers. This volume is intended not so much to prove what an upstanding place Seattle has become, but to celebrate that period—roughly the 1850s to the 1970s—when the city established itself as a distinctive and sometimes downright weird spot on the map.

So here's to Seattle: Long may it rain…er, reign.

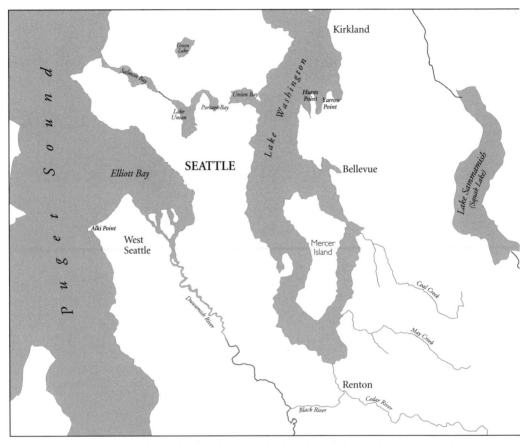

Overview of the immediate Seattle area, including Mercer Island and the communities of West Seattle, Kirkland, Bellevue, and Renton.

THE MARRYING KIND

W HAT MUST THOSE PEOPLE HAVE THOUGHT, as they huddled inside the
Unitarian church at Lowell, Massachusetts, in March 1864 and lis-
tened to Asa Shinn Mercer encourage the educated single ladies of
the town to sail off to Seattle and the howling wilderness that was the Pacific
Northwest? Yes, Mercer, the bewhiskered president of Washington's nascent
Territorial University, appeared to be honorable, and he certainly presented
his plan from the church's podium with sincerity. But the substance of his
scheme—to export young women of good moral standing from New
England to a rough-hewn place that didn't even appear on many maps—
seemed, at least on its surface, incredible.

Although there had been a great deal of westward migration preceding America's Civil War, and a large number of adventurers had hied off
to Northern California after gold was discovered there in 1848, this was
still a time when most folks didn't venture much beyond the horizon of
their birthplaces. For Mercer to propose that Lowell's lasses follow him to
the other end of the continent, where they would teach Seattle's growing
population of children and, perhaps, if all went well and Cupid's arrows
didn't fly awry, wed some of the town's overabundance of unmarried
men...well, the odds hardly seemed in his favor.

And yet, Mercer did succeed, opening a chapter in the history of
upstart Seattle that would gain it publicity—positive as well as negative—
across the Union. A chapter that was destined to be recalled a century later

in a short-lived TV series, *Here Come the Brides*, that made clear the lengths to which an isolated frontier settlement once went to add the gentle sounds of rustling skirts and feminine laughter to the crack and crash of tall timber being felled.

The original party of white settlers at Alki Point in 1851 had been fairly evenly divided, genderwise: seven adult men and five women, plus a dozen children—three boys and nine girls. Within a decade, however, as the number of whites living along Elliott Bay approached 200, the balance grew disproportionately masculine. Single, virile males outnumbered unwed women by a 9-to-1 margin, and a girl "who passed her sixteenth birthday without being married was considered an old maid," wrote Gordon Newell and Don Sherwood in their popular history, *Totem Tales of Old Seattle*.

Adultery may have been an option for some gents, but in a community of such modest size, maintaining the secret of an extramarital affair was probably as difficult as finding some accommodating white woman with whom to enjoy one in the first place. Abstinence was always an option, though not a popular one. So the taking of Native American wives or mistresses became a well practiced, if not widely favored, alternative. Local Salish girls weren't immune to the enticements of Caucasian bachelors, the ethics of their culture allowing for greater freedom in sexual matters than was condoned by Christian preachers. But sin was one thing; sanitation was quite another. Whites moving into this area had brought with them venereal diseases, and local gallants weren't happy to trade a roll in the hay for a case of the clap. Nor did the grooming habits of those willing native maidens recommend them as paramours for the pioneers. Frequent shampooings with urine kept the women's hair glossy, but it also left behind a scent that, combined with the odors of smoked fish and other seafoods from their diet, plus excrement (which some tribes used to insulate their homes), doomed many an amorous coupling. And that's saying something, when you consider that the loggers and sawmill workers in need of lustful release could, themselves, have benefited from closer association with soap and water.

It was just such ripe conditions that drew John Pennell (sometimes spelled Pinnell) to Seattle. "Tall, saturnine, and suave, wearing a waistcoat and a plug hat, he was a character straight out of Bret Harte," *American Mercury* magazine wrote of the man more than half a century after he debarked from a lumber schooner near Yesler's Mill in the summer of 1861. "A minister of evil, a trafficker in human flesh," as one source described him, Pennell had been the operator of a moderately successful brothel in San Francisco's Barbary Coast district. However, the raucous Coast—"on which no gentle breezes blow, but where rages one wild sirocco of sin," to quote the *San Francisco Call*—was overflowing with establishments in which a man might satisfy his need of female companionship, no matter how rarified or ribald his tastes. Seattle was virgin territory, by comparison, and Pennell intended to take advantage.

Reports are that he had his bawdyhouse built and bustling in less than a month's time. The unpainted, oblong structure of rough lumber wasn't much to look at, but its appearance mattered less than its location—just south of present-day Yesler Way, a quick walk from the mill and in clear view of ships (and their sailors) as they hove to in Seattle's harbor. If it was the first business of its breed in the Puget Sound area, it certainly wasn't the last. Pennell called his place the Illahee, a Chinook jargon word meaning "home place," though most locals referred to it as the Mad House. Or they called it the Sawdust Pile, because it had been raised on tideflats stabilized by the waste produced in Yesler's Mill. Naturally, the female employees there became known as Sawdust Women. They were Indian girls, procured by Pennell from local chiefs in exchange for Hudson's Bay blankets, the comeliest recruits fetching two or three woven spreads. With concerted scourings, haircuts, and liberal dousings of perfume, these women were remade into the hottest attractions north of the Columbia. Men came from many miles around just to lead them onto the Illahee's copious wooden dance floor. To supply the tunes, Pennell had imported a musical trio—a fiddler, a drummer, and an accordion player—from San Francisco.

The house rules were simple: a Sawdust Woman would dance, for no charge, with anyone who asked her. But following each spin about the floor, the man was expected to buy drinks for himself and his partner from a long, adjacent bar. (Ofttimes, the bartender substituted cold tea for whiskey in the woman's glass, to keep her sober, while still charging the whiskey price.) When a logger or miner or tangle-bearded trapper finally wearied of sashaying and socializing, and wanted to get down to more passionate pursuits, he would purchase a couple of additional libations and then lead his calicoed companion down a hallway, bordered by cube-like rooms where they could find a modicum of privacy. While these arrangements may not have measured up to the standards of the Barbary Coast, where upper-end "parlor houses" offered mostly legitimate theater performances, and roués were invited to take would-be starlets away after the show to velvet-curtained boxes for special encore acts, the Illahee was an exotic showplace on Elliott Bay.

As the *American Mercury* put it, Pennell had erected "the best mousetrap in the woods. Hobnails and calks were deepening all the paths to its door." Even some of Seattle's more respectable residents, while publicly deploring John Pennell's business as morally repugnant and a nuisance, privately conceded that the Illahee had its value. After all, those men who came from the hills in search of licentious merriment also spent money in the town's more legitimate venues.

Pennell consciously insulated himself and his enterprise from attack, either by anti-prostitution reformers or religious opponents of miscegenation, who argued that any opportunity for Caucasian males to engage in sexual congress with Native American women debased "the society of virtuous people." Not only had he established the Illahee far from family residences, but he was generous in contributing to municipal projects.

Folks concerned for the spiritual vigor of this community might have refused to truck with a man of Pennell's corrupted character, yet they could exert little or no influence over the randy roustabouts who comprised most of the Illahee's clientele. As long as there remained a significant disparity in numbers between the male and female populations of Seattle, men were prone toward commercial enticements of the flesh. The only way to combat that inclination would be to increase the quantity of eligible local women. But how?

The idea of importing brides for Seattle's lonely single men may not have originated with Asa Mercer, but it was he who brought that most unlikely plan to fruition. An idealistic Methodist, Asa was the brother of Thomas Mercer, who had arrived in the Puget Sound country from Princeton, Illinois, in 1852. Thomas had brought with him a pair of horses, Tab and Charlie, and he soon prospered as Seattle's first teamster. He would go on to make money from real estate, become a judge, and have the privilege in 1854 of naming both Lakes Washington and Union. (In turn, Mercer Island was named after him.)

Asa, a full quarter-century younger than Thomas, followed his sibling west in 1861, after graduating from Franklin College in New Athens, Ohio. He initially took the job of clearing brush from Denny Knoll, a hillock that used to rise from the area bounded roughly by today's 3rd and 5th avenues, and Union and Seneca streets. This was the designated site of Washington's future Territorial University, a plum project won for the town by Arthur Denny, then speaker of the Territorial House of Representatives, and the Reverend Daniel Bagley, an influential Methodist preacher who had traveled west with Thomas Mercer, but had settled in Salem, Oregon, before relocating to Seattle in 1860. Asa continued to work on that site, helping to construct the single, white, columned university building, and after its completion, he moved in as the institution's first principal—and, for a time, its entire faculty. The school welcomed its inaugural class of 16 students on November 4, 1861.

Unmarried himself, and with ample free time on his hands due to a shortage of funds that kept the school year short, Asa Mercer turned his mind to solving Seattle's "woman problem." In his popular history of Seattle, *Skid Road*, Murray Morgan suggests it was Asa's brother, Thomas, who put the notion in his head of seeking acceptable brides on America's East Coast. The thinking was that, with the Civil War raging on the other end of the continent, and thousands of able men heeding President Abraham Lincoln's call to fight and die for the salvation of the Union, "there must be a surplus of pure young ladies of high intelligence and moral character in those parts. It seemed reasonable to [Mercer]," explains *Totem Tales of Old Seattle*, "to import this surplus to a place where it would be appreciated; namely, Seattle."

The Seattle men he shared this idea with were enthusiastic about him immediately commencing to ship spinsters from afar. Asa Mercer also won encouragement from the territory's legislators, many of whom were bachelors. But his pitch to Governor William Pickering for funds to make any such expedition possible brought him little satisfaction. Pickering, an Illinoisan and the fourth man to hold his post in Olympia (replacing Richard Gholson, who had resigned after Lincoln's election in 1860, declaring that he was "unwilling, even for a day, to hold office under a Republican"), told Mercer that he ought to go ahead with his plans, but that there was no extra money in the public treasury to aid his cause. Refusing to be discouraged, Mercer decided to seek private monies instead. He went among Seattle's frustrated swains and told them that, for the price of ship and train passage (about $250 per person), they could help a virtuous New England woman make a fresh start in the Northwest. If it wasn't voiced outright, the message was clear that these females, in their gratitude, would wed whoever had given them this chance. While there is no record of exactly how much Mercer gleaned in this manner, it was enough to convince him to sail for Boston in early 1864.

Again, he hit a snag: The women of Massachusetts' capital evinced scant interest in leaving their civilized environs for a remote village that claimed far more pine stumps than proper stores. Mercer didn't give up, however. Venturing north to Lowell, the 25-year-old educator received a warmer reception. Not only because with that town's smaller population the war's draw on its young men had been more keenly felt, but because the local economy had suffered as a result of a cessation in cotton shipments from the South. Lowell's ladies were amenable to new opportunities, leading Mercer to believe he had hit a mother lode of marriage material. But in the end, only eight women, ages 15 to 35, could muster the determination (and maybe also the supplemental funds) to make the journey. On a chilly afternoon in March 1864, they—along with Mercer and Daniel Pearson, father to two of the girls who were headed west—took a train from Lowell to New York City. There they were joined on the steamship *Illinois* by two more women in their 20s and an older man, all from Pepperell, Massachusetts, plus a 16-year-old girl who intended to make San Francisco her home, but wound up going on to Seattle instead.

The *Illinois* departed New York Harbor on March 14, 1864, and landed 10 days later on the Caribbean side of the Panama Isthmus. After crossing by rail to the Pacific, Mercer's company boarded the S.S. *America* for a 15-day trip to San Francisco. Their original schedule had called for rapid transit from there via a monthly steamer bound for Seattle, but delays caused them to miss that connection. Instead, the group cooled their heels in San Francisco until April 28, when they secured passage on a northbound lumber bark called the *Torrant*. And it wasn't until the late evening of May 16 that the exhausted travelers finally reached Yesler's Wharf in Seattle, to be greeted by a paltry contingent of curious males who hadn't succumbed to either sleep or drink. A bigger celebration of Mercer's enterprise was held the next day, when the 11 "virgins" were applauded for "the self-sacrificing spirit" they had demonstrated by forsaking their "happy homes" for this "youthful country."

Mercer's confidence in his importation plans had been vindicated. By the end of that summer, most of the "Mercer Girls" were gainfully employed, several as teachers. And all but two—one of whom perished within weeks of reaching Seattle—soon wed, though as Morgan notes, "it is uncertain whether the maidens married the men who had financed Mercer's trip."

Front Street (now 1st Avenue), looking north from S. Main Street, 1865. The new Territorial University building stands on the distant hill. *UW Libraries, A. Curtis 32137*

Reward for Asa Mercer's pivotal role in this enterprise came in the form of his unanimous election to a one-year term in Washington's territorial senate. But he wasn't ready to get out of the bride-procurement business. Not yet. Not when he knew that 11 women barely made a dent in the town's sexual imbalance. Next time, Mercer figured, he'd round up hundreds of women for the westward trek—"Enough girls," Morgan explains, "to provide mates for every single man west of the Cascades." Furthermore, he hoped that, with the conclusion of the Civil War, he could convince President Lincoln, who he knew slightly from his growing-up years in Illinois, to provide him with the use of a transport vessel to carry those women back to Puget Sound.

So, after once again hitting up forlorn single men in Washington Territory for the price of a woman's passage west, the teacher-turned-legislator embarked for New York in early April 1865. Unfortunately, he landed in Manhattan on the very day that Lincoln was assassinated in Washington, D.C., by actor and Southern sympathizer John Wilkes Booth. "I was at sea without a compass," Mercer wrote later, mourning the death of his prospective ally in matrimony—just five days after Confederate General Robert E. Lee had surrendered to Union Army commander Ulysses S. Grant at Appomattox Courthouse, Virginia. Mercer didn't know Andrew Johnson, who replaced Lincoln in the White House, but after a few months in the nation's capital, he did manage to win the ear of General Grant, who

Running from Office

Politicians often insist that, while they may be castigated in the present, the future will treat them more generously. But that certainly wasn't the case for Mayor Corliss P. Stone (1872–73).

After moving from Vermont to Seattle in 1861, he built up a prosperous grocery business, helped organize one of the town's earliest electric companies, and invested in real-estate development. In 1872, Republican Stone was elected as only Seattle's third mayor. But three months before his term was up, he absconded to San Francisco with $15,000 (or well over half a million bucks in current dollars), taken from his merchandising partnership with fellow pioneer Charles H. Burnett. As Seattle's *Weekly Intelligencer* reported in March 1873, that money was to have been used in "making payment to creditors." However, the mayor apparently changed his mind, informing Burnett that he had appropriated the money "to my private use" and was leaving California for the East, having "abandoned all idea of continuing his business here," as the *Intelligencer* put it.

The historical record isn't at all clear on how Stone redeemed himself, but he must have done so, since he died of "heart disease" in Seattle in 1906 and was hailed by the press as a prominent capitalist. More recent histories, though, have portrayed Stone not only as an embezzler, but as a wife-stealer, perpetuating an 1873 rumor (refuted vociferously at the time) that Stone was accompanied to San Francisco by another man's spouse.

prior to the Civil War had served for one undistinguished year as a brevet captain at Washington's Fort Vancouver and understood the pain of isolation in the backwoods. Grant agreed to supply Mercer with a steamship, "coaled and manned, with a capacity to carry 500 women." But the offer was shot down by the U.S. Army's quartermaster-general, Montgomery Meigs, who declared any such use of federal property illegal. It was only the intervention of one Ben Holladay that kept Mercer's second recruiting expedition from collapsing at that point. A wartime speculator with his eye on building up a West Coast shipping empire, Holladay agreed to buy the surplus transport *Continental* and convey 500 beauteous belles to Seattle—for a fee. A desperate Mercer agreed, not realizing that the contract he signed with Holladay would be void if fewer than 500 passengers showed up for the voyage.

Downtown Seattle, circa 1875. *UW Libraries, A. Curtis 05320*

And far fewer than 500 did, thanks in part to the *New York Herald*. That newspaper's editor, James Gordon Bennett, ever on the lookout for sensationalistic material, apparently published an exposé of Mercer's recruitment campaign, implying that most of the volunteers would wind up in waterfront whorehouses, and that any women who managed to secure a legal mate in Seattle would find him detestable-looking, diseased, and ill-mannered on top of it all. Much to Mercer's dismay, the story was picked up by papers across the Northeast.

When the *Continental*'s day of departure, January 16, 1866, finally arrived, only a few dozen would-be brides walked up the gangplank with their possessions in tow. Mercer had managed to sell more of his 500 reserved spots to men and married women, but he still had only 100 passengers—nowhere near the count he had originally anticipated. Nevertheless, Holladay demanded full payment. Although he didn't get it, he did reportedly take every cent Asa Mercer had before allowing the ship to shove off. Mercer likely breathed a sigh of relief, thinking that his worries were over, at last. But three months later, when the *Continental* docked at San Francisco, he had another surprise: The captain ordered everyone off the ship, he would travel no further north. Seeking help, Mercer implored Governor Pickering to send money…but received in reply a telegram—sent collect—that offered nothing save for lofty wishes of good luck.

Transportation was ultimately negotiated with several captains of lumber ships, who thought that a trip to Puget Sound might be made more pleasurable by the presence of females aboard. But 36 of the 100 passengers from the *Continental* stayed behind in San Francisco, including 13 eligible women. Only 34 maidens from Mercer's second expedition made it to Seattle. That was three times as many as in his first contingent, but not nearly the number promised. Called to publicly account for this discrepancy, Mercer did his best. It helped that most of the damsels who had accompanied him from the East showed up to support him.

That old rapscallion, John Pennell, did his damndest to sooth the aggrieved men of Seattle. Breaking from his tradition of employing Indian prostitutes, he imported a handful of somewhat faded but still saucy roses, plucked off the Barbary Coast. These *filles de joie* were the first white harlots to work in the territory, and their arrival caused quite a stir—both in the press and the loins. Especially popular at the Illahee was a buxom bawd known as Flying Cloud, who supposedly had an exact illustration of that famous 19th-century clipper ship tattooed across her belly. "She would have done well in any seaport," observes *Totem Tales of Seattle*.

But it didn't take long after that for other, even grander palaces of pleasure to open down on the sawdust-covered southern end of town. By the 1880s, Seattle had an honest-to-badness tenderloin district south of Yesler Way, complete with saloons, gambling emporia, boxhouse theaters, and innumerable brothels of varying class, from the low-order "cribs" to the high-end "parlor houses" run by Rae Roberts, Lou Graham, and other flouncing madams. The days of Pennell and his Sawdust Women seemed ancient, and families that had spawned from the joyful union of naughtiness and necessity downplayed their pasts, seeking the same respect as those that were founded by wagon-training pioneers or had a Mercer girl—Seattle's equivalent of Mayflower maidens—sitting pretty in their family trees.

After 1866, Asa Mercer made no more trips to the East in search of suitable spouses. He didn't have to, for as Seattle grew in population, it became more attractive to families and even unmarried ladies who could get here without benefit of a special expedition. Besides, Mercer had other things to think about. Not long after he returned to Puget Sound that second time around, a notice appeared in the newspaper, saying that the Reverend Daniel Bagley had married Asa Shinn Mercer to Annie E. Stephens—one of his own "girls."

THE WHITE STUFF

F OR WINTER LOVERS, recent years in the Emerald City have been terribly disappointing, offering lots of bluster but only the most meager sprinklings of snow. Do you even remember the last time we had an honest-to-goodness, slip-and-slide White Christmas hereabouts? Yeah, think hard.

Yet there are still folks who curse and whine every winter, angry that they have to deal with thin slicks of ice atop local roadways. There are still office-goers who grumble about having to trudge through the barest slush on sidewalks. And schools seem to have developed the habit of shutting down if there is so much as a dusting of the chill white stuff on their monkey bars. This city has been without blizzard conditions for so long that we've forgotten how to tolerate winter's inclemency. To put it bluntly, we've become *weather wimps*.

Now try to imagine what would happen if Seattle were blanketed with 64 inches of snow—nearly five and a half feet—during a period of eight days. Don't worry, that probably isn't the prediction for this coming winter. But it was the reality for locals as they headed out for work and play in the earliest days of 1880.

In that year of the so-called Big Snow, there were 3,533 people living on the banks of Elliott Bay, 174 of whom were employed by just over two dozen local manufacturers. Only 29 years had passed since Arthur Denny and his cadre of Midwestern pioneers landed in a downpour at Alki to found a new town, and Seattle was still decades away from being a significant power, even among its West Coast brethren. It would be another two years before this place could claim its first chamber of commerce or its first major lynching (of a pair of murderous thieves). Seattle didn't experience its introductory taste of racial agitation until 1885, during which nativists tried to drive out 350 Chinese immigrants. Although a fire in 1879 had leveled a sizable chunk of the predominately wooden business district, the burg's greatest blaze wasn't due until 1889. A transcontinental rail connection to Elliott Bay didn't exist before 1893.

All in all, Seattle was still a very callow and remote spot in 1880. However, it did claim a newspaper of some distinction—the *Daily Intelligencer* (forerunner of today's *Seattle Post-Intelligencer*). And it was in the pages of that broadsheet where townspeople kept track of the devastation brought on by a snowstorm that whipped into this area without warning on Monday, January 5.

"It is safe to say that snow never before fell on Puget Sound…as it has fallen since Monday afternoon," the *Intelligencer* remarked three days later, in a report squeezed between an overview of coastal shipping and the tale of a San Francisco woman who had committed suicide after a negative horoscope reading. "For forty-eight hours there was no cessation whatever of the fall, and for thirteen or fourteen hours on Tuesday night and Wednesday morning it came down at the rate of two inches an hour. The writer has spent twenty-two winters in five different towns on Puget Sound, and until the present one never saw in any one of them a depth of snow on the level of two feet. Now, however, we have, averaging it through Seattle, a depth of four feet…"

The entire West Coast seemed to suffer a cold spell that month. The Oregon coast town of Astoria was barraged by hurricane-like winds that shook houses and toppled trees with such force that it sounded as if someone was firing cannon off the headland. The northern reaches of Washington's Olympic Peninsula were hit with snow that piled up to six feet deep in places. Even in usually balmy Southern California, trains were halted by snowdrifts as high as the windows of their engines. Old Man Winter was definitely flexing his muscles.

But Seattleites were blind to the vicissitudes of others, unable to reflect on how mild their winter experience was when compared with circumstances in, say, New England or Minnesota. All they saw was the snow falling…

and falling…

and falling…

and falling.

And the flurries showed no sign of letting up.

After a couple of days, *Intelligencer* editors forsook their amateur attempts at meteorology. "There is no telling the depth of snow a few hours ahead," the paper finally conceded. "We tried it yesterday and the day before, and wretchedly failed in both instances… On Monday evening we supposed from the appearance that the depth on Tuesday morning would be four inches, which was one-third the reality. On Tuesday evening we supposed the Wednesday depth would be two feet, instead of which it was four. We'll be safe this time the other way, and suppose this morning's snow depth at ten feet." In fact, it didn't amount to quite half that much.

Dozens of rickety barns huddled in the Duwamish, Green, and Cedar river valleys collapsed beneath this snow's accumulating tonnage, flattening cattle and horses that had sought sanctuary indoors. Blacksmith shops, wharves, and scores of smaller structures in town sagged and then

Yesler's Wharf after the January 1880 blizzard. Heavy snow has collapsed the roof of the small false-front building, while poles support the main facade from falling. *UW Libraries, UW 2295*

split asunder. Even in some larger buildings—including several hotels, Squire's Opera House (now the Grand Central Arcade in Pioneer Square), and a Cherry Street performance hall established by pioneer Henry Yesler—cracks opened in walls. Makeshift buttresses were arranged against any further damage. Men were recruited at a dollar an hour to shovel snow from rooftops (better wages than were paid in Seattle-area mines), and there was plenty of this work to go around.

Ships' masts lining the waterfront were mantled with snow and stood out starkly against the cloudy sky, like trees denuded of their leaves. Winds bellowed down from the hills, stealing hats off curmudgeons and separating parents from their under-ballasted young. Temperatures crashed into the single digits. Snow drifted up against buildings, and in many areas pedestrians and horse-drawn wagons were forced to share the middle of the street, with predictably confrontational consequences. Commerce crawled, and then it halted altogether. Nary a noise could be heard about town, save for the hypnagogic patter of snowflakes tumbling atop one another, and visibility was often measured in mere arm's lengths.

It didn't take long for Seattleites to feel isolated, and claustrophobic. They sought out any organized entertainment they could find, no matter how amateurish. Even a grade-school music performance enjoyed a packed house. Gents weary of taking heat before their home fires sought instead the warm embrace of those accommodating American and French cocottes who worked the red-light district south of Yesler Way.

One of the foremost amusements, though, was just watching pedestrians brave the slick surfaces and frigid gales that had become so familiar downtown. As the *Intelligencer* put it, "The average citizen walks nowadays as though he were drunk."

"The [side]walks of Seattle were never in a more slippery condition than at present," the paper observed four days after the white deluge began. "Paths have been cut through the deep snow in every direction, and are wide and hard, and would be excellent were they only level." Another problem was that those walkways tended to be cut rather close to drainage ditches, into which near-sighted strollers were wont to tumble.

Each new day brought more reports of demolished buildings and a somewhat higher degree of despair that the town might eventually vanish under a snowcap. By day six of the storm, tempers were seriously frayed, and one editorialist wrote testily that "if anyone has anything to say about our Italian skies . . . shoot him on the spot." By then, however, other people had started adapting to the situation. Industrious men made snowshoes.

A chairman of the local street committee supervised construction of a giant road plow, hitched it behind a team of six horses, and reopened many of the business district's main thoroughfares. After that, he plunged off north to Lake Union to rescue residents who, like members of California's ill-fated 1846 Donner Party, had been trapped by the unexpected snow and were rapidly going hungry.

Finally, on Monday, January 12, rain replaced most of the flakes cascading down from the heavens. Within a few days, Seattle had kicked back into gear, though the slush would hang around for weeks more. With sunshine again gracing their shoulders, *Intelligencer* editors mulled over the events of the eight-day snowstorm and determined that it really hadn't been that bad. After all, though there was quite a bit of property damage, not a single human life had been lost.

Later years would remind Seattleites that their town could really pack a potent winter punch. In February 1884, for instance, Lake Union froze over and 18 inches of snow fell in a single day. In January 1916, with temperatures in the 20s, skaters took to the ice on Green Lake, while on First Hill, the copper dome of St. James Cathedral collapsed beneath 30,000 pounds of flaky precipitation. But there has been nothing since to rival the Big Snow of 1880.

Even so, Seattle residents will begin grousing the moment any new winter's first snowflakes start falling. And drivers will honk their horns and swear and swerve on those occasional snowy days that residents of America's Midwest or Northeast would consider positively mild. 'Twas ever thus. Even in the wake of the Big Snow, the *Intelligencer* observed that Seattleites liked to overstate their winter hardships. "People will growl," the editors wrote, "and paying attention to them when they do is useless. They would not be content in the Garden of Eden, and we cannot expect them to be on Puget Sound."

Ghosts of Christmas Past

I t is so easy nowadays to take the holidays for granted in Seattle, even to feel a bit Scroogeish in the face of earnest attempts to put you in the mood for buying and receiving gifts. Yuletide advertisements begin appearing even before Halloween candy has disappeared. Suddenly all the wind-denuded trees downtown sparkle with tiny lights, as if fireflies were crowded locust-like upon their branches. Both classical and pop renditions of the season's most familiar tunes, from "God Rest Ye Merry Gentlemen" to "Rudolph the Red-Nosed Reindeer" to "Up on the Rooftop," begin spilling from every jeweler's shop and bookstore. It takes but a short while before you're ready to scream at the next announcement of precisely how many shopping days are left before Christmas.

But it wasn't always so...

Seattle pioneers celebrated their first local Noël in 1851, counting their blessings out on Alki Point. Led by Midwesterners Arthur and David Denny, Carson Boren, and William Bell, the 24-member party had spent months traveling cross-country, enduring malarial fevers, only to arrive at their promised land in a torrential downpour on November 13. Most of their subsequent energies were spent building cabins and securing food supplies. Christmas might well have come and gone amidst more quotidian activity, yet the settlers decided they needed the optimism that a real celebration might bring.

While some neighboring Native Americans watched in bewilderment, those early Seattleites huddled together in one of the cabins. They must have made a motley sight. "Not since they left Illinois had they had an opportunity to mend and sew," wrote Roberta Frye Watt, granddaughter of Arthur Denny, in her book, *Four Wagons West*. "They had no new material, but they made over and freshened up what they had. The men turned shoemakers and soled and patched the well-worn shoes. On Christmas Day, everyone appeared bright and gay in clothes that were whole."

Few familiar trappings accompanied the affair. "There were no turkeys, no mince pies, no fruit, no candy, no nuts, no candles, and no Christmas trees," the *Seattle Post-Intelligencer* recalled in 1908. History says that wild goose was served, along with dried apples and clam juice in place of milk for the children. "There were presents, but so different from the present day. Those presents had been made by the mothers after dark, ...by the

Santa arrives at Pioneer Square, November 30, 1907. *MOHAI SHS 15,307*

light of lamps which burned whale oil. There were new dresses for the girls, made of heavy, coarse stuff, new trousers for the small boys, made from cast-off clothing of their elders; there were heavy woolen stockings, knit at odd times. The fathers took a hand and made coarse shoes for the youngsters from the home-tanned leather. Every present for that Christmas was a necessity."

Jolly Old Saint Nicholas finally made his debut at Seattle in 1859, long after the pioneers had moved east across deep Elliott Bay to a hilly, well-treed claim on its far side. Just prior to December 25 of that year, George F. Frye, a genial and bearded German immigrant who would go on to build the town's first luxurious theater (an unfortunate casualty of the Great Fire of 1889), gathered up all the candy he could find, along with oranges, apples, and assorted trinkets. On Christmas morning, he "descended upon all the homes where youngsters reigned supreme," according to the *P-I.* "Santa Claus, rigged out in blankets more like an Indian than in the accepted form of costume, was the most welcome visitor who had appeared in the settlement in many a day." It was also in 1859 that baker Jacob Wibbens baked the hamlet's first cupcakes, announcing that each one contained a prize—everything from a 20-cent silver coin up to a $20 gold piece. Within a short time, his stock was gone, "many people buying more cupcakes than they could eat in three months of Christmas days," by one account.

The tradition of a public Christmas tree apparently began in 1864, when a sturdy evergreen—lit with handmade tallow candles—was unveiled in Yesler Hall, a crude performance space on Cherry Street. Kids who showed up for the festivities received not only presents, but the first white popcorn served in Seattle.

By the time the 19th century rolled into the 20th, residents demanded more elaborate holiday entertainments. Every year they gathered around the totem pole at Pioneer Place Park to greet Kris Kringle in his four-wheeled "sleigh." "The patron saint of childhood," reported the *Seattle Times* in 1907, "afforded the eyes of young America a spectacle that will never be forgotten when, mounted on the seat of his sleigh of state, he drove his real live reindeer, Dancer and Prancer, through the principal streets of Seattle." The bewhiskered Kringle would conclude his run in front of the Garvey-Buchanan department store on 2nd Avenue, near Seneca Street, and be followed from there up to a second-floor "Toyland" by every youngster with a wish for something special under his or her tinsel-covered tree. Adults, meanwhile, were treated to seasonal sales downstairs. It was a real disappointment for Seattle families when proprietors Garvey and Buchanan shut their emporium and retired Santa around 1911.

Some of the innocence of those days has been lost since. Children aren't so easily convinced anymore by the legend of Saint Nick, and parents cringe at the cost of preparing a big Christmas dinner. Yet as you watch families downtown clutching wrapped presents to their breasts and the sound of hand-rung bells finds your ears, it's still possible to remember the gaiety of Christmases past—even if none of them ever found you sipping clam juice with your turkey.

STROKES OF GENIUS

EGIN AT THE END: March 30, 1915. At just after 5 P.M., an automobile
driven by chauffeur Paul Kumai and bearing five passengers—each
of them later recalled in the press as "members of prominent families"—wheeled noisily along the old Pacific Highway on a cliff slope parallel to the Duwamish River. The passengers had spent that cool afternoon
in Tacoma, attending sessions of the Washington State Historical Society
(of which they were all members), and were finally headed home to Seattle.

When questioned later by police, the Japanese chauffeur insisted that
he couldn't have been traveling more than 18 miles per hour.

The accident occurred just below Allentown, a tiny municipality south
of Seattle, where the trestled stretch of the highway took an abrupt swing
across the Duwamish River. Just as Kumai started to approach the bridge,
he spotted a pair of boys in his path. His fist went to the horn. At the same
time, he jerked the steering wheel left, throwing his startled passengers
against the car's right-hand side. Maybe if the load had been lighter, or if
he had known the road better, or if he had more experience with this car
(he had driven it for only four days), Kumai could've recovered from the
turn. Instead, the vehicle pulled only slightly to the left, enough to save
the boys but not enough to keep it on the pavement. Brakes screamed before
the car tore headlong through the highway railing, somersaulted once—
perhaps twice, depending on which account you read—and crashed, wheels
down, into the roaring watercourse 30 feet below.

Amazingly, Paul Kumai and the owner of the auto, Emily Carkeek,
an Englishwoman and wife of Seattle developer Morgan Carkeek, were

thrown clear of the wreck. Kumai quickly swam to rescue his shouting employer, depositing her on top of the car that showed barely above the river level, and then dived for the other four passengers, whose lives he could see evaporating in bubbles from beneath the automobile's roof.

Of the passengers trapped in the vehicle, only one, a former owner of the *Seattle Post-Intelligencer* named Thomas Prosch, was removed alive— and he died shortly after being pulled to shore. The others were past saving: Prosch's wife, the former Virginia McCarver, daughter of the man who founded Tacoma; Margaret Lenora Denny, offspring of Seattle pioneer Arthur Denny; and one Harriet Foster Beecher, artist.

Although Emily Carkeek would miss all of those who died, a *P-I* reporter who drove her back to Seattle that afternoon wrote that "she kept calling for Mrs. Beecher, and we were unable to quiet her."

Since the 1910s, Harriet Beecher's name hasn't always hung so readily on the lips of Northwesterners. Her paintings—many of them haunting landscapes, others portraits with a precision about them that suggests the work of her contemporary, John Singer Sargent—were exhibited during her lifetime at world's fairs and received plaudits from West Coast art critics at the turn of the last century. But more recently Beecher's work often is overlooked in studies of Washington's contributions to fine art. More attention has been paid to the labors of 20th-century artists such as Mark Tobey, Jacob Lawrence, and Morris Graves, and less to those of painters—many of them women—who helped establish the Northwest's fine-arts tradition during the latter half of the 19th century.

Many of the region's early artists were self-taught, but some studied at the finest academies in Europe. Their work is united by a common fascination with the giantism and ruggedness of the local environment. Unlike Eastern landscape painters of the time, those of the Northwest School placed more attention on capturing the raw beauty of nature and less on investing scenes with religious or moral baggage. From John Fery's oil painting of a Seattle waterfront dominated by Indian canoes to Frederick Ferdinand Schafer's striking *Mt. Baker from near Victoria, B.C.*, we're left with a record of the pre-developed Northwest that no journalistic account can surpass.

Beecher was one of those who had received professional training. Born Harriet Foster in Mishawaka, Indiana, in the 1850s (accounts of her birth date vary), she moved to San Francisco at 21 to take her first drawing class at that city's School of Design, later known as the Hopkins Institute. Leaving the institution five years later, and after picking up several prestigious awards for her creations, Beecher studied with the German portraitist Oscar Kunath. At some point during the 1880s, she spent a winter in New York studying watercolor with master George Smillie and oil portraiture with Abbott Thayer. She also sought instruction from William Keith, "The king of landscape painters," in San Francisco.

In 1878, "Hattie" Foster had met Herbert Foote Beecher, son of the often-controversial Brooklyn, New York, preacher Henry Ward Beecher and nephew of Harriet Beecher Stowe, who wrote *Uncle Tom's Cabin*. According to the Beecher family records, Herbert had been dispatched west by his father to learn the sheep business. However, after an unsuccessful term as bookkeeper on a sheep drive—it left him "with a taste for adventure, but not for sheep"—he signed on as a ship's purser with the Oregon Railway & Navigation Company, making the run between San Francisco and Portland. Herbert later relocated to Puget Sound. He wed Hattie in 1881.

One account penned during her lifetime says that, after Harriet's marriage, "several years elapsed with no art progress." Yet in 1881 she opened what may have been Seattle's first art studio, in a two-room cottage on stilts. Located across the street from the old Arlington Hotel on Commercial Street (now 1st Avenue South), the studio's back door opened onto the beach, where camping Indians often provided Beecher and her pupils with a source of inspiration.

Beecher's first teaching experience, as she describes it in one of her sketchbooks, sounds frustrating: "I found all [my students] most interested in home beautification, which consisted chiefly in decorating furniture, mirrors and screens—with flowers, birds and butterflies. [But] they are willing to study from nature, which is pleasant." Her patience paid off, though. Several of her students—including Emily Inez Denny—rose to fame, and their works show Beecher's influence.

Beecher spent a year giving lessons in painting and sketching at the Territorial University before Herbert Beecher—by this time the honorable "Captain" Beecher—bought a mail-shipping route and moved his wife and two children to Port Townsend. In 1885, President Grover Cleveland appointed Herbert collector of customs for Port Townsend, but the appointment wasn't confirmed, reportedly as a result of Captain Beecher's campaign to curtail the highly profitable smuggling of opium and Chinese laborers into Washington from British Columbia. He took, instead, a commission as special agent of the U.S. Treasury Department for Oregon, Washington, and Alaska, and in 1889 formed a commercial shipping company serving the West Coast.

Her relocation to Port Townsend provided fresh material for Hattie's appreciative eyes. Many of her watercolors depict Olympic Peninsula scenes or camps of the Makah and Clallam tribes. Fully costumed Indians can be found in some, but Beecher's pieces often exclude people or reduce them to just a few dismissive brush strokes.

The artist once said that she had no favorite subjects, that "I like best whatever I am doing," but judging by her pre-1890 *oeuvre,* it was the bounty and power of nature and the effects of light that most enthralled Beecher. The natural world best allowed her to "use color freely and affectionately," as she often reminded her pupils, "instead of scantily and intellectually." Her 1882 portrayal of a storm-shrouded steamer seeking distance from a threatening cliff draws all that's possible from the nuances of a gray day. Another piece shows the coast of Puget Sound near Port Townsend. The tide is going out, and has attracted what looks like a boy and a girl eager to collect shells. Again, the people are tiny, confined to the left side of the picture, while hills and spiny trees and the undulant Sound dominate.

The painter continued to teach during her time in Jefferson County, adding a studio to her family's uptown hillside home. But she didn't confine herself to the northwest corner of Washington. Beecher traveled frequently between Port Townsend and San Francisco from 1888 until 1913, painting or sketching the sights she saw along the way. Some of her sketchbooks survive, held by museums and by her grandson Henry Ward Beecher's widow, Doris, who lives at Shilshole in Seattle. These books are often only half filled—a gallery of faces she'd seen, or a travelogue of pencil and pen drawings that commemorate her passage around Rooster Rock on the Columbia River and her visit to Oregon's Mount Hood. Watercolors from Beecher's California journeying show Chinese children, a windy afternoon at Monterey, and a lake fingered exquisitely by moonlight.

Any surface seemed ripe for Hattie Beecher's rendering of the world. She even adorned plain tin containers with landscapes of fields and trees, and dying streambeds, then gave them to friends. And she lost no opportunity to practice her art. In Doris Beecher's Shilshole home hang two tiny impressionistic landscapes, neither of which shows the attention she gave her larger pieces, but both demonstrating some skill. "These were apparently done while she was cleaning her palette knives," explains Doris. "Amazing, isn't it?"

In the late 19th century, somebody with Hattie Beecher's talent and energy wasn't to be ignored. Even if she was a woman.

Visitors to the Chicago World's Columbian Exposition of 1893 were struck not only by the enormity of the buildings and their overwhelming whiteness, but also by the number of exhibits. There was a Vaseline display, a wire exhibit, a scale model of the Brooklyn Bridge shaped completely of bars of soap, a door-screen display, and colorful examples of needlework, "the art which began when Eve sewed fig-leaves to the Garden of Eden," according to a magazine of the time. The Washington Building alone was crammed full of enough material to keep a wide-eyed fairgoer occupied for hours. There was a miniature farm; the skeleton of a prehistoric mammoth; fish displays; stuffed elk, deer, and bear; and art. Like so many of the states represented in the Windy City, Washington wanted to show off its art. Thirty-six of the 150 paintings sent from Washington to the fair were by Harriet Beecher and her students.

This was but the first occasion when Harriet Beecher's name would be noticed at a world's fair. Twenty-two years later, her oil painting of Washington pioneer Ezra Meeker was hung at the Panama-Pacific Exposition in San Francisco.

Beecher's later years won appreciative notice by Puget Sound's few early 20th-century art critics. They described her as not only "an artist of distinction," but also as a "charming, cultivated woman, who commands the admiration and affection of a large circle of friends and acquaintances

Indian camp on beach; watercolor by Harriet Beecher. *MOHAI 1924.709.1*

not only in her home town [Port Townsend] but in Seattle, where she is so well known and appreciated." Beyond these sorts of notes, however, the volume of surviving commentary regarding Hattie Beecher's personality is regrettably small. Ezra Meeker must have talked with the artist for hours as she translated the valleys, ridges, and plains of his face onto canvas, yet Meeker historians can come up with nothing that he wrote about the experience. Even Emily Denny, who recorded much about her own education as an artist and might have been expected to write appreciatively and at length about Beecher, leaves us with a single dispassionate comment: "I received, in 1882, some sound advice from the artist, Mrs. Hattie Foster Beecher. Then I worked harder."

By the year of her demise in 1915, the Beechers had been back in Seattle for more than 10 years. The city's art scene was heating up. The Society of Seattle Artists was formed in 1904, with Hattie Beecher as a charter member. Beecher—who had long applied her training in portraiture to little more than making tiny pictures of local Indians that she exchanged for handmade baskets—was finally concentrating her brushwork on people by painting portraits of her family and locally prominent figures. She had an eye for the play of light across a lady's gown, and worked for hours to make skin tones just right. Even her most formal subjects exhibited a soft edge that probably wouldn't have been evident in a photograph. Most of Beecher's models seem to have been captured in a wonderful moment of wistfulness, their attention divided in a distinctly human manner. Her two renderings of Ezra Meeker show distinct sides to the man—one, the wily adventurer and writer who would live to age 97; the other, a more tired, bent-shouldered gent in long white mane, whose strength and weakness are both revealed in tiny dark eyes behind metal-framed specs.

One of Beecher's last portraits was of herself. Now hung in the entrance hall of Doris Beecher's condominium, the small painting shows the artist in a flowered hat, little round glasses perched atop her nose, and a light-blue jacket and white shirt adorning her bosom. At the time of this rendering in 1914, she was between 55 and 60 years of age. Gone is the curly brown hair of her youth; in its place a neat gray coiffure. This was Beecher at the height of her renown: Beecher the artist, Beecher the critic, Beecher the consultant to fairs and museums. Aspiring artists consulted her for advice. She'd begun an illustrated history of Washington. Although her self-portrait shows scant sign of a smile, she could have been excused for showing one. This was her time.

A year later she stepped into a chauffeur-driven car for what was supposed to be an easy round-trip to Tacoma.

Bloodstained Boat

Mercer Island's first recorded murders were brought on by a logging rights dispute. On February 8, 1886, James Manning Colman, a former King County commissioner and land-title investigator, left his Kennydale home to row across Lake Washington to Rainier Beach, planning from there to catch a trolley in Seattle bound for Olympia. With him went a houseguest friend of his 12-year-old son. In the state capital, Colman expected to file charges against one George Miller, who had illegally claim-jumped some of Colman's timberland on southern Mercer Island. Colman had demanded several times that Miller relinquish his claim without going to court, but Miller's response was loud and harsh: "Get off this place. If you come back, I'll kill you."

Knowing of this threat, Colman's wife was understand-ably dismayed when her husband didn't return home that night. And the news only got worse: Colman's bloodstained boat was found unattended, and later the bodies of the ex-commissioner and the boy were pulled from a lake at the south tip of Mercer Island. Both had been shot. George Miller was immediately arrested, for witnesses had seen him out in his rowboat around the time of Colman's disappearance. Surprisingly, Miller was acquitted in his first two trials, and was only convicted in a third. After two years in prison he appealed his case and was released. Only on his deathbed did Miller own up to the killing of James Colman, and it's said that, after Miller's funeral, the murder weapon was finally found on the property that Miller had long ago taken from his victim.

Residence of Agnes Colman, widow of James M. Colman, 411 Columbia Street, October 17, 1932. *UW Libraries, A. Curtis 59760*

In the fall of 1885, anti-Chinese feelings led to four months of mob riots aimed at driving the Asians out of Seattle. Government officials, the state militia, and some Seattle citizens upheld the law and protected the Chinese. Nevertheless, many were driven from their homes. *Harper's Weekly (March 6, 1886); UW Libraries, UW 5863*

EMPIRE BUILDER

I T NOW SEEMS INEVITABLE that James A. Moore—real-estate broker, builder, and promoter extraordinaire—should have died of "heart strain brought on by overwork," as the *Seattle Times* reported in 1929. He was a free-spinning dynamo of business activity. Moore never did anything small if he could do it large, never did anything large that he couldn't outdo at the next opportunity. The *Times* had long been impressed by his "restless energy and indomitable desire for the achievement of vaster results," as well as by his vision. "Mr. Moore," the paper opined in 1909, "had the shrewdness and foresight, coupled with that most necessary element, courage, and the capacity to do great things, to set about the work of aiding Seattle to be the foremost city on the Pacific Coast."

But he was a dreamer who dreamed too big, constantly pushing ahead, constantly unraveling behind.

It was Moore who developed much of Seattle's Capitol Hill neighborhood, not to mention University Heights, Rainier Beach, Madison Park, and the Latona section of Wallingford. He participated in the city's extensive regrading endeavors and raised the Moore Theater and Hotel, which still shoulders up from the corner of 2nd Avenue and Virginia Street. He tried winning the contract to build the Lake Washington Ship Canal, operated coal mines to the east of Seattle, developed gold digs in Alaska, and, regrettably, tore down what was certainly one of the largest and most elegant hotels ever erected in Seattle—an edifice that, were it still standing today, might well outshine the comparatively youthful Four Seasons Olympic.

Among the papers Moore had with him when he died in a San Francisco hotel room, inconspicuous and having suffered a run of bad luck, was one scrawled with a statement usually credited (with slight difference) to famed Chicago architect Daniel H. Burnham: "Make no little plans; they have no magic to stir men's blood. Make big plans; aim high and hope and work."

Make big plans; aim high. It was Moore's credo. It was Moore's downfall.

A rather solid gentleman with heavy, dark brows and an enviable mustache, James A. Moore (or J.A., as he was affectionately known) was the namesake of and fifth-generation removed from the founder of his Scottish-Irish clan in North America. The original was an emigrant from the north of Ireland, who began wresting a life for himself from the virgin soil of Nova Scotia, Canada, in 1650. His male progeny were mostly merchants, boat builders, and shipmasters. The Seattle developer's father, Andrew K. Moore, was born on Nova Scotian land that had been in his family for almost two centuries. Politically conservative and an elder in the Congregational Church, Andrew was also prominent in shipping and shipbuilding, at one time owning more than 40 sailing vessels. With the former Isabel McClellan, his wife of Highland Scottish heritage, he gave life to six children, and by family tradition, named his oldest son James.

The future Northwest business tycoon was born in Nova Scotia on October 23, 1861. Once out of high school, he joined his father in the maritime business, but soon needed to strike out on his own. In his early 20s, James Moore settled in Denver, Colorado, where he became a heavy mining operator and, in 1885, married Eugenia Genevieve Jones. Within the next two years, they set off for a new home in Seattle.

At that time, the town was still caught between its metropolitan aspirations and its frontier roots. It claimed the largest theater north of San Francisco—Frye's Opera House, on Front Street (now 1st Avenue), a mansard-roofed pile opened in 1884 by German-born builder and real-estate speculator George F. Frye. He had come west over the Oregon Trail in 1853 "to find a land free of Negro slavery," as he put it. Seattle also hosted Washington's Territorial University (today's University of Washington, founded in 1861) and was building up trade with Alaska. Grand hotels dotted the surrounding hills, schools were opening, and an iron-and-steel works was planned for Lake Washington's east side. Local burghers were determined to establish a major railroad link to the East, though their decade and a half of efforts hadn't yet brought success. The closest Seattle had come was in 1872, three years after its official incorporation, when the Northern Pacific Railroad appeared interested. Alas, when NP directors finally announced the pot at the end of their new steel rainbow, it was Tacoma, Seattle's chief rival to the south. (Henry Villard, president of the Northern Pacific, did lay a spur line in 1883, connecting Seattle with Tacoma and Portland, Oregon. But it only helped reinforce the city's second-class status, and train service along the tracks was discontinued after a year, leaving the unused line to become known as "the Orphan Road.")

On the other hand, the Moores had arrived at Elliott Bay just five years after angry vigilantes stormed the county courthouse, seized two men suspected of killing a popular merchant in the course of a robbery, and hanged them summarily from a tree near what's now Pioneer Place Park. And only a single year had passed since Seattle had experienced its sorriest episode of racial violence. In February 1886, mobs of white laborers—upset at a dearth of employment and convinced that low-wage Chinese immigrants were "stealing" their jobs—invaded Chinatown and herded almost all of its 350 to 400 occupants toward steamships bound for San Francisco. Martial law was declared to halt this expulsion; however, at least half of the town's Chinese wound up leaving anyway, fearful of the consequences if they stayed.

But Moore preferred to focus on this town's potential and dismiss its unfortunate growing pains. He understood that averages of 150 new residents were arriving *each week* in what was already being touted, with unwarranted braggadocio, as "the Queen City of the Sound." They all had to be housed and their businesses had to be headquartered, and on those simple facts he commenced to build his fortune.

In 1887, he launched the Moore Investment Company. It began buying up and developing large tracts of open real estate around Seattle, using venture capital raised from deep-pocketed local entrepreneurs as well as East Coast mandarins with whom the gregarious J.A. had struck up business associations. In addition, with the help of Edward C. Kilbourne, a dentist and early developer of the Fremont neighborhood, Moore incorporated the Lake Union Transportation Company, which operated small steamboats from the south end of Lake Union to what might otherwise have seemed, in those horse-drawn trolley days, like far too distant residential developments, such as Latona, Edgewater, and Brooklyn (which eventually grew into the University District)—all created out of Moore's ambition. His "vision" even extended beyond Seattle. In the late 1880s, for instance, he platted and marketed an addition to Port Townsend, on Washington's Olympic Peninsula.

By 1900 (the year of his father's death, at age 74), Moore was considered a major real-estate operator. Among his advantages was that he refused to respect obstacles that might have hindered a lesser dreamer. For example, to ensure the success of his neighborhood-building schemes, Moore willingly loaned money to prospective buyers. In 1899, he promoted home sales in the Renton Hill area with an advertisement that promised "very easy terms," adding: "We will loan purchasers sufficient money to build with at 7 per cent." Raising investment capital with his left hand, he spent it with his right to improve properties that didn't even have buyers yet. C.T. Conover, a newspaper columnist, onetime chamber of commerce publicist, and businessman, recalled many years after Moore's death finding that the developer had spent $150,000 on one tract to put in "cement sidewalks, paving, sewers and water—before opening the sale. This was a previously unheard-of procedure." Ah, but Moore was impatient to bring his plans to fruition, and he knew that the more inviting he made his properties look, the easier they'd be to sell. Especially during the early 20th century housing boom that followed the Klondike gold rush.

Among his coups was the acquisition and development of a large chunk of present-day Capitol Hill, located northeast of downtown Seattle. Much of that area had already been platted, and 140 acres had been purchased by the city, later to be split between Volunteer Park and Lake View Cemetery. However, 160 acres adjoining the park—identified on early maps simply as "the Woodward Tract"—were still dominated by underbrush and wild fauna. Not until 1901 did Moore acquire that land in what the *Seattle Post-Intelligencer* called "one of the largest deals in unimproved residence property ever made in the city of Seattle."

As Jacqueline Williams explains in her book *The Hill with a Future: Seattle's Capitol Hill, 1900–1946*, this extensive acreage had previously belonged to Selim E. Woodworth, a San Francisco resident who had served as a midshipman during the Mexican-American War (1846–48). To encourage enlistment in that cross-border conflict, the U.S. government had issued bounty land warrants, giving soldiers and sailors ownership of "land anywhere in the public domain" as compensation for military service. Although Woodworth had received 160 acres in Washington's King County, he and his family chose instead to settle in Northern California. However, they retained ownership of that property for almost half a century, until Moore convinced Woodworth's heirs to sell. The developer paid $225,000 for the Woodward Tract—a fraction of what he expected to raise by parceling out the property (as well as an adjoining 40 acres he had bought) to individual home buyers.

The *Seattle Argus* called the Woodworth Tract the last of the "high-grade resident properties to be platted." Moore ensured "high grade" by prohibiting construction on this land of any home worth less than $3,000—a large sum at the time, but then Moore wanted his development to rival First Hill as the address for Seattle's *nouveau riche*. Still pricier abodes were erected along a once-gated stretch of 14th Avenue directly south of Volunteer Park, nicknamed "Millionaire's Row." It was here, in 1902, that J.A. completed work on an impressive new home for his own family—a French Empire-style mansion of sandstone and brick, designed by William D. Kimball. (The house still stands, at 811 14th Avenue East.) That Moore expected great things of this neighborhood is only emphasized by the fact that he dubbed it "Capitol Hill," either after an exclusive section of Denver or because he hoped that the state capitol might be relocated from Olympia to a five-acre section of his property. (Moore actually persuaded a King County representative in 1901 to introduce a bill in the Washington Legislature calling for a study of the capitol's move to Seattle, but it went nowhere.)

Interestingly, the name "Capitol Hill" had earlier been applied, if briefly, to another parcel of property in which James Moore would take an interest: Denny Hill, which used to climb north of Pine Street between 2nd and 5th avenues, then rolled downward across pioneer William Bell's land claim (Belltown). It was there that Arthur Denny, one of the original Seattle settlers—who'd gone on to serve in a variety of civic and government positions and achieve wealth through his extensive land holdings in the city—had reserved six acres just west of 2nd Avenue and Virginia Street, again with the thought that the territorial legislature might choose it as the site for Washington's capitol building. However, Denny would change his mind on this matter, and advocate Olympia or Vancouver as the state

From near Union Street, looking north up 3rd Avenue toward the Denny Hotel, 1891. *UW Libraries, UW 12077*

capital, after he was convinced that it would bring Seattle greater prestige to have a territorial university located here instead.

In the late 1880s, the usually conservative Denny decided that what really belonged on that high view corner was a first-class hotel. Plans drawn up by New York architect A.B. Jennings showed an opulent, five-story Victorian structure with 240 guest rooms, a broad staircase winding up from the 2,100-square-foot lobby to a grandiose second-floor dining room, plus towers, peaked roofs, and balconies scattered all over the $200,000 "castle." Work started in 1889, superintended by ex-Portland architect Albert Wickersham (who would later design Pioneer Square's sophisticated Maynard Building). In the wake of Seattle's Great Fire, as new downtown construction reached a fever pitch and the city drew both visitors and new investors, it was presumed that the Denny Hotel would be in the position to prosper. But its interior was only partially completed in 1893 when the United States was clobbered by its up-to-then worst economic depression. Work on Denny's project suddenly stopped, sending all parties into court with competing litigation. Meanwhile, the structure was shut up and left to decay for most of the next decade, a dark and looming reminder of unfulfilled expectations.

The hotel finally welcomed its first guest in May 1903—President Theodore Roosevelt, who had sailed north from Tacoma for a short stop in Seattle during a whirlwind tour of the West. By then, however, the building had changed hands. James Moore was its new—and very proud—owner. He'd spent $100,000 to repair, appoint, and landscape his renamed Washington Hotel, advertising it as "the Grand Hotel of the West" and insisting that "a trip to Seattle without a stop at the Washington is no kind of a trip to brag of at all!" Moore personally handed T.R. and his entourage the keys to their rooms.

Nonetheless, Moore's handsome hostelry was doomed from the outset. City engineer Reginald H. Thomson, who was determined to flatten out downtown Seattle's topographical irregularities to spur the spread of commercial development, had his eyes on the corner of Second and Virginia.

Moore, meanwhile, envisioned even greater things for that particular corner. He proposed erecting a new and elegant theater on 2nd Avenue below the hotel, onto the roof of which would spill the Washington's expensively manicured gardens. He wanted to expand the Washington, too, further asserting its place in the local tourist trade. To save his guests having to climb Denny Hill to their rooms, he already had created a tram to carry them up the slope and was looking for new attractions. Moore was familiar with Thomson's contention that the hill (and its "castle") should be regraded out of existence, in order to create more level land on which to build and ease the extension of streets north from the business district. But Moore preferred less radical approaches, perhaps extending thoroughfares through tunnels beneath the hill.

By 1906, though, Moore was tired of jousting with the determined Thomson. He would let the building that Arthur Denny had started and that he had finished be torn down. Moore proposed, instead, putting up a New Washington Hotel (now known as the Josephenium) at 2nd Avenue and Stewart Street. It was a sad night for the young city on May 7, 1906, less than three years after T.R. had checked in, when James and Eugenia Moore held a last good-bye party for their original Washington Hotel, attended by many of the town's distinguished residents. All turned out in their finest silks and diamonds, and the hotel was equally resplendent. "The lobby and grand ballroom were draped with scotch broom, Easter lilies, ferns, palms, rhododendrons, roses, and carnations. Red tulips shaded the lights," writes historian Paul Dorpat in *Seattle, Now and Then*.

A year and a half later, on December 28, 1907, the resilient Moore again welcomed the elite, only this time to a happier event—the opening of his Moore Theater, at Second and Virginia. (It was tucked into the north end of the seven-story Moore Hotel, which had opened eight months before, immediately north of the New Washington Hotel.) Designed by Englishman

Edwin W. Houghton, the theater was hailed by the *P-I* as "the finest play-house in the great domain West of the Mississippi River." More than 2,500 people crowded into the theater on opening night, including Washington Governor Albert Mead and Seattle Mayor William Hickman Moore. They had all come ostensibly to see a comic operetta called *The Alaskan*, which had been penned by Joseph Blethen, the elder son of *Seattle Times* editor-publisher Alden J. Blethen, but were no less curious to observe the play-house itself, which with its terra-cotta detailing, stained glass, and mosaic lobby floors had reportedly cost $350,000 to build.

Following addresses by the governor and mayor, J.A. left his private box for the stage, where he delivered what can only be termed "off-the-cuff" remarks. "In anticipation" of speaking at this event, Moore said he had "wrote out a very good speech. I wrote it out on my cuff and I laid out that cuff tonight to wear. [However,] Mrs. Moore is a careful sort of woman and she discovered what she believed was a soiled cuff and took it away. So I come before you speechless." The *Times* reported that Moore "was given an ovation previously unequaled in the city."

The flamboyant Moore was not shy about exalting his stature. He adver-tised himself as a "Capitalist, Financier, Promoter and City Builder." His influence could be felt in almost every corner of Seattle, and even as far away as Washington, D.C. In 1906 the developer won Congressional au-thority to organize a private company that could finish construction of the Lake Washington Ship Canal, opening the city's "inland sea" to Puget Sound through a series of locks. It was only the intervention of Hiram M. Chittenden, Seattle district engineer for the Army Corps of Engineers, that quashed Moore's plans. Chittenden contended that J.A.'s $500,000 pricetag to do the work was too low and that his completed canal wouldn't last.

Moore initiated a project to irrigate lands in Washington's Franklin County using technology that was very similar to today's Coulee Dam ir-rigation system. (The U.S. government put the kibosh on that plan when it refused to help.) He operated coal mines in southwest Washington and gold mines in Alaska. In 1909, after taking so many risks and winning, Moore sunk his entire fortune of approximately $15 million, plus $750,000 he'd conjured up from back East, into a steel mill at Irondale, six miles south of Port Townsend. Using three blast furnaces and a pair of rolling mills, his Western Steel Company could convert iron ore from the nearby Chimacum area into 300 tons of steel per day. As the *P-I* editorialized, "The making of steel on Puget Sound will bring about an industrial development of undreamed proportions, will mean more to Seattle and the state… than even the discovery of gold." Building lots in Irondale sold at one point for $1,000 apiece, but "on Moore Street they went for twice that much," according to *City of Dreams*, edited by Peter Simpson. The town soon boasted 1,500 residents, with plans to house 20,000. Another of Moore's gambles seemed to be paying off. But as *City of Dreams* recounts:

The steel mill was a losing proposition. Chimacum ore was of poor quality, and it soon ran out; ore was expensively imported from British Columbia and China. Prices dropped. The mill closed in 1911, although it reopened for eighteen months during World War I. The facility that had employed six hundred men could not compete with eastern rivals.

His wealth lost, Moore sold some personal effects for $1,000 and departed Seattle for Florida, where in 1915 he platted the first real town in the Everglades area, at the southwestern corner of Lake Okeechobee. He called it Moore Haven, and perhaps it was indeed a sanctuary for him, far from his previous business debacle and the death of his beloved wife, Eugenia, in 1908.

The town took off quickly, prospering from sugar cane farming and the catfish industry. Moore managed to convince some heavy national hitters, including orator-politician William Jennings Bryan and Judge Alton B. Parker of New York, who had run unsuccessfully for president against Roosevelt in 1904, to invest in Moore Haven. The seat of Glades County was relocated there. But after only two years, Moore's money began to run low. He was forced to sell off most of his holdings to a developer of Atlantic City. And then disaster struck, though this time it spared Moore himself. In 1926 a tremendous hurricane swept west from Miami across the Everglades, destroying a dike on Lake Okeechobee and flooding Moore Haven. Some 200 people drowned. Many victims were never found or identified. The town of Moore Haven still exists, now with a population of about 1,300 that still recalls the horrible night.

That memory stuck with James A. Moore, too. It drove him from Florida to San Francisco, where he lived with his second wife, the former Elsie Clark. On May 21, 1929, Moore was in residence at that city's grand Palace Hotel, likely dreaming up another venture of bold dimensions, when death suddenly snatched him up. He was 67 years old. Ironically, the man whose wealth had done so much to turn Seattle from a village into a city hadn't left enough money at the ready to pay for his own burial.

Frontier Equality

Although Seattle became infamous for mistreating its Chinese residents during the 1880s, the town's predominately white population exhibited scant racial intolerance toward African Americans in the late 19th century. This, however, may have had more to do with the small number of blacks here than it did with liberal attitudes or especial open-mindedness.

History records Manuel Lopes as the earliest black Seattleite. Born in 1812 in the Cape Verde Islands off Africa's northwest coast, Lopes was reportedly enslaved or otherwise kidnapped and brought across the Atlantic to New England, where he took up work as a sailor (probably on whaling vessels), shipping mostly out of New Bedford, Massachusetts. He arrived on the banks of Puget Sound in 1852 (or 1858, by some accounts), and it wasn't long before Lopes became a fixture in the town's annual Fourth of July parades, thanks to his ability to play a snare drum. He also gained distinction as an entrepreneur, opening both a restaurant and a barbershop on Commercial Street (today's 1st Avenue South), the latter containing the first barber chair to be transported around South America's Cape Horn.

Lopes' commercial enterprises reflected a pattern that would be followed by later self-employed African Americans. By 1870, six out of 13 black men in town listed themselves as barbers—a more prestigious occupation than other jobs open to them, such as hotel waiter, porter, or personal servant. A few local African Americans actually made a handsome living cutting hair, mostly for white customers. (Ironically, black barbers discriminated against African Americans, fearing that whites would eschew shops that catered to an integrated clientele.)

The second-most-common black-owned businesses in early Seattle were restaurants. It was in such a venture that William Grose (often spelled Gross) initially earned recognition. Born in 1835, Grose was the son of a free black restaurateur in Washington, D.C. Fifteen years later, he joined the U.S. Navy, traveling to the Arctic and Japan before he left in order to follow tens of thousands of other men west to the California gold fields. While there, he also helped to funnel blacks escaping from the slave-owning South into settlements in western Canada. After serving as the steward on a mail ship operating between Olympia, Washington, and Victoria, B.C., Grose put down roots in Seattle in 1860 or '61, making him only the young town's second African-American resident. (He was soon followed here by his wife, Sarah, and their two children.) In 1876, Grose opened Our House, a restaurant and hotel at the foot of Yesler's Wharf (formerly located at the western extreme of Yesler Way) that was popular with white Seattleites, including many of the pioneers.

A big man—6 feet, 4 inches tall and weighing 400 pounds—Grose had a comparably large influence on his adopted city. It is said that future mayor and shipbuilding magnate Robert Moran, who reached Seattle in 1875 from New York with only 10 cents in his pocket, consumed his first local meal at Our House—on credit. Many years later, Moran would recall how Grose "staked" him the funds necessary to create Moran Brothers Shipyards, by then Seattle's largest such enterprise.

Grose was instrumental, too, in establishing the town's first residential enclave for upwardly mobile African Americans. Already well on his way to becoming the 19th century's wealthiest black Seattleite, in 1882 Grose plunked down $1,000 in gold to purchase a 12-acre tract from Henry Yesler on the hilly, thickly forested, northeast edge of town (near what's now the intersection of East Madison Street and Martin Luther King Jr. Way). He built a fine home there, and after the Madison Street Cable Car line was extended east to Lake Washington in 1889—the same year that the Old House hotel, which Grose had sold, burned to the ground in the city's great fire—he started selling off lots to African-American professionals and businessmen. By 1900, when blacks numbered 406 among Seattle's more than 80,000 residents, "East Madison had the largest concentration of black homeowners in the city and represented the aspirations of a nascent African American middle class," according to Quintard Taylor in *The Forging of a Black Community: Seattle's Central District from 1870 through the Civil Rights Era*. Meanwhile, working-class blacks concentrated along Yesler Way and Jackson Street in the hills above Pioneer Square. (This residential segregation has largely persisted ever since.)

In 1879, when Southern blacks were migrating to the West, the *Daily Intelligencer* (forerunner to the *Seattle Post-Intelligencer*) opined, "There is room for only a limited number of colored people here. Overstep that limit and there comes a clash in which the colored man must suffer." Yet, African Americans mostly faced such condescending attitudes in Seattle, rather than outright racial barriers. Black males in Washington were allowed to vote and sit on juries without restrictions (rights extended as well to black women by the Territorial Suffrage Act of 1883), and in 1890 the state's first legislature prohibited racial discrimination. Yes, black workers often had to deal with venal white employers and labor unions hostile to their participation; but when there was race-borne violence in or around Seattle, it usually targeted Asians or Native Americans, rather than blacks. This more-or-less agreeable climate led Horace R. Cayton, editor of the *Seattle Republican*, the city's most prominent black-owned newspaper at the close of the 19th century, to suggest that "the colored people of this country should make a bold strike" for Seattle and the surrounding Pacific Northwest, where "thousands of Negroes...stand up like men and compete with their white brothers."

The welcome mat, though, started to be withdrawn in the first half of the 20th century, as more and more black workers came to take jobs in and around Seattle, fomenting housing and employment discrimination, denials of service to black patrons at cafes and theaters, and eventually, racial turmoil. Despite Cayton's dream of a new frontier for African Americans on Puget Sound, blacks now comprise only about 10 percent of Seattle's population.

Native Americans selling baskets on 2nd Avenue, circa 1912. *Webster & Stevens MOHAI 83.10.PA2.1*

5

THE SINFUL SEAMSTRESS

LOU GRAHAM PROBABLY would've had a hardy laugh from her obituaries, had she lived long enough to read them. "She spent her life in procuring and using girls and women for the purposes of prostitution," began one particularly acrimonious screed, published by the *Seattle Mail and Herald* in 1903. "She amassed a large fortune by selling the innocence, honor, virtue and souls of women. She died in a drunken orgie at San Francisco, where she had gone to look after the expansion of her trade in souls. Her remains were brought back to [Seattle] for burial, and a minister was found who would say over her polluted remains the rites of a Christian burial, and express the hope that at last her soul should find the reward of the good."

And that was just the wind-up. "So far as men may know," the paper continued, "she never for one moment expressed sorrow for the awful life she led. Never once has the tear of repentance made a furrow through the rouge she wore on her brazen cheek. Never once has she contemplated forsaking her hellish occupation for the sake of her life. Shameless, sordid, seared by crimes against nature, and nature's God, her soul steeped in the blood of innocence, she lived her life and died."

Of course, the lady known as Lou didn't try to sell herself as anything but what she was—a whore of uncommon perspicacity, a madam with extraordinary business acumen, and a genial entertainer who, according to the historian Bill Speidel, was "the most important woman in the first fifty years of Seattle's history. That her virtues were generally considered vices in the Gilded Age's pious ideology was of little concern to Graham.

She arrived in Seattle shortly before the Great Fire of 1889 and not long after the end of a disastrous civic reform campaign—one that had managed to close gambling joints and send strumpets packing, but at a terrible cost to the city, which then depended on such vices for most of its revenue. At the time, Seattle hosted either as many as 2,500 "fallen women" (an estimate provided by religious do-gooders) or as few as 250 (a deliberately low-ball count from the chief of police, who knew on which side his bread was buttered). A number of these ladies (black and white) were Americans, but others were French, part of a huge influx of European harlots to America's West Coast in the 1890s; and a significant portion— perhaps 200 by the early 1900s—were Japanese.

"To all the lonely camp-men," explained H.L. Mencken's *American Mercury* magazine in 1932, "the name of the town evoked an image of a girl in red stockings and a short skirt, with a sparkling glass in her hand, paint on her cheeks, and the divil in her eyes." On the Pacific shore, only San Francisco's Barbary Coast had a tougher, more salacious reputation than Seattle's tenderloin.

It was mostly eccentric harridans and slippery male pimps who had controlled the local demimonde since the 1860s. Lou Graham, though, was of a distinct breed. She was boldly public with her business, but never crass—no barkers perched outside her parlor house touting the traffic in human flesh and convenient affections (that trick was left to the crowded, low-class "crib houses" and the bawdy theaters called "box houses"). Censorious, Bible-clutching matrons despised her, but not just because she symbolized sin; she also exuded sophistication and integrity, qualities that would have made her a more suitable guest at a high-society tea than a subject of ridicule. She never married, but men adored her. What's more, they *respected* her. Thirty years before women were given a permanent right to vote in Washington, Lou exercised real political muscle in Seattle. Legend has it that city burghers periodically solicited her street-won wisdom.

Today, a century after prayers were said over her "polluted remains," this city has all but forgotten the woman known as Louise Graham. History texts rarely mention her name, despite the fact that after she died most of her fortune went to help build Seattle's public school system. Only a modest plaque on what was once her grand four-story parlor house, still standing in the Pioneer Square area, commemorates her time on earth.

Yet Lou Graham was unquestionably the queen of Seattle's whores and buggy days.

At her birth in Germany, on February 9, 1857, she was christened Dorothea Georgine Emilie Ohben, although her family Bible listed her as "Elise." The *Seattle Star* noted that she "was a member of the prominent Oben [sic] family of Hamburg, Germany," and had two estranged sisters and a brother, but Seattleites didn't know any of this until she passed away and conflicting claims were made upon her $250,000 estate.

She stood about five feet, two inches tall and was plump in a manner that was much admired a century ago. Blue eyes shone from her roundish face, and her jet-black hair was teased out like a great soft helmet. Her closets overflowed with pricey dresses and plumed hats. She had a weakness for ostentatious carriages and collected jewelry as addictively as Imelda Marcos did shoes. A posthumous assessment of her property shows that Graham had a particular fondness for diamonds; not only were they embedded in myriad rings and necklaces and brooches, but also in a pair of gold garters. "She could be regal as she swept into a room," Speidel wrote in *Sons of the Profits*, "or tell the latest off-color joke with a bonafide twinkle in her eyes."

In 1888, Lou Graham paid $3,000 for the southwest corner lot at Third Street South and South Washington Street, diagonally across from Seattle's first Catholic Church, Our Lady of Good Help. This put her on the edge of Seattle's red-light district, which rolled out south of Yesler Way and between 1st and 3rd avenues. Newspapers referred variously to this malefic quarter as the Lava Beds or Whitechapel, with the moral border streets of Yesler and Washington sharing another, special moniker: "the Deadline"—as in a statement made by the *Seattle Telegraph* that "There is no law south of the Deadline. Anything goes."

Lou Graham's business was the crème de la crime, the most orderly disorderly house in town. Her prices were fair ($2 for an afternoon's dalliance upstairs, $5 if the man chose to spend the night), and any gallant forced to seek the services of a physician after visiting her place could be sure she'd cover the fee. Graham's "hostesses" (only the uncouth called them prostitutes, and if arrested, the ladies listed their occupation demurely as "seamstress") were expected to be both seductive and intelligent. "Conversation in Lou's parlor ranged from the political to economics to the opera, conducted over good drink with pleasant companions against a background of fine music," once explained a Washington magazine called *Tavern Topics*. "As a bonus, private booths and suitable libation were always available without charge to representatives of Seattle's city government and their guests . . . 24 hours a day. According to history, more business was conducted at Lou's than at city hall." To avoid scandalizing sporting nabobs or their wet-eared progeny, and because cops already had their hands full with less savory Lava Bed habitués, Graham and her beauties were left pretty much to their own affairs.

With the Establishment's unofficial blessing, Lou's bagnio became a gold mine and paid the city off handsomely through taxes and other fees. When fire devastated 30 central city blocks in 1889, most of her competitors didn't have the funds to rebuild. But Graham could spend $25,000 for an expanded lot and replace her leveled wood venue with a new four-story brick edifice. Bedrooms were upstairs. The first floor was dominated by a parlor, decorated with Turkish rugs, gold brocade wallpaper, china cuspidors, and an upright maple piano, as well as a few delicately suggestive oil paintings of women's nude backsides, and lamps shaped like voluptuous nymphets. "No young businessman was really considered a man about town," Speidel wrote, "until he could discuss with ease the interior decorations of Lou's establishment . . . and some of the finer points of the distinguished young ladies who were their mentors in that particular phase of their education."

Graham displayed her girls to best advantage—and often to the shock of Seattle's beau monde. Carrie Goldsmith, Amber Clark, Lottie Robinson, and her other employees "weren't allowed to solicit on their own," longtime real-estate mogul Henry Broderick recalled in the 1960s, "but they got plenty of publicity. When a madam like Lou Graham made an addition to her staff, for instance, she'd go out in a smart-looking phaeton pulled by a team of spanking horses and ride up 2nd Avenue with a newcomer so that everybody would know there was a new girl in town."

It was all part of the currency of image making. Lou wasn't just a successful madam, she was the dream of the successful madam, one or two sizes larger than reality. She built a grandiose mansion on Capitol Hill, at 2106 East Madison Street (unfortunately, it was bulldozed away in 1966), where Chinese servant Lee Gow fulfilled her whims. She diversified her holdings, buying stocks, bonds, and property all over western Washington. During the devastating national depression that began in 1893, Graham made loans that "saved the fortunes of many of our first families," according to Speidel. Her generous pledge of $100 helped a local shipyard win the important contract to build the U.S. Navy's battleship *Nebraska* in 1898. Lou Graham may have been the patron saint of sin, but she was no common criminal.

So local sachems were flabbergasted in 1891 when, during the city's latest round of moral cleansing, Lou was actually arrested.

The mistake was made on Valentine's Day by a rookie constable named Long, who later told a judge that he hadn't known Graham's reputation. Lou, who is said to have appeared for her court hearing "in the richest of raiment . . . adorned with a sealskin sacque and bedazzled with diamonds and other jewels," watched contentedly as, one after another, Long's fellow officers disavowed knowledge of what went on inside the brick building at Third and Washington. Savvier newspapermen watched in amazement as the city establishment made good on its unspoken promise to protect Madam Graham.

Less than three minutes after being asked to decide Lou's case, her jury returned to a courtroom packed with men—many of them Graham's regular clients—and declared that by the evidence they had heard, she was "not guilty" of running a cathouse.

She died in San Francisco on March 11, 1903, at the age of 46, but apparently not in a "drunken orgie." Her death certificate lists the proximate causes as "strangulation of intestines, syphilis hepatis." Robert L. Ferguson, a collectibles dealer and author of *The Pioneers of Lake View*, who has researched tales of early Seattleites such as Lou Graham, says she had traveled to the Bay Area for a mysterious medical procedure and probably contracted some form of blood poisoning or peritonitis on the operating table. Her train trip home was in a coffin. She's buried in an obscure corner of Capitol Hill's Lake View Cemetery. Many years after her demise, a Lake View administrator added yet another twist to her story, claiming that an unmarked grave next to Lou's contains her unacknowledged son.

The only part of Graham's empire that still remains is her four-story palace of sin, now the Washington Court Building, at 221 South Washington St. Where women once cavorted in the warpaint of the world's oldest profession, lawyers now have their offices. Some would say that the building's occupancy has gone downhill.

Hot Times in the Old Town

Seattle had been an incorporated city for a scant 20 years when, on June 6, 1889, fire threatened to reduce its business district (today's Pioneer Square) to a mephitic smudge on the eastern shore of Puget Sound. So violent was the conflagration, it sent up a roiling column of purplish smoke that could be spotted from Tacoma, 32 miles to the south.

The disaster began in the basement cabinet shop of Victor Clairmont, at the corner of Front (today's 1st Avenue) and Madison streets. Around 2:40 P.M., one of Clairmont's assistants was heating a pot of glue over a stove, when the adhesive suddenly caught fire. Dashing water onto the flames only spread them, igniting wood shavings on the floor and forcing the cabinetmakers to flee. Within half an hour, whole blocks of Seattle were alight, the fire fed by the town's wood-frame construction and its occasional infiltration of a liquor store or saloon, where exploding whiskey barrels spread high-proof fuel hither and yon. A fire hose cart as well as Seattle's first steam fire engine were rushed in to help. However, hydrant pressure was too low to adequately combat the calamity's progress. Wet blankets and gunnysacks were thrown over building roofs, in hopes of curbing the inferno's spread. The measure did save some structures, among

Mid-afternoon on June 6, 1889. By nightfall, most of the business district was destroyed. *UW Libraries, UW 9454*

them Henry Yesler's dark mansion on 3rd Avenue, but it didn't preserve Frye's Opera House, the elegant four-story, mansard-roofed entertainment venue (modeled, it's said, on San Francisco's 19th-century Baldwin Theater) that sat right across the street from where the blaze began.

Ironically, the city's fire chief was off in San Francisco attending a convention on advanced fire-fighting methodology. When it became obvious that his young acting chief, James Murphy, wasn't up to this fight, Robert Moran, a shipyard owner who was then completing his first one-year term as the city's mayor, took command, ordering the demolition of buildings in front of the fire and marshaling 200-man bucket brigades to retrieve water from nearby gullies. Brave efforts, all. But not good enough.

While alarm bells rang and steam whistles shrieked, the rickety offices of dentists and boot makers and chandlers vanished into the holocaust's maw. Prisoners shuffled anxiously through the streets, shackled together in flight from their burning jail cells. Flames danced about the stilts supporting mudflat-anchored shacks and chased horses into madness down cluttered alleyways. Sawmills smoldered, then finally burst with heat. Ships tethered to endangered docks cast off desperately out into Puget Sound. A saloonkeeper, hoping to save his 100 barrels of whiskey, floated them out into nearby Elliott Bay (he later recovered only two), while burly larrikins on the waterfront threw a wake for their town over another 50-gallon keg of spirits. Twenty tons of rifle cartridges at a hardware store suddenly exploded, sending rubberneckers diving desperately for cover. Other shots came from policemen, who aimed their pistols at looters plundering vacated banks and commercial emporia.

Inside the wooden county courthouse (later to become city hall), at 3rd Avenue and Jefferson Street, Judge Cornelius T. Hanford was in the middle of conducting a murder trial. Though everyone in the courtroom could hear the clanging outside and smell the smoke, Hanford refused to adjourn, not wanting to separate his jury, which was supposed to be isolated until the trial was done. "But justice was not being served," Murray Morgan wrote in *Skid Road*:

The witness on the stand, a businessman, could not keep his mind on the questions he was being asked. The merchants on the jury peered anxiously through the smoke toward their stores. The crowd thinned until only the officials

Destroyed wharves near 2nd Avenue and Columbia Street in the aftermath of the June 6, 1889, conflagration. *UW Libraries, A. Curtis 36929*

were present. With the flames mounting the Trinity [Church] belltower only a hundred feet away, Judge Hanford closed the court and told the bailiff to let the jurors go their separate ways until the following Monday. Before they could get out of the room he drafted some of them to try to save the courthouse.

Seattle's Great Fire of 1889 lasted 12 hours, and by the time its fury was spent, 30 central city blocks—a total of 64 acres—had been leveled. Amazingly, not a single person is known to have died in the catastrophe.

Even the optimism of locals came through intact. As the *Seattle Times* reported four days later, "Everywhere confidence in the future of this city is maintained... The heaviest losers are the most cheerful."

It isn't hard to understand why. Before 1889, Seattle was something of a pestilential hodgepodge—violence-ridden, rat-infested, and poorly constructed upon mudflats so low to the water that when tides washed in, sewage backed up, and geysered out of toilets. The big blaze gave civic boosters and planners a chance to completely reinvent the town, this time in fireproof brick, stone, and iron, rather than wood.

Among their first orders of business was to hoist the city well above the waterline. No more erupting johns for status-hungry Seattleites. The post-fire business district would sit an entire story higher than its predecessor, letting gravity do its proper job of waste disposal. Of course, this meant some hefty regrading of land. Tons of dirt from precipitous slopes on the town's eastern edge had to be scraped down to fill in mudflats. In the meantime, new structures were designed to accommodate the anticipated change in street elevation. Each was given a double set of entrances—one at Seattle's original ground level, the other on the second story, at which height new streets and sidewalks would ultimately be laid.

There was just one problem—and it was a doozy. Streets were raised throughout this neighborhood well before pedestrianways could be realigned to match them. Thus, ostentatiously gowned Victorian ladies and their gentlemen escorts, after shopping along one side of a thoroughfare, were forced to scale tall ladders (eight to 30 feet high) in order to cross intersections. Strolling downtown at night was a particular hazard, as streetlights were few and far between. Seventeen people and an unrecorded number of horses are said to have perished in Seattle by plunging from curb to sidewalk during that first regrading era.

Interestingly, when engineers finally got around to lifting the sidewalks, they simply mounted them atop heavy arches, abandoning intact a subterranean network of original walkways and formal entrances. This "underground Seattle" was condemned in the early 1900s, and for many years it harbored the city's criminal contingent, including rumrunners who hauled their illegal intoxicants through the torch-lit tunnels, literally under the noses of the local constabulary. Then, in the 1960s, popular historian and author Bill Speidel began taking regular and irreverent public tours through those dusty, cobwebbed corridors. The calamity that had once reduced Seattle to ashes had left it with a prime tourist attraction—"a city beneath a city."

Pioneer Square with northern Tlingit totem pole at intersection of Yesler Way, James Street, and 1st Avenue. The Fisher-designed Pioneer Building stands at left. *UW Libraries, UW 8571*

ELUSIVE ARCHITECT

N HIS SPIRITED HISTORY, *Sons of the Profits*, Bill Speidel recalled a New York newspaper reporter visiting Seattle just after the Great Fire of 1889 had leveled 30 downtown blocks in what is now the Pioneer Square district. While surveying the pungent hillocks of wreckage and interviewing people charged with rebuilding the nascent metropolis, the scrivener encountered an intense-looking Scotsman—a man in his 40s, with brown hair neatly parted almost in the middle, and a well-trimmed mustache hung beneath a short blade nose.

Learning that the man was an architect, the New Yorker asked him innocently, "And which building are you designing?"

"With no little astonishment," Speidel wrote, the reporter noted for his readers that Elmer H. Fisher "was designing and supervising not one but fifty-four downtown buildings."

Fisher seemed to have a knack for popping up in cities just in time to find plentiful employment. His arrival in Victoria, British Columbia, in 1886 coincided with one of that provincial capital's big growth spurts. Soon afterward, he opened an office on the B.C. mainland, in Vancouver, just in time to help with reconstruction following a tremendous fire there, which killed 20 people and reduced some 1,000 buildings to ashes in just 45 minutes. From Vancouver he moved on to a stint in ambitious Port Townsend, designing at least three of the most prominent structures along that burg's main downtown thoroughfare.

Elmer H. Fisher. *UW Libraries, UW 12609*

There were other architects practicing in Seattle right after the 1889 blaze. But Fisher may have been more skilled or just more aggressive than his competitors when it came to self-promotion. Indeed, Seattle's charred downtown wasn't even cool yet when he began advertising his services on the front page of the *Post-Intelligencer.*

Claiming an office full of draftsmen and a resume that may have come liberally padded with overstatement, Fisher scored "the bulk of the work" in post-fire Seattle, according to *Incidents by the Way,* the 1935 autobiography of architect John Parkinson, one of Fisher's Seattle contemporaries.

Fisher's brick and stone creations bristled on the skyline all the way from Jackson Street north to Belltown. Thanks to his flurry of commissions in Pioneer Square, it was Fisher who established that neighborhood's now-famous architectural vernacular, synthesizing some of his more Victorian philosophies about facades with the weighty Romanesque Revival look that had come into vogue immediately following the 1886 death of its chief practitioner, Boston architect Henry Hobson Richardson. The paradigm of Fisher's style was his Pioneer Building (1889–91), commissioned by business leader Henry Yesler on the same land where, in 1863, he had established this area's first sawmill. With its rusticated stone base, Roman archway, and round arches over the fifth-floor windows, the six-story Pioneer Building was so remarkable that even the American Institute of Architects in Washington, D.C., sat up and took notice. Upon its completion, the AIA labeled it "the finest building west of Chicago."

Fisher was not averse to championing his own influence. In an October 1889 *P-I* interview credited to him (although he is never actually named), the architect contended that "Seattle's fronts will compare favorably with those of much larger cities than this."

It wasn't long before Elmer Fisher was being touted in Eastern architectural journals, courted by Seattle capitalists who wanted their new office blocks to win national plaudits, and even solicited for product endorsements. Only two weeks after Seattle went up in smoke, a *P-I* ad featured him among notables recommending Hall's Safe & Lock Co. of San Francisco. "I am very much gratified," he pronounced, "on opening

my No. 88 fire proof safe…to find everything in a state of perfect preservation, not a paper showing the least sign of being in the great fire of June
6. My tracings and plans are as good as new; have ordered another safe of
you by telegraph, same size. Ship at once."

Fisher's fortunes seemed assured. Yet in 1894 he apparently fled Seattle
for Southern California, later gave up his practice there in order to settle
some bills, and perished in utter obscurity in 1905, leaving behind no will,
no death certificate, and no known grave.

What happened to Elmer H. Fisher? It's a mystery that may never be
fully solved. But it is just one of many surrounding this man. Seattleites
who think they know Fisher through his work would be surprised to discover how little they can learn about his life. Were it not for his involvement in a well-documented scandal—one that may have made him a pariah
in Emerald City social circles—we might know nothing of the architect
except what he leaked through a few brief profiles. And even those are highly
suspect, calling into question his bona fides as a trained architect.

The most oft-repeated gospel on Fisher is that he was born in Edinburgh,
Scotland, in the early 1840s, and at the age of 17 immigrated to the town
of Worcester in central Massachusetts. It was in Worchester, Fisher claimed,
that he studied architecture, at least in part while working for a firm called
"Boyd & Son." However, Fisher's name doesn't appear in the Worcester City
Directory between 1857 and 1865, the most likely years of this tutelage.
And Preservation Worcester, which catalogues that city's architectural resources, has records on a firm called E. (Elbridge) Boyden & Son, which
designed some of Worcester's signature buildings during the 1850s, '60s,
and '70s, but finds no mention of an Elmer Fisher ever working with the
Boydens.

"It may be that Fisher fabricated a good part of his professional history," says Jeffrey Karl Ochsner, editor of *Shaping Seattle Architecture: A
Historical Guide to the Architects*. "The fact that he worked in a leading firm
in Worcester, then disappeared for years before resurfacing in the hardware business halfway across the country—well, it's sort of peculiar. But
by the time he got to the Pacific Northwest, who was going to check his
background thoroughly enough to question him?"

The first proof I have been able to find of Fisher's existence in the
United States comes from the 1874 city directory for Minneapolis,

Minnesota, where he is listed as a cabinet maker living in rooms just up the bank from the Mississippi River. Booming Minneapolis was a touchstone for many of Fisher's design contemporaries, and it's possible that he had the chance to learn from some of that city's established architects, though there's no proof he ever worked for them. Instead, he went from crafting furniture to making sashes and decorative moldings, then moved on to become a market clerk. In 1879, an "E.H. Fisher" is described as "deputy sheriff." His last Minneapolis listing is in 1880, although the 1881 directory records a "*Mrs.* E.H. Fisher" left behind at the address he had just vacated—raising the question of whether Fisher was married before his only confirmed wedding at Seattle in 1893.

Unfortunately, written background information that ought to have accompanied Fisher's application for a King County marriage license, and which might have shed light on his experience at walking down the aisle, is—like so much of the paper trail that should've accompanied this man— missing.

By 1883, Fisher was in Denver, Colorado, advertising himself as an architect for the first time. Within another year, he had joined a partner, Joseph H. Corrin, and together they were taking on any carpentry or building jobs they could find. "Because Corrin & Fisher were very likely constructing projects of their own design, Fisher may have designed some Denver buildings," Ochsner notes in a 1992 issue of the University of Washington's *Journal of Architecture.*

Again, though—"there are no buildings that I can find listed here by Corrin & Fisher," says Jim Bershof, a longtime Denver designer who worked on the AIA's *Guide to Denver Architecture.*

Elmer Fisher left Denver in 1885, but he didn't go alone. Sometime during the previous two years, he had made the acquaintance of Mary H. Smith. Fisher would later testify that he "understood [Smith] to be a woman of unchaste life," who "had recently been the mistress of one Johnson and also of one O'Neil or Neal." Yet this seems not to have deterred the architect from taking her as his own mistress. According to Mary Smith herself, in October 1884 he went one step further by entering into "a verbal agreement" with her, "whereby they agreed to take one another as husband and wife and to live together with one another as husband and wife as long as they should live." This partnership lasted "about three years," during a brief residency in Butte, Montana, and a move to British Columbia. It would blow up in his face later on.

Evidence of Fisher's involvement in Vancouver is sparse. The only building there that historians can definitively attribute to his pen is the famed Byrnes Block, an Italianate 1887 creation still standing at 2 Water Street in what's now the vintage Gastown district. Victoria is somewhat better endowed with Fisher works, including the small 1887 Willes Bakery (537 Johnson Street), the 1888 W.G. Cameron Building (579–581 Johnson Street), and the 1888 Craft and Norris Block (1319–1329 Douglas Street), which was built as an ornate Victorian-Italianate dry-goods headquarters, but has since been stuccoed over and deprived of its original parapet details. These last two structures were born from what may have been Fisher's more successful partnership with William Ridgway Wilson, a China-born and London-trained architect who came to Victoria in 1887, opening his office with Fisher a year later. The team of Fisher & Wilson has been credited not only with commercial properties, but also with residences in southwestern B.C.

W.R. Wilson would practice in Victoria until the early 1940s. But Elmer Fisher had his sights set farther. In 1887, the *Victoria Colonist* announced that Fisher would design a huge waterfront office building in Seattle, commissioned by prosperous steam-mill operator and fellow Scottish immigrant James M. Colman. However, Fisher's fanciful four-story proposal was finally passed over in favor of a still-grander, five-floor model by architect Stephen J. Meany, which in turn was discarded after the 1889 fire to make way for the more functional Colman Building (designed by August Tidemand and completed in 1904) that still stands today on 1st Avenue.

Fisher turned instead to Port Townsend, which had interested him since 1887 and by the next year was flourishing in anticipation of a direct railroad connection to the Columbia River (never to be built). He designed a trio of cynosures along Water Street—the Italianate James & Hastings Building (on Tyler Street), the N.D. Hill Building (now housing the Town Tavern, on Quincy Street), and the grandest of the three, the much-ornamented Hastings Building (on Taylor Street). At the same time, Fisher had opened his practice in Seattle.

Critics can go on endlessly about the purity of Fisher's architecture in Seattle. Author Ochsner says that Fisher's work suggests that he may have learned his art as much from studying widely published illustrations of the latest American buildings, as from any formal or practical education. "How much

Finding Fisher

Although downtown no longer is as thick as it once was with Elmer Fisher's distinctive brand of architecture, several of his most significant buildings still stand for observation by persons with interests in Seattle architecture and history:

- **Austin A. Bell Building**
  2324–2326 1st Avenue
- **Bank of Commerce** (Yesler Building)
  95–99 Yesler Way
- **Barnes Building** (Odd Fellows Hall)
  2320 1st Avenue
- **Korn Building**
  115–119 Yesler Way
- **Pioneer Building**
  600–610 1st Avenue
- **Schwabacher Building**
  105–107 1st Avenue South
- **State Building**
  300–312 Occidental Avenue South
- **Yesler Block** (now Mutual Life Building)
  603–605 1st Avenue

did Fisher know about design?" Ochsner asks. "It may not have mattered. With the number of buildings his firm produced, he had to be very dependent upon his staff."

The Fisher office flourished in the first two years after Seattle's Great Fire. In addition to the Pioneer Building, Fisher designed the nearby, darkstone Bank of Commerce (a.k.a. Yesler Building, 1890–91), from the balcony of which President Benjamin Harrison pontificated during his 1891 flag-waving tour of the Northwest, and the adjacent Schwabacher Building (1889–1890) that housed one of Seattle's earliest hardware and mercantile stores, managed by Bailey Gatzert, the city's first Jewish mayor (1875–76). Fisher is credited as well with designing the State Building (1890–91), a broad-shouldered Chicago School edifice on Occidental Avenue South; the tiny Korn Building (1889–90) on Yesler Way; and at least the beginning work on the Mutual Life Building (originally the Yesler Block,

1890–91), which later was enlarged by Robert L. Robertson and James E. Blackwell.

Of course, his architectural efforts were not confined just to Pioneer Square. Farther north on 1st Avenue between Bell and Battery streets, Fisher designed the Barnes Building (a.k.a. Odd Fellows Hall, 1888) and, in Victorian Gothic, the neighboring Austin A. Bell Building (1889–90), the latter assigned to Fisher by the wealthy son of Belltown founder William Bell. "He also received commissions for buildings in Kent, Ellensburg, Bellingham, and Yakima," Ochsner noted in *Shaping Seattle Architecture*, "but his practice focused primarily on commercial work in Seattle . . . He was so busy he refused all but a few residential projects."

Sadly, many of Fisher's constructions have been victims of modernization, perhaps the most notable sacrifice being a grand pile of red brick and stone that he built for businessman/judge Thomas Burke. Owing a debt to the design of Chicago's famous 1888 Rookery (the judge allegedly insisted on such imitation), the 1889 Burke Building was torn down during the Nixon administration to make way for the far less interesting Henry M. Jackson Federal Office Building, at 2nd Avenue and Marion Street. All that remains are the main granite-columned entry arch and some detail work, scattered over a surrounding plaza.

Elmer Fisher's own downfall began about 1891. In July of that year he took over as proprietor of the Abbott Hotel, a three-story "traveling men's quarters" that he had designed for the corner of Pike Street and 3rd Avenue. Then he turned over his office to Emil De Neuf, one of the architects who had worked with him during the building boom. Despite all the money that Fisher must've made from his profuse commissions, he complained in his letters about a barren bank account. Chances are he was overextended in some real-estate ventures and other projects, including his investment in a company producing steam for downtown offices.

Things, though, seemed to be looking up for him when, on February 14, 1893, he married Charlotte Mollie Willey, a widow and the daughter of a local clerk. But no sooner had the couple returned from their honeymoon in Portland than scandal struck.

Evidently furious over these nuptials, Mary Smith, the architect's inamorata from Denver, brought a breach of promise suit against Fisher, contending that he owed her $10,000 in damages for abandoning her five years before when he left Victoria for Puget Sound. She said at that time she'd been "in a very sickly and delicate condition," and that Fisher had promised to come back for her when she was recovered and his business

Austin Bell's Folly

"**W**eary of Life." That's how the *Seattle Post-Intelligencer* headlined its story detailing the final, tormented hours of Austin Americus Bell, who went to his grave in 1889 leaving behind claims to significant portions of today's Belltown neighborhood, a "handsome and affectionate wife" as the *P-I* described her, and an unfinished showpiece of a building that still stands as a monument to his abiding misery.

Austin Bell took his first breath on January 9, 1854, becoming only the second white male born in Seattle. (Orion Denny, the number-two son of Arthur and Mary Boren Denny, had been delivered in these parts just a year before.) Austin's parents were William and Sarah Ann Bell, former Illinois farmers who'd been among the pioneers landing at Alki Point in 1851. In spring 1852, William and his wife staked out adjoining 160-acre donation land claims at the north end of what would become downtown Seattle. However, after their log cabin homestead there was looted and burned by Native Americans in 1856, during the so-called Battle of Seattle, the Bells fled to California. William Bell eventually took up residence again on the shores of Elliott Bay in the early 1870s, following his wife's demise and a marked appreciation in the value of his Seattle property. He set about making improvements to that acreage, including putting up the Bell Hotel, a four-story, mansard-roofed landmark at the southeast corner of Front and Bell streets. The hotel was completed in 1883.

As Arthur Denny told the press in 1889, William's son, Austin, ventured back to Seattle in 1875 after having "learned the job-printing business and worked at it for several years in San Francisco and other places in California." For a few months, he was an owner and editor of the Seattle *Evening Dispatch* (one of several newspapers later combined to produce the *Post-Intelligencer*), but then left town again to start another, unsuccessful newspaper in central Washington's Kittitas Valley. Following that experience, Austin apparently moved south again, and in 1884, married Eva Davis of Vacaville, California. Following the 1887 death, though, of William Bell—who during his last five or six years was invalided by his deteriorating mental health—Austin returned to Seattle to bury his 70-year-old father and claim his share of an estate worth $400,000.

He and Eva moved into a Belltown house at the corner of 2nd Avenue and Blanchard Street, and Austin began to plat and improve the property that was now his to

"Monument to an Unhappy Man"—the Austin A. Bell Building. *UW Libraries, UW 8531*

been a robust man, and during his final decade, had "been vainly endeavoring to repair his shattered health," according to friends. Denny confided later that Austin was desperately afraid he would succumb to the same mental decay that had afflicted his father.

It was apparently this fear that led to the tragic events of April 24, 1889. After a night of fitful sleep, Bell arose that morning at 6 A.M., "ate a hearty breakfast, and appeared to be cheerful," according to the *P-I*. At 9:30, he left his house and walked the block or so to his office, at 2222 Front Street (now 1st Avenue). About an hour later, after writing a note to his wife, "full of endearment and keen regret," Bell put a .38-caliber Smith & Wesson revolver to his right temple and pulled the trigger. He was 35 years old, about the same age his father had been when he'd first settled in Seattle.

Though devastated by her husband's suicide, Eva Bell decided to finish the Victorian

sell. He also began planning the erection of a five-story brick apartment building next door to his father's hotel (which by then had been renamed the Bellevue House), to be designed by the not-yet-renowned Elmer H. Fisher.

By most accounts, the sedate and mustachioed Austin—who within only two years of his return to Seattle was worth a reported quarter-million dollars—led "a model life." However, he'd never

Gothic edifice that Fisher had designed on his behalf. She insisted on only one significant change—that Bell's name and the year of his death be incorporated into the façade, moving the *Seattle Times* to describe the Austin A. Bell Building (2326 First Avenue) upon its completion as a "Monument to an Unhappy Man."

"Bell's Folly," as that structure would subsequently be dubbed, had to survive fire, the removal of its most decorative cornice elements, and decades of neglect. Not until 1999, after most of what lay behind the historic façade was rebuilt, did Bell's "monument" regain some semblance of its original luster, reopening as a handsome condominium complex.

obligations were less "complicated." She admitted that he'd sent her money later when she moved to Yakima and Spokane (he pegged the sum at "several thousand dollars"), but insisted it wasn't enough to make up for the savings she had turned over to him at the time of their "marriage."

Fisher countered that, despite occasions in Victoria when he had "introduced her as his wife to avoid public scandal," their relationship had been a mutual convenience at best, and a commercial arrangement at worst. "During his residence in Colorado," Fisher's lawyer wrote, "the defendant had sexual intercourse with the plaintiff, for which he paid her a pecuniary consideration." Furthermore, Fisher insisted that in exchange for a tract of land in Yakima and $400 "in gold coin," Smith had released him in December 1892 from "any claim or demand…by reason of any fact connected with their past relations." He even produced the document confirming that arrangement, with Smith's signature at the bottom.

The case quickly became a source of outrage, gossip, and titillation. This was, after all, still the repressed Victorian era, and though sex-related stories weren't unheard of in Seattle newspapers, rarely did they involve someone of Fisher's renown—the man who had literally lifted the city from its ashes! When the suit's conclusion finally came in September 1893, it seemed positively anticlimactic. After four hours of deliberations, a jury agreed with Fisher "that he had paid the woman many times over the price of her shame," as the *P-I* phrased it.

Earlier that same year, Fisher had tried to reinvigorate his architectural practice, opening offices in one of the buildings he'd designed on 1st

Avenue (then Front). But business was slow. "Had the Mary Fisher case affected his reputation?" muses Jeffrey Ochsner. "It's clear that he was no longer able to attract the kinds of clients he had." The final blow, though, probably came with the nationwide depression that began in 1893, which economically devastated the already struggling Northwest, and clobbered so many men like Fisher who'd leveraged themselves in real estate.

A once-promising career in Seattle had turned sour. Elmer Fisher didn't stay around to be listed in the 1894 city directory.

Fisher's final years cannot be fully reconstructed. He may have spent some time working with one or more architects in San Francisco. By the mid 1890s, though, he was in Los Angeles where he set up an office in the renowned Stimson Block at Third and Spring streets, owned by former Washington lumber baron T.D. Stimson and designed by an ex-Fisher employee from Seattle, Carroll Brown. His talents weren't in great demand, however. In June 1896, he was forced to sell his desk, cabinets, and other furniture to Stimson for $1, probably for back-payment of rent. Fisher thereafter took work again as a carpenter.

The last note on Fisher comes from the autobiography of architect John Parkinson, who had relocated from Seattle to L.A. in 1894 out of frustration at the paucity of commissions available in a town dominated by Elmer Fisher. After Fisher's move south as well, Parkinson wrote, he "worked for me as an outside Supervisor and died there in 1905."

Is that true? Repeated calls to Los Angeles' oldest cemeteries don't turn up any record of his burial. Los Angeles County can't find a death certificate. The oddest conclusion yet comes from Robert L. Ferguson, author of *The Pioneers of Lake View*. He was told by one knowledgeable California architectural historian that Fisher was cremated after death, and that his ashes were stored inside the San Francisco Columbarium, an 1898 edifice located in the Richmond District near Golden Gate Park (and now operated as a non-denominational cemetery for cremated remains) that Fisher may have helped design.

Naturally, operators of the Columbarium, which has had some serious setbacks over the years, claim to have almost no records of who is stored in their 20,000-plus cubicles. And the man who told Ferguson this story? He died not long ago.

Will Fisher's mystery never end?

Hotel Calkins on Mercer Island, circa 1890. *UW Libraries, UW 4815*

GO EAST, YOUNG MAN

B Y TODAY'S STANDARDS, Mercer Island's Hotel Calkins might seem diminished from its historical stature, in the same way that a child's perception of his parents often dwindles as he matures. But at the height of its operation in 1890, skyscrapers were just being invented and Seattle's new buildings only sometimes were taller than the trees they displaced. The inn must have been an impressive, almost magical sight—especially if you approached it aboard a tiny ferry chopping across Lake Washington. It was three stories in height and an architectural amalgam of a Swiss chalet and an American railroad station, with dormers, turrets, and chimneys punctuating its tile roof, and broad, elegant porches girdling its lower levels. Surrounding the hotel were landscaped grounds, with roses, fountains, and cypress trees dancing in the wind.

It is a sad, perhaps even cruel irony, that the only thing remaining today of all this elegance is a brown-painted sign that identifies a tiny wedge of lawn and footprinted sand as "Calkin's Landing," just to the south of where eastbound Interstate 90 blasts onto Mercer Island. The hotel once had a dock on this site. But now there's just a roped-off rectangle of water where it's presumably safe to swim, and there are boundary signs on either side of the green that are supposed to put the fear of God into any visitor who so much as thinks to set toes upon the neighbors' private property.

That this sign is so carelessly mispunctuated only emphasizes how thoroughly locals have forgotten the man after whom the pocket-edition park was named—Charles Cicero Calkins, an entrepreneur, real-estate gambler, and inveterate dreamer who encouraged Seattle's expansion eastward, but then couldn't wait around these parts long enough to see his vision for a prosperous Mercer Island become reality.

Arriving in Seattle in the 1880s, Calkins determined that Lake Washington's only isle should shed its scratchy pioneer roots to become an ordered haven from the strictures of urban existence. It should be modern and self-sufficient, he reasoned, but also elegant and proud of its easy access to water and completely lacking in dirty industries—the Newport, Rhode Island, of Puget Sound, if you would. And at the nexus of this "East Seattle" resort would stand an exquisite hotel, tucked into the island's northwest corner and surrounded by acres of fruit trees, swimming beaches, yacht clubs, and parks, where tourists could find the simple sort of escape that even in those fairly stressless days was much sought after.

The press gushed over Calkins' plans. "East Seattle is not excelled as a place of residence in this section of the Pacific Northwest," proclaimed *Pacific Magazine* in its December 1890 issue:

> Mr. Calkins has commenced an arboretum that promises to be the grandest display of flowers and shrubbery on the American continent. Already something like 700 varieties of flowers have been planted, with a prospect of three times that number by April 1, 1891. Everything that money, taste, and industry can do will be done to promote the beauty and comfort of East Seattle… An electric railway is to girdle the island, steamboats are constantly plying to and from points on Lake Washington, and the magnificent steamer, *C.C. Calkins*, is being run for the special accommodation of the residents and visitors to East Seattle.
>
> Before another year goes by, the plans of Mr. Calkins will all be fully developed, and then, no matter what the other attractions may be in or around Seattle, East Seattle and its arboretum will be the leading place of interest in Western Washington, so far as beauty and loveliness of surroundings are concerned.

The electric railway was never built, of course, and the rest of Calkins' project was barely out of diapers when he suddenly abandoned it, chased out of Washington by financial and family tragedy—both of which would haunt him as he tried to make a new life in the American Southwest. As a result of his short tenure here, he figures but briefly in most Seattle history books—when he's mentioned at all. He is absolutely unknown to most Eastsiders and a mystery even to those few who've plumbed the still-too-shallow archives of this area's heritage.

The buildings that he raised on Mercer Island have either gone up in flames or fallen before the wrecking ball. His name apparently survives in only two places on the island—at Calkin's Landing and at Calkins Point, which marks the northern tip of Luther Burbank Park in an area where he erected a luxurious home for his family. Calkins lived an enviably long life (he was 98 years old when he died in 1948), but he left no diaries or other writings that relate his experiences on Lake Washington.

None of this, however, should diminish the historical importance of Charles Cicero Calkins—or "C.C." as he preferred to be known.

"Calkins wanted to have people come out to his resort and spend the weekend, get a taste of the good life without going too far away," says Judy Gellatly, author of *Mercer Island: The First 100 Years*, a largely anecdotal, yet fairly complete look at its subject. "But in the course of that, he also created the island's first community—what still today is called East Seattle—and he improved ferry access to the island. If he hadn't had such troubles in his life…well, there's no telling what he might have done."

C.C., after all, was never one to dream *small*.

On a blustery winter's morn in 1888, a sinewy, rather angular and serious-looking gentleman in his late 30s, his six-foot frame wrapped in a dark coat, strolled slowly south along Seattle's Front Street. The air wheezed with a fog that hadn't fully escaped from what was then the city's business heart, and whistles screeched from steamships trying to navigate safely to wharves along Elliott Bay. Yet the man seemed oblivious to this day's weather—save for the fact that he periodically fingered his black handlebar mustache, just to ensure that the oppressive dampness wasn't wilting its carefully twirled ends before he reached his office.

Seattle, he thought to himself, was finally becoming an honest-to-goodness city—an average of 150 new residents arrived each week. Maybe it wasn't yet Chicago, a town familiar to him from years before; maybe it wasn't even Denver, where he had done business for a short spell, but Seattle portrayed civic ambition and a boastful confidence in the region's future.

Front Street, with its rising crop of office buildings, entertainment palaces, and other commercial emporiums, represented this evolution in microcosm. Its very clutter—with street vendors hustling their wares, carriages and streetcars dodging for the right-of-way, and crews working to cover over rutted mud with precise wood planking—bespoke prosperity. The man in the mustache could feel the energy of the place, and was made confident by it. So with a final check of his heavy pocket watch against a sidewalk clock, and a quick glance at the cloth banner waving gently above him—CALKINS, MOORE & WOOD, Real Estate Exchange—C.C. Calkins entered his office at the corner of Front and Columbia.

C.C. Calkins. *Pacific Magazine (December 1890)*

He had spent a long time crawling up the economic and social ladder to sit where he did that morning. Calkins was born on February 13, 1850. Although his death certificate declares that he took his first breath in Chicago, his generally more complete university records say he was actually born in Antioch, Illinois, a small town just north of the Windy City. C.C.'s father, David M. Calkins, was an immigrant farmer from Wales with a gift for the blarney that was his most memorable feature. His mother was the former Margared Marshall, a woman reared in Nova Scotia, but as an adoring C.C. would remark later in life, "full with the air of the Scottish highlands," her family's ancestral stomping grounds. The Calkins family didn't have the kind of money to turn a banker's head, but David owned enough acreage to provide a decent life for C.C. and his several other sons.

C.C.'s brothers became farmers, like their dad, or they turned to the proselytizing ways of preachers. But neither of those occupations was enough for C.C. So probably in his 20s, with all the schooling behind him that was available in Antioch, C.C. started saving for a college education. He planted tobacco, a substance that he neither smoked nor chewed during his life, but that was much in demand in 1870s America when Southern tobacco plantations were still recovering from the Civil War. And in about 1878, he left home for Madison, Wisconsin, to sign on there as a boarder in Mrs. J. Cook's home, present the requisite "credentials of good moral character" before University of Wisconsin officials, and finally begin his first term at law school.

It was a two-year program, heavy on lectures and reading, with weekly moot court practice. As Madison was the state capital, the university could invite not only local circuit court judges, but also exalted justices from the Wisconsin Supreme Court to drill its aspiring attorneys in the mazework of jurisprudence.

By the time C.C. walked down the aisle to receive one of 32 bachelor of law degrees conferred by the University of Wisconsin in 1880, he'd soaked up, as best he was able, the complications of criminal law and evidentiary procedure, the nuances of torts, wills, and copyrights, and—something that would prove invaluable to him later—he had sat before two different judges to learn everything he could about real-estate law. He spent his last year at Madison clerking at the offices of William Freeman Vilas, a prominent member of the local bar and former treasury secretary under President Ulysses S. Grant, who would go on to become U.S. postmaster general and secretary of the interior.

In other words, few people doubted that Charles Cicero Calkins would make one hell of an attorney.

Unfortunately, one of them was Calkins himself.

The 1885 Colorado census lists C.C. Calkins as living just north of Denver in Longmont, a town founded 14 years earlier as a "subscriber's colony" for Chicago residents who wanted to move west. Calkins' college sheepskin was still barely warm in his hands when he arrived in Colorado, but by 1881 he was already important enough to be mentioned in Denver's *Rocky Mountain News*. The extent of his operations there isn't clear—although newspapers mentioned on several occasions that he'd gone to assess diggings in which he presumably had some financial interest, and on February 15, 1881, the *News* reported that he'd been elected a trustee of the Highland Ditch Company, a water-supply enterprise drawing its resources from Longmont's St. Vrain Creek.

Those were still heady times to be staking a claim on the future of central Colorado. The Pikes Peak gold rush was over, but that excitement had spurred an orgy of mining across the state. Lead, silver, iron—minerals of every sort were being prodded from the ground, sifted, assayed, and smeltered, often by men who'd already been hardened to mining life by the 1849 California gold rush. Gamblers, gun toughs, and "pretty waiter girls" had been followed to Denver, Leadville, and other central Colorado towns by speculators, accountants, and respectable ladies in pricey peacock plumage.

This was a life-changing period for Calkins in many ways. On May 30, 1881, he journeyed back to Wisconsin to marry a Southern belle, Nellie L. Jencks. C.C. was 31 years old, and if records are correct, she was 18. In 1884, Nellie gave birth to their first daughter, Grace, but unfortunately the little girl didn't live long past infancy. A second child, Ruby, was born in 1886.

It was also in Colorado that C.C. boarded the economic roller coaster he would ride until his last day on earth. Up and down, up and down, went his fortunes over the following six decades. Like so many men of his time, he hitched his fate to the mercurial fortunes of the maturing country at large. He was a dervish of ambitions barely restrained, and constantly unmaking himself. Calkins might collect half a million dollars trading in real estate one year, then lose it all the next, pack up his family, and move into modest digs until luck came bounding back his way, then raise his standard of living all over again, swing another big deal, and—well, you get the idea.

"In a few years," explained *Pacific Magazine* in 1890, as it looked back on Calkins' Colorado days, "he made a fortune and then spent it to pay the debts of those whose paper he had endorsed."

C.C. landed in Seattle in September 1887 with only $300 in his pocket. It wasn't much of a grubstake, but Calkins made the best of it. "In about 10 days he was the owner of 21,000 acres of land and was in debt $19,000," *Pacific Magazine* continued. "In a few days more, he disposed of 700 acres of this land, and after wiping out his indebtedness, had $170,000 worth of property left. About 16,000 acres of land passed through his hands in less than four months."

Mercer Island was only barely settled in the mid 1880s. Surveyors had gridded it for occupation under the Homestead Act of 1862. But it was mostly hunters, trappers, and boating berry-pickers who spent any time there. Prospective residents came slowly, until the '80s, when rumors began boiling up about a canal connecting lakes Union and Washington, and a Navy yard to be installed on Mercer Island's northwest corner.

Calkins may originally have been interested in the island for the same reason that so many others were—because it looked like money could be made, and maybe heaps of it, from operating a business in close proximity to a heavily used military construction zone. But by 1889, when he purchased pioneer Gardiner Proctor's 160 acres of homestead and some adjoining acreage on the island, the U.S. Navy had pretty much decided that a more convenient operations site could be found elsewhere. (The yard eventually became a political football, tossed between Seattle and Tacoma, before it finally landed in Bremerton's lap.)

Instead, C.C. raised $130,000 in 1889—from his own real-estate business and also probably from investors—to clear and prepare a town-site on the corner of the island where the Navy had once thought to locate. Another $30,000 went into his hotel. In spite of this project's significance and extent, not a word was published in local newspapers during its construction. Today, it's hard to say how long it took to build or even the exact date of its opening. But once the Hotel Calkins was finished, the trumpets started sounding.

Seattle Illustrated, an expensive chamber of commerce publication of 1890, described the building's attributes in effusive detail:

The hotel is beautifully furnished, and was laid out, adopting the latest improvements which are so pleasing and necessary in hotel appointments. Tiled flooring, costly hearths and mantels, handsome wall decorations, perfect sanitary appliances, electric system of lighting, and wells, and to crown all, an observatory for the grandest mountain and water scenery in America. Upon the grounds over $50,000 have been spent. Walks, mazes, flowers are in profusion. Over 12,000 trees, Monterey and Italian cypress, arbor vitae and shade trees are on the ground. A greenhouse 20 x 160 contains the finest collection of flowers outside of California, there being 635 varieties of roses alone. The water front has been boulevarded, and is a delightful strolling and boating resort. On the grounds are twenty-five fountains, one with a sixty foot bowl. At an elevation of 165 feet above the hotel is a reservoir holding 1,500,000 gallons of water and fed from eight large springs of pure, fresh, soft water. Twenty-five arc lights of 2,000 candle power, mounted on eighty foot towers, illuminate the surroundings. A bathhouse holds 100 boats and twenty-eight dressing rooms for bathers, also a complete system of Turkish baths. A fine church and college are to be located, and within a short time the conveniences of old established cities will afford to the residents all the comforts that can be wished for.

The inn's first floor, according to historian Gellatly, "contained an immense reception room or ballroom, a big hall with a grand staircase, a fine kitchen, very large dining room, and several small parlors. The two upper floors contained large parlors and 24 rooms for guests."

Credit for this structure's exuberant design belonged to John Parkinson and his partner, Cecil Evers. Parkinson was an English-born architect who, after working in Canada, Minnesota, and California, arrived in Seattle in January 1889. In addition to the Hotel Calkins, he created a variety of local schools, among them Fremont's B.F. Day School and what's now the Interurban Building in Pioneer Square. (Parkinson later relocated to Southern California, where he gained renown with his work on the Los Angeles City Hall, the Los Angeles Coliseum, and that city's exquisite 1939 Union Station.)

Tourists came from far and wide to study the hotel's detailing and marvel at its grand lobby staircase. Even President Benjamin Harrison, when he swung through Seattle in May 1891 during a grand tour of the West, included in his itinerary a boat trip around Lake Washington and a stop at the spectacular Hotel Calkins.

No less impressive was the community surrounding the hotel, as *Seattle Illustrated* portrayed it:

> Mr. Calkins' original intention was to make East Seattle an extensive floral and residence park, and with the improvements already placed, it needs but a short time for nature to transform what was the ancient forest into what may be rightly termed the floral depot of the Northwest. The nature of the soil encourages the growth of tropical plants, while the semi-tropical flowers and shrubs flourish in luxuriance. The palm house and rose house will be a revelation to even the old inhabitants, and a comparison can only be found in such places as Shaw's Gardens, St. Louis, Woodward Gardens, San Francisco, and the statuary will rival the famous Sutro Heights of San Francisco.

Calkins and his fellow planners were so strict in their vision of East Seattle that they required prospective residents—whether they wanted year-round or just summer homes there—to submit plans for review before they could begin building on the town's 50-foot lots. Examples of "correct" design could be found in a row of identical porched cottages that Calkins constructed just north of the hotel, along what is today 60th Avenue.

Transportation improvements begun in 1888 quickly made it easy and even trendy for Seattleites to visit Mercer Island on Sunday afternoons. They could board one of the Lake Washington Cable Railroad cars that left every four minutes from the junction of Yesler and Commercial streets downtown, rumble five miles or more over the wooded stomach of Seattle to Leschi, and then transfer to the 78-foot steamer *C.C. Calkins*, which had been launched on March 21, 1890. The *Calkins* ran 13 trips each day from East Seattle to Leschi, and four a day from Leschi to Meydenbauer Bay (Bellevue). On Saturday evenings, the boat made a special sightseeing excursion around Mercer Island under the direction of Captain George Rogers and later, Captain John L. Anderson.

Charles Cicero Calkins finally seemed to have found his niche, to have shed the misfortunes of Colorado. His hotel never did attract a great volume of summertime guests, but the surrounding resort community thrived. Part of a storage warehouse, put up originally to house goods off-loaded from steamers, had to be converted into a school for the children of Calkins'

employees and other East Seattle residents. Additional acreage was platted for sale, and Calkins named new thoroughfares after people he felt had influenced his life—Ruby Avenue after his daughter, for instance, and Vilas Street for his early mentor.

After moving to the island, Calkins had erected a big log residence for his family on a homestead in the island's northeast corner—where Luther Burbank Park now stretches. But with the hotel in operation, they finally replaced their cabin with a brick mansion, surrounded by graveled walks, lawns, and orchards. "Mr. Calkins built a fine large barn and two smaller buildings just like it close by," remembered Florence Guitteau Storey, whose father had worked for Calkins from 1888 to 1892, and who in 1958 recorded her memories of early Mercer Island for the local historical society. "Behind the mansion he built a six-sided building to house a planting [and] potting shed, and a reservoir on its third floor. Attached to it was a long greenhouse. Beyond the greenhouse was a fancy birdhouse—red and white, almost a copy of the big hotel. The birdhouse was so large that I had no trouble walking around the lowest veranda."

Then, sometime in the spring of 1890, Nellie Calkins and her surviving daughter, Ruby, boarded a train for the East, stopping first in Atlanta, Georgia, then traveling north to New York. The trip was probably taken to visit family and show off the new child, but the time apart may also have been salutary for C.C. and Nellie. Husband and wife were having trouble together after little Grace's demise. Calkins, a man who would say a prayer at his dinner table, but wasn't an avid churchgoer, was troubled by Nellie's "strong religious tendencies" and her "nervous condition and temperament." She thought him distant, a situation that was surely exacerbated by Calkins' consuming attention to his business projects.

C.C. did join Nellie and Ruby in Chicago for three days, beginning on June 30, but then went off to see former associates in Madison, while his wife and daughter headed back to Georgia.

Nellie and Ruby had taken Room 207 at the Kimball House, Atlanta's premier hotel of the time—a six-story, 400-room mix of Old Dutch and Queen Anne styles at the corner of Pryor and Wall streets. After supper on Saturday night, July 12, Nellie instructed Ruby's nurse to put the child to bed, while she went to listen to an orchestra that was playing elsewhere in the hotel. About 9 p.m., the nurse finally left Ruby, apparently asleep and being cooled pleasantly by an open window beside her bed, and went off to tell Mrs. Calkins that all was well.

Just minutes later, as Nellie was returning to her room, she was confronted by one E.T. Moss, looking frantic and holding in his arms an "almost lifeless burden." It seems Ruby had rolled across her bed and right out the window to the stone pavement of Pryor Street, one story below. Moss was sitting with some chums on the sidewalk, and saw the accident.

"The child received several frightful gashes upon its head, and had its right arm broken," the *Atlanta Constitution* reported the following day. "Everything that could be done for the injured child and terrified mother was rendered by the physicians and hotel proprietors."

Ruby Calkins died at about midnight. She was 3 years and 9 months old.

Good things come all too infrequently, but bad things have a way of tumbling over one another. That was certainly true for C.C. Calkins. His Seattle real-estate office at the corner of Front and Commercial, once a symbol of hard-won success, was destroyed in the Great Fire of 1889. (A parking garage now occupies the site.) And Gellatly writes, "before Mrs. Calkins could rejoin her husband on Mercer Island" after Ruby's death, "their mansion burned to the ground."

The couple likely found temporary lodging in the Hotel Calkins. C.C. opened a new real-estate office in the city on 2nd Avenue, and started spending time off the island. Nellie gave Ruby's clothes away, some of which had been convent-made. She gave the child's toys away, too, but she couldn't get rid of the memories so easily. Mercer Island reminded her of all that she had hoped for and all she had lost. So, not long after returning to Washington, Nellie moved into the Vendome, a hotel on Front Street in Seattle.

In the summer of 1891, C.C. filed for divorce from his wife of 10 years, claiming abandonment. Even Nellie, in her reply to Calkins' court action, recognized the "entire difference in their desires, tastes, thoughts, ideas and conduct of life, temper and disposition." The passing of their two daughters had wrenched a gap between them that they were unable or unwilling to bridge. After two months of litigation, a split was declared.

And then things *really* turned sour. Following an explosion of prosperity and speculation, the U.S. economy slowed in 1891; then it crashed in May 1893, taking C.C. down with it. People suddenly stopped weekending on Mercer Island. Calkins couldn't peddle the land he still had available and couldn't collect for some that he had already sold. He mort-gaged the hotel for $120,000. The steamer *C.C. Calkins* was laid up near Kirkland, while C.C. himself tried to put his financial ship back together. (The *Calkins* never did regain its glory. It was partially destroyed by fire in 1898, after which its hull was scavenged for a new vessel.)

In about 1894, the man who had invented Mercer Island left Lake Washington, never to return.

His stately hotel was taken over initially by Dan Olden, a furniture store owner from Seattle, but the place couldn't be kept open. "It was empty for years," Florence Storey remembered later.

[My brother] Ollie and I knew a window we could push up and climb through. We visited every room again and again. The ceilings of all rooms except the kitchen were plastered in fancy ways, with cupids and baby angels and flowers with scrolls and curlicues all painted. The walls were covered with wonderful wallpaper with pictures in panels. The grand stair-case was a sight to see. One could imagine fine gentlemen and ladies parading the veran-das and balconies, going up and down the wide stairs.

The inn, as well as other property once held in C.C.'s name, were purchased again in 1902 by businessman Eugene C. Lawson and leased to a Major Cicero Newell, who used it for a while as a school for delinquent boys. Residents of East Seattle were dismayed by Newell's operation. After news spread that he had his pupils chained to fences as a disciplinary tech-nique, the major had to hightail his school to the old Calkins homestead. By fall 1902, he had departed the island altogether, taken command of children for the Boys' and Girls' Aid Society in North Seattle, and was again being warned by police to cease and desist from chaining, tying up, or otherwise hobbling his youthful charges.

Soon after Newell's escape, the Hotel Calkins was reborn as a private sanitarium, run by one Dr. Murray and specializing in narcotics treatments. ("Investigate Before Going Elsewhere," proclaimed a newspaper ad for this Murray Cure Institute. "Cures Drunkenness, Opium, Morphine, and Other Drug Habits.") When Murray died in 1905, the hotel was transformed yet again, this time into a boarding house, before it finally got a second chance in 1907 to accept summer hotel guests, when Dr. J.J. Leiser of East Seattle purchased it.

One year later on the evening of July 1, 1908, flames clawed angrily through the roof of the renamed Hotel Mercer and the old observatory tower was choked in smoke. Leiser and some of his employees scampered onto the roof, seeking to extinguish the blaze with buckets of water. Gar-den hoses sprayed desperately up from below. But a stiff east wind encouraged the conflagration, forcing a dozen coughing guests and others who'd been trying to pack furniture out of the hotel to abandon the effort. Leiser, surrounded by tenants and friends, could only watch as the building crackled and tumbled upon itself.

Although rumors blamed the fire on a disgruntled Japanese houseboy, who after a scolding had supposedly stuffed a chimney with oily rags to cause a revolting smoke, Fire Marshall Gardner Kellogg chalked up the disaster, instead, to a defective flue. Leiser's loss was estimated at $28,000, but the building was not insured.

The voice on the other end of the telephone line was clear and just a little husky—not at all what you'd expect from a ghost.

"Hello," she said, "this is Ruby Calkins."

I'd spent the month before this call trying to track down what happened to C.C. after he departed the Northwest. I checked with the University of Wisconsin alumni office, which knew at least that he died in Los Angeles in 1948. That led me to his obituary in the *Los Angeles Times*, to property records in Southern California, to historians all over the Southwest, and finally to a woman who, as far as I knew, had perished in a childhood fall from a hotel window in 1890.

After the Panic of 1893, Calkins moved from Washington to Southern California, where he continued to exercise his passions for mining and real-estate development. Records list him in 1902 as a resident of L.A. But he had business interests just north of there, in the Mojave mining district of eastern Kern County. This was lucrative territory, according to Larry Vredenburgh, a geologist with the Bureau of Land Management in Bakersfield and co-author of a book about California's desert mining history. "Gold was first discovered [in Kern County] in 1894," Vredenburgh explained, "but it wasn't until 1900 that things really picked up"—about the time Calkins entered the picture.

More than $23 million in precious metals were extracted from a 70-square-mile area around the town of Mojave. Calkins owned all or part of 11 mines in that district, including the oldest of the bunch—the Exposed Treasure Mine, a quartz vein opened in 1901 and purchased by Calkins only two years later. After his death, the L.A. *Times* called C.C. "one of the largest gold mine operators in Kern County."

So much for the good news. The bad is that, in 1907, Calkins—in an eerie reflection of his speculations on Mercer Island—bought the entire subdivided, 640-acre townsite of Rosamond, California, from the Southern Pacific Railroad. It cost him $13,000, and there was still a $5,000 mortgage on the site. Calkins' idea was to develop this town in the southeast corner of Kern County as a place where workers and their families could live during construction of the massive Los Angeles Aqueduct, a project that would tap water from the Sierra Nevada as a cure for drought down south. C.C.'s venture failed, as Rosamond was considered too far away from the construction zone. Mojave became the focal point for workers, instead, and Calkins lost his town and his money when the mortgage holder foreclosed.

C.C. married not once, but twice more after Nellie. Wife no. 2 was Kate A. Calkins, whom he wed just around the turn of the last century, and who relished the desert mining business as much as he did. But Kate died painfully in the early 1920s, perhaps from complications of edema or, as it was known then, dropsy. After that, he tied the knot with Ida Mae Sirr, from Calgary, Alberta. Although C.C. was at that time in his mid 70s, Ida was only in her mid 30s—perfectly capable of bearing him his third child in 1926. Perhaps because it reminded Calkins of his youthful hopes, they named the little girl Ruby.

When I found Ruby Myrtle Calkins in 1992, she was 66 years old. A bookkeeper for a dye-making company in Los Angeles (she has since retired), she had never married and still lived in the West 59th Street house that she shared with her mother Ida before her death in 1968. Her memories of C.C. were of a man grown old and gray, his eyes debilitated by cataracts during the last five years of his life, but still courtly and still a dreamer. He had shaved off his mustache by the time she knew him and gravity had reduced his once-imposing presence, but his hands and feet were big and powerful as they would be on a man half his age.

"Some people thought of him as a diamond in the rough," Ruby said of her father. "But he was always very outgoing, very affectionate, and he loved my mother very much. If I ever felt ill or my mother was sick, he was always there to rub our backs or do something to make us feel better. He was never really sick himself, maybe because he was so careful about his food. He said he'd eaten poorly as a younger man, and that he now wanted to make up for it. He never drank, never smoked, and I never remember…well, I guess he did use the name of the Lord in vain occasionally, just to emphasize something…

"He loved to talk about his age, which would upset my mother terribly, because she worried that people would think I wasn't his child at all…

"He was friendly; he'd take his hat off to anyone. He always kissed ladies' hands, though not like a rake or anything. But he wasn't a person who needed a lot of people around him. There was nothing he liked better than to go out to the desert and stay out for a while. He went through a phase where he was always doing paintings of the desert, of formations and rocks. He didn't do them in oils, or anything, but in something like poster paint. My mother liked to paint, too, so the two of them would sit in their room and paint. His pictures were lost during our moves. They're all gone now . . .

"Does it bother me that I was named after a dead girl? Not really. But I never liked my name. And my father never called me Ruby. He used to call me 'Doodledinks,' or 'DeeDee,' for short."

C.C. couldn't stick around long enough to tell his second daughter Ruby the details of his younger life. What she knew was from passing conversations only. She knew that Kate Calkins died in the same big Victorian house on West Adams Boulevard where Ruby was born. She knew that Ida and C.C. met when the Sirrs moved into an apartment next door to Calkins' house. She knew about East Seattle and the old Hotel Calkins, but she never had been up there to look over the land her father once commanded like the first Marquis du Mercer Island.

Financial troubles plagued C.C. Calkins to the end. He continued making money from his mine holdings, but it wasn't substantial or regular enough for him to provide an easy living for his family. Ruby told me about her family moving several times, leaving one rental house in search of a less costly one. C.C.'s final home was at 2121 South Gramercy Place— what's now the middle of the Santa Monica Freeway. It was there, on May 31, 1948, that C.C. got mixed up on the basement stairs and fell. "He was able to get up, and nothing seemed amiss," Ruby recalled. "But he died later in his sleep." Official cause of death—arteriosclerotic heart disease, brought on by general hardening of the arteries, from which he had suffered for two years. He is buried at Inglewood Park Cemetery in Inglewood, California. His death certificate misidentifies him as *Cicero Charles Calkins*.

With Calkins went almost a century of observation, knowledge, and ambition. His life spanned from well before the Civil War to after World War

II, probably the most exciting stretch in all of American history. He out-lived two wives, two children, and 20 U.S. presidents. He never fought in any war, but he had his own battles.

Other people over the last century have had high hopes for Mercer Island. In 1911, engineer Virgil Bogue suggested that Seattle "acquire Mercer Island and set aside this 4,000 acres as an island park—a people's play-ground, worthy of the city of millions which will someday surround Lake Washington." More than a decade later, Bellevue real-estate mogul James Ditty proposed building a bridge to link Seward Park with Mercer Island, and erecting an observation tower on the island and airports at both its north and south ends. But C.C.'s notions about developing the island were born well before those two schemes and have had a more lasting impact.

If the Hotel Calkins still stood today, it probably would be a gentrified boutique inn for the moneyed classes—a spectacular tourist draw, on the order of Rosario Resort or Lake Quinault Lodge. Instead, it's only a memory trapped forever between the crinkly edges of black-and-white photographs. The lake that Calkins once gazed out on each day is now nine feet lower, thanks to the 1916 opening of the ship canal that joins lakes Union and Washington to Puget Sound.

Maybe people today can't even punctuate his name correctly on a park sign. But as Gellatly remarks in *Mercer Island: The First 100 Years*, "Calkins' dream of a non-industrial, non-commercial, almost purely residential is-land became the ideal of many property owners who followed after him. The island's biggest industry today is residential property, and developers seek to attract buyers by offering individually designed, handsomely land-scaped homes."

C.C., it seems, had the right idea after all.

He Moved Mountains

While C.C. Calkins was trying to build up Mercer Island, Reginald Thomson was doing his damnedest to knock Seattle down—literally! As the city's chief engineer, it was his responsibility to tame the original irregular contours of downtown, smoothing out steep hills and

Reginald H. Thomson. *Kurt E. Armbruster collection*

filling in valleys that inhibited commercial expansion and slowed transportation. His efforts weren't always appreciated—taxpayers and pundits often complained that Thomson's "improvements" were too expensive and overly disruptive. Yet for 20 years, he worked to give Seattle a face-lift like none it had experienced before, or is likely to endure again.

Born in 1856 into a Scottish community at Hanover, Indiana, Reginald Heber Thomson graduated from Hanover College 21 years later with a doctorate in philosophy. Soon after, he followed his father to northern California, where the elder Thomson became principal of Healdsburg Institute (today's Pacific Union College), while "R.H." taught mathematics. Thomson first reached Puget

Sound in September 1881, when Seattle had little enough to brag about. Nonetheless, he saw potential and stayed here to work as a surveyor involved in canal digging between lakes Washington and Union (one small step along the way to creating the Lake Washington Ship Canal). Three years later, he was named city surveyor and charged with building the town's first sewers. In 1892, after he'd made a brief detour into railroad construction in both western and eastern Washington, Seattle was much in need of an experienced planner and recruited Thomson to the position of city engineer.

An intense, serious-minded man who sported a full beard and wire-framed glasses, Thomson wasted no time in tackling a to-do list of increasingly difficult projects. He expanded the town's sewage system, installed some of its first sidewalks and paved thoroughfares, realigned wharves and piers jutting into the Sound, and laid 30 miles of pipe—part wood, part steel—out to the Cedar River watershed, located in the Cascade foothills southeast of Seattle, in order to provide city dwellers with a more abundant source of potable refreshment. Before this system went into service in 1901, Seattleites had drawn their water from a reservoir on Beacon Hill filled with water pumped out of Lake Washington. Thomson's confidence in the Cedar River as being adequate to fulfill the needs of a growing population has been vindicated—Seattle and surrounding King County *still* exploit that watershed today.

In addition to tapping the Cedar River for tap water, Thomson used it to generate electricity. The City Light Cedar Falls hydroelectric plant began operating in October 1904. Within five months, the electric current was lighting Seattle streets, and by September 1905, City Light was serving private clients, as it continues to do so today.

Until Thomson's regrading of Seattle streets began in the late 1890s, the incline of some roadways leading out of down-town was as great as 20 per-cent—too steep for horse-drawn conveyances. The engineer

Regrade work along 4th Avenue, November 20, 1908. *UW Libraries, A. Curtis 11442*

wanted to reduce those slopes to around 5 percent, and used manual and steam shovels to do the work, as well as hydraulic sluicing methods that had proved their value in mining operations. His department's earliest success came in 1898, when 1st Avenue was regraded all the way from Pike Street to Denny Way. Thomson then went on to lower the incline of Pike and Pine streets from 2nd Avenue east to Broadway, before tackling his largest endeavor—the flattening of mammoth Denny Hill between 2nd and 5th avenues, and Pike Street and Denny Way. That project was executed in two main stages over 30 years and caused the destruction of James A. Moore's grand Washington Hotel. It also led to some of the oddest photographs ever taken of the city, showing manmade buttes—some topped by teetering houses—left temporarily behind during the excavations. These "spite mounds," as

Denny Hill regrade, circa 1910, showing "spite mounds." *UW Libraries, UW 4812*

Thomson's critics called them, didn't all disappear until 1911.

Thomson also attacked the southern end of downtown, regrading Dearborn Street and lowering almost 50 blocks between Main and Judkins streets and 4th and 12th avenues. Meanwhile, his crews created Westlake Avenue, a level approach to Lake Union. By the time Seattle finished its regrading, 16 million cubic yards of dirt was displaced, with most of it emptied onto the tideflats south of the city, creating new real estate for development, which now is the home to King Street Station as well as sports arenas.

Still unsatisfied, Thomson quit his city engineer post in 1911 to organize the Port of Seattle. He pushed the city to acquire Smith Cove (today occupied by piers 90 and 91) and lobbied in Washington, D.C., for money to build locks on the Lake Washington Ship Canal. On top of all this, he served as a member of the Seattle City Council from 1916 to 1922, built a hydroelectric plant in Eugene, Oregon, surveyed power plant locations in southeastern Alaska, and consulted on the construction of the first Lake Washington floating bridge. He died in January 1949 at the age of 92.

Asked late in life whether he'd accomplished everything he hoped to in Seattle, Thomson answered: "No."

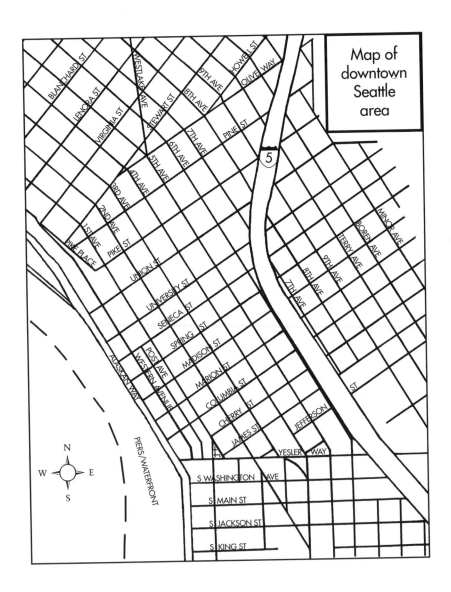

Map of downtown Seattle area

8

THE OTHER GREAT DEPRESSION

T WAS MID-AFTERNOON on Monday, November 22, 1893. James L. Wheatley, an intelligent-looking chap from South Dakota with thin dark hair and a mustache, walked into the lobby of Seattle's Queen City Hotel at 112 2nd Avenue. He'd been staying there for about a week, while scouting desperately for a job in his chosen field of railroading.

Approaching the desk clerk, Wheatley asked when his rent for Room 19 would run out. "Today," replied the clerk.

"I will not need it any longer," said Wheatley, very calm, very businesslike, "so don't hold it for me." And with that, the guest wheeled about and trod upstairs to his room.

Fifteen minutes later, that same man—now with his coat tightly buttoned up, a polka-dot scarf ringing his neck, and a small cap on the back of his head—came bounding back down the steps. He "walked rapidly" into an apothecary at the corner of 2nd Avenue and Washington Street and, "without the least indication of undue excitement" (according to a newspaper report of the time), approached the counter to announce, "I have taken a drink of carbolic acid to commit suicide."

The druggist eyed the gentleman in astonishment. "When did you take it?" he inquired.

"Just now in the Queen City Hotel. I have been out of work, and despondent because I could not get employment and wanted to die. Now I want to be saved, because I regret my actions."

In less than three minutes, and despite a dose of sweet almond oil as an antidote, Wheatley went into convulsions and perished.

Newspapers across the Pacific Northwest were peppered with such tales of monetary woe from late 1893 through the following year. They told of men who turned to suicide because they'd been scratched from the payrolls of suburban factories or lost their small businesses; of women, abandoned by out-of-work spouses, who were caught stealing from markets or were booted from their apartments for lack of cash; of city treasurers who one day loaded up their bags with public funds and disappeared. The national economy was coming apart at the seams and some Northwesterners were coming apart with it.

"Everyone is in a blue fit of terror," New York novelist Henry James wrote at the time, "and each individual thinks himself more ruined than his neighbor."

The Panic of 1893 wasn't the first economic crash to humble the United States. An earlier "panic" in 1819 had been precipitated by sluggish sales of frontier land and a contraction of credit following the mammoth Louisiana Purchase. The most serious fall prior to 1893 came just 20 years before, after the collapse of mogul Jay Cooke's banking house forced a 10-day shutdown of the New York Stock Exchange just to check the decline.

But the Panic of 1893 and the depression that followed in its wake marked the first time that the Northwest had been crippled by a widespread financial downturn.

At the time, this still-remote region was only beginning to emerge as a center of population and commerce. It had grown too swiftly and too recently to boast adequate defense against widespread fiscal upheaval. The consequences were predictably grim. As Archie Binns remarked in *Northwest Gateway: The Story of the Port of Seattle*, "men who thought they knew about storms and how to weather them went over like straw men. And when they picked themselves up they were empty handed."

By the close of 1893, more than 15,000 assorted business ventures, and 642 banks, had gone belly up across the nation. As railroads, mines, streetcar lines, and deluxe hotels sank in red ink, the laboring ranks were devastated. Twenty percent of American workers (between two and three million men) lost their jobs by January 1, 1894. Unemployment, 3 percent of the workforce in 1892, skyrocketed in just two years to 18.4 percent. Troubled families descended on banks, withdrawing their savings and shoving those institutions into ruin.

Jobless workers fled Seattle, Everett, Spokane, and especially Tacoma hoping to find work elsewhere, *anywhere*. Thousands set off east in the spring of 1894 to join up with the so-called Commonweal Army of Jacob S. Coxey, an Ohio businessman who was organizing laborers from around the country in a mammoth protest march on Washington, D.C. Despite relatively swift legislative action from both President Grover Cleveland and Congress, tremors touched off by the Panic of 1893 would reverberate throughout most of the rest of the decade.

Adversity forced economic as well as political changes in the Northwest. While small industries crumbled in droves, large ones innovated in order to survive and prosper later on. The Populist Party, which had organized nationally as a third party only in 1891, drew delegates from all over Washington to its convention at Ellensburg in 1893. After the depression, that party became a significant force in the state, winning the governor's office and a raft of legislative seats in 1896.

The Panic marked a painful, bitter end to what Mark Twain dubbed "the Gilded Age," that period of extravagance and prosperity that followed the Civil War. Few observers had seen this crash coming or could have known that its devastating affects on the Northwest would continue until the Klondike gold rush began in 1897. Even fewer might have guessed that the political aftermath of America's Other Great Depression would still be felt in the Northwest even a century later.

Seattle in 1893 was still recovering from the great fire that four years before had leveled 30 blocks of its original downtown. Rebuilding was fast and furious, with office termitaries that might once have been raised in wood now reaching skyward in fireproof brick and rusticated stone. Streets were being widened and paved with brick, rather than the creosoted fir planks that had served for many years. There was talk of erecting a permanent, Gothic-style city hall on Yesler Street. The new Rainier Hotel, a timber castle with a broad, wraparound porch, rose magnificently from the northeast corner of Columbia Street and 5th Avenue, while Arthur Denny's huge, multi-turreted hotel was taking shape high above the corner of 2nd Avenue and Virginia Street. Streetcars crawled over the hills, while cargo ship sails billowed along the waterfront. Seattle was staking its position among important American metropolises.

The city had been snubbed in the 1870s by the Northern Pacific Railroad, which chose Tacoma over Seattle as its western terminus. But in June 1893, "Empire Builder" James J. Hill's Great Northern Railway finally opened easy access from Elliott Bay to the rest of the United States. Meanwhile, local pioneer David Denny was creating the most ambitious urban railway system the city had yet seen, and real-estate hustlers were busy touting "a streetcar at your door." Other entrepreneurs ran up ponderous debts, trusting that their high-risk ventures would realize handsome returns in a surging economy.

Boosters called the Puget Sound area "the boomingest place on earth." Even right after stocks started crashing in the spring of 1893, the *Seattle Post-Intelligencer* proclaimed "brighter prospects" ahead for the city. "The so-called 'panic' in Wall Street really amounted to nothing but the pricking of a number of inflated industrial bubbles," the paper scoffed. "Outside of the professional Wall Street gamblers, and the speculating dupes who never learn wisdom by experience, no one was harmed. The country on the whole will be better off for the liquidation that has taken place."

Such words would soon taste very sour.

The depression of '93 was partly the fault of federal policy. Under President Benjamin Harrison, who occupied the White House from 1889 to 1893 (between Cleveland's two nonconsecutive terms), a Republican-controlled Congress had profligately spent away a $100 million treasury surplus, passing legislation (including orders for a brand-new navy of armored ships and a nationwide assortment of harbor improvements) designed to gladden the hearts and fill the wallets of wealthy industrialists. In 1890, it also passed the Sherman Silver Purchase Act, which obligated the government to pay gold in exchange for millions of ounces of coinable silver being mined from western states. Unfortunately, this act assigned a value to the silver that was radically beyond what public markets paid. The results were a serious undermining of U.S. gold reserves and skyrocketing inflation.

At the same time, the country was wobbling under the rapid shift from an agrarian economy to an industrial one. The U.S. Census of 1890 found that, for the first time, the majority of Americans didn't live and work on farms. Ambitious men instead swarmed into towns such as Seattle, Tacoma, and Portland, confident that through the alchemy of being in the right place at the right moment, they could convert bantam grubstakes into dynastic fortunes. But the bigger cities were already overwhelmed with annual immigrations from Europe, and disparities were growing between the capitalist classes and the laboring ones, inspiring strikes and worker violence.

James J. Hill had spotted trouble on the horizon as early as 1890. He told his son-in-law, wealthy lawyer and highway builder Sam Hill, that the United States was on a collision course with "a panic that it will take five years to get over." But most observers ignored the warning signs, blithely confident that the marketplace would correct itself without government intervention.

Their confidence was dashed only 10 days before Democrat Grover Cleveland took his second oath of office as president, on March 4, 1893, when the Philadelphia and Reading Railroad went bankrupt. In April, the new Treasury secretary, John G. Carlisle, confessed that the nation's gold reserves had dipped below their traditionally acceptable level of $100 million. On May 4, the National Cordage Company, an important rope trust, failed, touching off a next day Wall Street selling panic—"Industrial Black Friday." Seven weeks later, on June 27, the price of silver caved to 77 cents an ounce, down from 92.2 cents just a week before. Suddenly the value of an American silver dollar was a paltry 58 cents. Historian Bernard A. Weisberger put it nicely: "The band music of inauguration day was more or less drowned out by the noise of the roof falling in."

In the summer of 1893, the Panic chased almost everything else off the nation's front pages—talk of a Nicaraguan ship canal, rumors of a giant serpent plying Puget Sound, the ousting of Hawaii's Queen Liliuokalani from her throne, illegal opium imports from Canada into Seattle, and the sensational double ax-murder trial of Lizzie Borden in Massachusetts. Chicago's grandiose World's Columbian Exposition, a last gasp of the Gilded Age, opened on May 1 to celebrate the 400th anniversary of Christopher Columbus' arrival in the Western Hemisphere. With its soaring domes, monstrous dynamos, and the first Ferris wheel, this "Great White City" was supposed to make people forget life's distresses. Instead, it focused attention on the yawning gulf between the monumental visions of capitalists and the impoverished reality of America's masses. When the fair closed after six months, some 100,000 unemployed Chicagoans stood waiting in charity soup lines.

Thundering west from Wall Street, the Panic blasted San Francisco, then spread its carnage up the coast. In Washington, as elsewhere, a run on banks ensued. Depositors desperately withdrew their savings. They converted money into gold when possible, or buried or hid it when they couldn't. Credit became impossible to procure. Construction stopped. Banks tried to collect mortgage payments, foreclosed on creditors who couldn't pay, and then went out of business themselves. Within a year, 11 Seattle banks bolted their doors.

Bellingham's First National Bank, the Bellingham Bay National, and several other lending institutions bit the dust while that city's new town hall stood half finished, the clock faces in its tower inoperable for a lack of funds needed to buy the workings. Centralia's population cascaded from a high of 5,000 in 1891 down to 1,200 in 1893, and many families were reduced to living on potatoes and watery gravy. For six years, one could buy a business block in Centralia for $10 at public auction; north end mansions went for the price of the hardware they contained.

Dreams of making Union City into "the Venice of the Pacific" dried up. Located on the leg of land connecting the Kitsap and Olympic peninsulas, Union City was booming just before the Panic took hold, back when residents and investors thought the town would be on a Union Pacific Railroad line to Port Townsend and the ocean. Originally, "land sold for a thousand dollars an acre," Murray Morgan wrote in *The Last Wilderness.* "The town's lone mill couldn't saw lumber fast enough to meet the demand for new houses." A strike against the Union Pacific in April 1893, in league with credit shrinkages, led to the railroad's failure and the town's virtual demise. It's own future suddenly in doubt, Port Townsend stopped dead, its grand edifices preserved in historical amber, waiting to be rediscovered by preservationists nearly a century hence.

Meanwhile, plans to create a huge mill town on the northeast shore of Lake Washington, as envisioned by English industrialist Peter Kirk and a group of Seattle investors, were just taking shape when the Panic closed its fist over the country. Envisioned was the largest steel mill west of Pittsburgh, surrounded by a bustling community of brick buildings. Stock had been sold, trees were cleared, and ironworkers came from Britain to take new jobs in Kirkland. A group of deep-pocketed investors, including billionaire John D. Rockefeller and Leigh S.J. Hunt, owner of the *Seattle Post-Intelligencer*, had sunk between $750,000 and $1 million into the development corporation, only to lose it all in the Panic. Hunt lost his newspaper as well.

"The Panic of 1893…crumbled cities like Everett for which confidence was the only adhesive in the foundation of the community life," Norman

H. Clark observed in his Everett history, *Mill Town*. Three of that burg's five banks went under. When the Northern Pacific Railroad, which owned and worked hundreds of thousands of acres of land-grant timber around Everett, went into receivership in 1893, it cut off a lumber trade that had been slowing for the previous two years.

Eastern capitalists, who had wanted to create a "New York on Puget Sound" at Everett, sold much of their stake to Rockefeller, hoping that would secure confidence in Everett's future. But by 1894, the New York plutocrat had taken his money out of city lands, a local hotel, street railway, nail factory, and paper mill. "Thus cut away from their eastern resources, most of these enterprises sank in a few months, or at most a few years," Clark wrote.

After 1893 wages in Everett fell to 40 percent of what they'd been previously. "A family could rent a house for ten dollars a month," Clark recalled, "though one man shot his landlord for trying to collect that amount."

In Seattle, pioneer Arthur Denny had been struggling since the Great Fire of 1889 to complete his lavish $200,000 hotel on what was then a hill east of 2nd Avenue, at Virginia Street. Unfortunately, the '93 depression stalled work on the structure, sent all parties to court for years, and left the hostelry to decay for more than a decade.

Arthur's brother, David Denny, had an even harder time. In 1889 he'd become convinced that electric trolleys were the ideal means of opening up Seattle's outlying districts to residential development. With his second son, David T. Denny, and under the corporate moniker of the Rainier Power & Railway Company, the elder Denny began in 1890 to construct three extensive sections of a rail network north and east from city center. Even when he lost money on these ventures, it seemed not to bother Denny, who, with a net worth of $3 million, was one of the richest men in town. In 1893 he bought out other rail lines to more populated neighborhoods, but the Panic derailed Denny's streetcar empire. It also spelled disaster for his holdings in real estate and a sawmill on Lake Union, the largest of its kind in King County. Three years of litigation and foreclosures followed. Finally, the banking firm of Dexter Horton & Company, where brother Arthur served as senior vice president, fell in with other creditors to force David Denny's bankruptcy.

Land values in Seattle plummeted by as much as 80 percent during the Panic. Fifth Avenue's magnificent Rainier Hotel was shut down (though it would later reopen as an apartment building). The depression caused hundreds of smaller businesses to fail all over King County. It ended dreams of turning Belltown into hot commercial property. It endangered Woodland Park, which had been heavily landscaped and improved by Nova Scotian owner Guy Carleton Phinney. When Phinney died in September 1893, he left maintenance of the property to his beleaguered wife, who was happy to sell out to the city in 1899.

Many people fled town with their last savings in their pockets; some vanished with *other people's* life savings in their pockets. In September 1893, Seattle city treasurer Adolph Krug hopped an early morning train to Canada, taking with him about $225,000 in public funds. At the end of November, the president and cashier of the Buckley State Bank of Tacoma skipped with $30,000.

Tacoma's fate during the Panic was even worse than Seattle's. The Merchants National Bank went into a "temporary suspension" on June 1, 1893, from which it never recovered. Tumbling close behind were the Tacoma National Bank, State Savings, and Traders' Bank. Of 21 banks operating in Tacoma when the Panic began, only four survived the year.

The Tacoma Hotel, an impressive brick building overlooking Commencement Bay, went into the hands of receivers. Designed by renowned New York City architect Stanford White, it sadly would be destroyed in the 1930s. On Cliff Avenue, a chateau-like tourist hotel under construction by the troubled Northern Pacific was abandoned. It later was gutted by flames and then transformed into present-day Stadium High School.

Murray Morgan, in *Puget's Sound: A Narrative of Early Tacoma and the Southern Sound*, recounted the dismal tale of Paul Schulze, a well-educated, German-born manager of the Northern Pacific's Land Division and a heavy stockholder in many of Tacoma's largest enterprises that went bankrupt during the Panic's premiere year:

Schulze's house at 601 North Yakima was mortgaged beyond its worth. He owed thirty-five thousand dollars alimony. His debts exceeded $300,000, not counting the more than a million it was later discovered he had embezzled. His assets were about five thousand.

Schulze solved his problems by withdrawing $35,000 from an account he did not have in San Francisco. After a last spasm of affluence, he returned from [Tacoma's exclusive] University Club to the big house that dominated the double block on Yakima Avenue, dined alone by candlelight, burned his private papers in the kitchen stove, stirring gently, said an ambiguous goodbye to his Chinese cook ("I am going on a long trip"), wrote a letter to his mistress, and shot himself through the temple.

Not even in death could the once-upstanding Schulze find distance from his shame. Although his "last wish was that his ashes be sent to Germany," Morgan explains, "he was buried in Tacoma."

Prodded by President Cleveland, Congress repealed the disastrous Sherman Silver Purchase Act in October 1893, and the Treasury Department subsequently floated four bond issues, collecting enough gold so that government gold payments wouldn't have to be suspended.

But the Pacific Northwest felt the depression's reverberations throughout the 1890s. Declines in the price of silver and elimination of the Sherman Act caused mines to close all over the West. It ended a mining explosion in Washington's Okanogan County, shutting down camps at such places as Ruby, Conconully, and Loup Loup. "Never again," wrote Bruce A. Wilson in the Washington historical magazine *Columbia*, "would mining attract such an influx of people, give birth to towns of consequence, or so dominate the local economy."

Lumber interests were hurt when nervous railroads from the East cut shipments from Washington by a full third. Three-quarters of the shingle plants operating in the state in 1893 were closed two years later. Large lumber concerns, such as Pope & Talbot and the Stimson Mill Company, saw much of their market dry up during the Panic and suffered still more when tariff schedules eased the flow of Canadian lumber into the States.

In Kent, farms continued to be foreclosed upon. Poorhouses throughout western Washington went bankrupt. Many Everett children simply didn't report for school during the mid 1890s, some because they couldn't afford books, others because their schools couldn't afford to stay open. Cash became so precious in Everett that at one point the Merchants' Protective Association actually began publishing the names of people who spent their money in Seattle; the *Everett Times* endorsed running such "traitors" out of town.

Railroads consolidated in the mid '90s, with Hill's Great Northern coming out a winner. After securing majority rights in the Northern Pacific, the Empire Builder in 1900 sold 900,000 acres of NP land-grant timber at $6 an acre to German immigrant Frederick Weyerhaeuser—the largest single timberland transaction up to that time in American history. The sale would become the basis for the Weyerhaeuser Company's broad influence in the 20th century.

President Cleveland's Secret Surgery

President Grover Cleveland, a former mayor of Buffalo and onetime governor of New York, had earned the sobriquet "Grover the Good" for his honesty in office. Yet, in the midst of the depression brought on by the Panic of 1893, he committed an act of deceit for what he believed was the good of the nation—an act that would remain secret for almost a quarter century.

On May 5, 1893—the very day that stocks began plummeting on Wall Street, "Industrial Black Friday"—he detected a quarter-size "rough spot" on the roof of his mouth. A biopsy specimen showed it to be severely cancerous. His close friend Dr. Joseph Bryant, a distinguished New York surgeon, recommended removal. Cleveland acquiesced, but according to Bryant, the president said that he would undergo the surgery only at a time and place that would offer "the best opportunity of avoiding disclosure" and prevent "even a suspicion that anything of significance had happened to him." Cleveland feared the impact on an already beleaguered U.S. economy if he was known to be so ill. He also worried about the consequences of leaving his vice president, Adlai E. Stevenson, a persistent compromiser and acknowledged silver sympathizer (and grandfather of the 1950s presidential candidate), in charge of the nation just as Congress was holding a special session to repeal the notorious Sherman Silver Purchase Act.

So, on June 30, Cleveland—unbeknownst to Stevenson or most other members of his Cabinet—slipped out of the White House and, together with Dr. Bryant and his Secretary of War, Daniel Lamont, took a train for New York

Politicians proclaimed that better times lay ahead, but millions of men who'd been ousted from their jobs by the Panic couldn't see them coming. Thousands left Seattle and Tacoma aboard railroad cars, convinced that conditions couldn't be as bad everywhere. Some had formed grumbling "tramp gangs" that petitioned authorities for food along their eastbound routes and shared what they could get, while others just went it alone.

In the spring of 1894, Jacob S. Coxey, the prosperous owner of quarries and a scrap-iron business in Massillon, Ohio, decided to unify these disgruntled workers behind his own banner. The Ross Perot-like Coxey was something of an economic zealot (he'd named his son Legal Tender).

The Other Great Depression 91

City. There the trio boarded the *Oneida*, a yacht owned by the president's wealthy banker friend, Elias Benedict. The press was kept in the dark about Cleveland's absence from Washington, though it was known that first lady Frances Cleveland and their daughter, Ruth, had gone to Cape Cod for the summer. "Should word of his having left the city get out," Alyn Brodsky wrote in *Grover Cleveland: A Study in Character*, "reporters were to be told he had joined his family for a brief rest."

The next day, the corpulent, 56-year-old Commander-in-Chief was anaesthetized as the *Oneida* pulled out for a leisurely spin around Long Island Sound. Conscious of the scandal that would erupt were the press to discover what was going on aboard the boat, Bryant told its captain, "If you hit a rock, hit it good and hard, so that we'll all go to the bottom." The operation—conducted in a specially prepared surgical theater, with attending physicians all sworn to secrecy—took about an hour. Cleveland's cancerous ulcer and upper left jaw were surgically removed, leaving no external scars to provoke questions later.

After convalescing for a few days, the president reunited with his wife and family at Cape Cod, and not long after that he was fitted with a prosthetic jaw and a rubber plug in the roof of his mouth. The country was told, through the press, that Cleveland had merely been treated for a couple of insignificantly ulcerated teeth. Rumors that something more serious had occurred were officially squelched. Not until 1917 was the true story reported.

At the Panic's peak, he'd petitioned Congress to lend scrip to local communities, which would then be distributed to the unemployed in return for labor on a new interstate highway system and other public works projects. When Capitol Hill turned thumbs down on his proposal, Coxey decided to deliver "a petition with boots on"—a peaceful march on Washington, D.C., that would prove just how serious Americans were about improving their nation's fiscal profile. Seventeen "commonweal armies" of the jobless were organized around the country.

Fifteen hundred displaced laborers from Seattle and Tacoma were reportedly prepared to march in April 1894. Hundreds of them left Seattle on April 28 to meet up with fellow protestors at Puyallup. Deputies were hastily sworn in to maintain peace and to guard railroad property from these Washington "Coxeyites," who said they planned to ride the rails, commandeering trains when money wasn't available. They were encouraged by reports on April 30 that 350 Ohio Commonwealers had reached the outskirts of Washington, D.C., where—led by Coxey's daughter, Mame, dressed as Peace on a white horse—they were ready to approach the Capitol.

Despite cautions from Washington Governor John M. McGraw, saying "I look on this movement as wholly unwise," by early May an organized body of about 250 people left Puyallup aboard freight trains. The rest, reported the *P-I*, "have degenerated into an unorganized body of tramps" traveling eastward by heel and toe. Public sympathies were with the Coxeyites; well wishers brought them food when they stopped in small towns.

Jacob Coxey's bizarre arrest in D.C. on May 1—for walking illegally on tended grass—robbed some steam from the national march. So did a fight between railroading Commonwealers and deputies in North Yakima on May 9, after which 153 alleged free-riders were arrested, 30 of them receiving 60-day sentences at McNeil Island Penitentiary. The sheer distance from Washington state to Washington, D.C., further discouraged Seattle's "Industrial Army." Few Northwest marchers actually reached Pennsylvania Avenue, but one who did was Frank P. "Jumbo" Cantwell. A bouncer and prizefighter, he'd started his cross-country trek with 1,260 men and finished it by helping to draft a "Bill to Provide Work for American Citizens." However, this well-intentioned bit of legislation soon died in Congress.

The populist message to do away with business-as-usual politics was heard, even if all of the populists themselves weren't. In 1895 the Washington Legislature passed the Populist Party's "Barefoot Schoolboy Law," which ended the practice of financing schools locally and guaranteed at least minimum state support for educating all children. A year later, John R. Rogers was elected as the state's first Populist governor, with a new legislature dominated by a fusion of Populists and Democrats. However, writes Richard C. Berner in *Seattle, 1900-1920*, "little of their reformist platform was passed into law. They were unable to create a state railroad commission even though such action occupied the highest place on the Populist agenda . . . In the next decade, Republicans regained control of the state legislature and were able to frustrate Governor Rogers' feeble efforts to establish a railroad commission." Rogers died in 1901, the first year of his second term.

The Panic of '93 induced an unusual alliance of Populist and Prohibitionist forces. In 1892 organized Prohibitionists had run a full campaign ticket in Washington, covering offices from governor on down to state printer. With the Panic, the Populists swallowed up the nascent Prohibition Party, although they didn't pick up their uniting cry. Fearing to offend any potential voters, the Populists didn't launch anti-alcohol legislation. Who knows? If it hadn't been for the '93 Panic, Washington might've adopted Prohibition even earlier than it did. (The Evergreen State finally went "dry" in 1916, four years before passage of the U.S. Constitution's 18th Amendment.)

Seattle's release from the crash came in 1897 with the Klondike gold rush, when Elliott Bay became the frenzied embarkation point for miners headed to the precious-metal bearing rivers of northwest Canada. The city did everything it could to make up for lost time. In 1898 the business community collected $100,000 to support Moran Brothers Shipyards, so that the shipbuilding firm could win a contract to build the U.S. Navy battleship *Nebraska*. City engineer Reginald H. Thomson began an aggressive regrading project that eventually leveled 94 acres of downtown land for construction. Seattle's biggest boom would follow its biggest bust, lasting until about 1910.

National journalist Ray Stannard Baker well understood the city's Panic-driven determination when he wrote in 1903, a decade after the depression began, that "In Seattle, everything seems to have happened in the last 10 years."

A case could be made that the Seattle region resented the balance of the country for stumbling economically just when the Pacific Northwest was getting used to walking—and ever since it has been bolder, more self-sufficient, and more liberal. Manifestations of this could be found not only in capital-intensive development, but also in Washington's passage of women's suffrage in 1910, a decade ahead of most other states.

Many lessons were *not* learned in that first great depression, however, particularly about the perils of being overly dependent on natural resources and distant markets. The Northwest did, however, learn a big lesson in politics, setting the foundations for a progressive tradition that endures to this day. But for the privations and passions of the 1890s, the Pacific Northwest might not be so progressive as it is now.

(OUNT OF YARROW POINT

"[Hunt's] adventures would fill a book."—Bill Speidel, *The Wet Side of the Mountains* (1974)

"I would be much happier if my life remains a closed book."—Leigh S.J. Hunt, 1905

READERS OF THE *Seattle Post-Intelligencer* on June 1, 1888, could have been forgiven for thinking that the storied Second Coming had happened while they slept—or, perhaps, that Ponce de Leon's fountain of youth had finally been uncovered in Florida and its waters were being bottled for quick shipment to the West.

"GOOD NEWS," the paper trumpeted, and it followed that headline with no fewer than 14 double-deck subheads and an article consuming all five news-columns on the front page. This concentration of coverage was almost unheard of locally. But then, it wasn't every day that a frontier broadsheet, and in particular its brash and ambitious young owner, could take so much credit for influencing the future of the region.

"It is with pleasure," the report began, "that the *Post-Intelligencer* makes the positive announcement this morning that Mr. Peter Kirk, of the Moss Bay Iron and Steel Company of Cumberland, England, has selected a site on Lake Washington near this city for the location of extensive iron and steel works." The paper explained that this was only the beginning of Eastside development, that a new town surrounding the works—inevitably christened "Kirkland"—would soon rise, bringing more Americans to Washington Territory. And it predicted giddily that, with the foundry in operation producing steel for shipment to South American and other Pacific markets, and with the other heavy industries it would inevitably attract to Puget Sound, Seattle "could not well help being a second Pittsburg [sic]."

Kirk had been touring the western United States for most of two years, and, until just before this announcement, Tacoma had counted on the English industrialist setting up shop on Commencement Bay. Thus, part of the *P-I*'s "pleasure" in Kirk's decision derived from a sense of revenge—justice's scales were being rebalanced 15 years after the Northern Pacific Railroad had chosen the City of Destiny instead of Seattle as its western terminus.

But the paper also had its own reasons to celebrate. For months, its publisher had waged a propaganda campaign to convince Kirk that the keys to success awaited him on Lake Washington's northeast shore. The *P-I*'s optimism was singularly resilient. Even as the mill owner was debating his possibilities at Tacoma, the *P-I* announced prematurely in March 1887 that Kirk had investigated "inexhaustible" iron deposits found recently in the Cascade Range near Snoqualmie Pass and "would erect in the heart of King County large Bessemer steel works similar to the works partly owned by him in England." It was this very sort of impudence that lately had helped raise the *P-I* from struggling obscurity to becoming "the leading paper of the gestating State," as it was described by an 1890 city guide.

Nowhere in all of this "good news" was any responsibility for Kirk's decision attributed to the activist at the helm of the *Post-Intelligencer*, Leigh S.J. Hunt. Nowhere was it mentioned that the publisher maintained a mansion on Yarrow Point within reach of Kirk's mill site, or that he was planning on becoming the largest single landowner on the Eastside, which would pay off handsomely if Kirkland and its foundry prospered. However, anyone who was savvy to the mill negotiations of 1888 couldn't have failed to recognize Hunt in a quote from Peter Kirk himself. After reiterating his faith in the Eastside, Kirk told a *P-I* reporter, "I might add that the advantages of this situation have been industriously kept before me by one of your citizens during the past six months."

This wasn't the first time, nor would it be the last in his long, sometimes troubled life, that Hunt sought to twist arms and grease the wheels of commerce or politics to win his way. From his early days as a newspaper mogul and Republican Party boss in Seattle, through his gray years as a real-estate baron in Las Vegas, Hunt was recognized as an energetic opportunist and large-scale visionary—an empire builder whose peripatetic pursuit of challenges was barely interrupted by obstacles that might have broken the confidence of lesser men.

His resume would've made any would-be world-beater envious, as it included not only his Seattle career, but also his roles as a college president in Iowa, a gold-mine operator in Korea, a cotton magnate in the Sudan, and a counselor on Asian affairs to President Theodore Roosevelt. Hunt even inadvertently helped spark off the Russo-Japanese War of 1904–5.

Hunt's exploits were so remarkable, and his impact on the Eastside and Seattle so great, that it's odd his name should be absent from most local histories and that the only Eastside testimonial to his passing is Hunts Point, a lightly-developed peninsula on which he never lived.

Perhaps we can attribute these slights, in part, to the mixed reviews that Hunt received in life. On the one hand, his speculative instincts and his persuasive powers often awed observers. "He was a sphinx," longtime Seattle newsman C.T. Conover wrote of Kirkland's founder in the 1920s, "but [he] had an uncanny power over men and women and could get their financial support on any project he chose to pursue."

He could be ruthless, too. The evening *Seattle Press*, which clashed so often with the *P-I* over political issues that it was easy to forget they were both GOP organs, once remarked that "while Colonel Hunt"—as the *Press* had derisively nicknamed him—"is tall and divinely fair, he is . . . 'devilish sly' and keeps as many cold decks up his sleeve as Bret Harte's heathen Chinee."

Hunt, leaping from one enterprise to another and one nation to the next, his fortunes rising and falling all the way, was never an easy person to figure out. Perhaps the best assessment comes from Laurance B. Rand, a history teacher in Kent, Connecticut, who also happened to be Hunt's great-grandson and biographer. "He was a genuine frontiersman, always ready to take the risk and lead the way, but bored by the notion of mere proprietorship," Rand explained. Hunt wanted adventure, the thrill of the chase, the ultimate gamble. Easy success was anathema to him. As Hunt himself wrote to a Seattle friend in 1901, "ordinary business does not interest me."

Most of all, what the self-styled Count of Yarrow Point wanted was to leave behind some commercial legacy, something by which he'd be remembered. That was the good news that Leigh S.J. Hunt most desired—good news that he never received.

Photographs of Hunt in his prime are rare, and there are even fewer detailed descriptions of the man. But the old *New York Press* captured him well in a brief profile from 1891 near the upswing of his power curve, and at the height of his Eastside imperium—"He is nearly six feet in height, with a face as absolutely destitute of whiskers and as youthful in appearance as usually seen on a boy of 15. It does not thereby lack masculinity, but has lines that show decision of character and executive force. Heavy hair of jet black crowns Mr. Hunt's head, and is usually topped by a small, narrow-brimmed felt hat, with low crown and slouchy tilt."

He favored bow ties and double-breasted jackets, and was almost as economical with words as he was with drink. He had blue eyes. He carried a gold repeater pocket watch. C.T. Conover, who worked for him at the *P-I*, called him "self-contained" and "taciturn." For a man who performed on such a public stage, Hunt was ardently protective of his privacy. Informed in 1904 that he was being considered for the U.S. vice presidency under Roosevelt, he said he "hated" the notion of elective office and would prefer to influence from behind the scenes, thank you very much.

He would've hated this story, too. He spurned all biographers. As the Count of Yarrow Point remarked late in life, he didn't believe in "the idea of passing in the market of men for more than my face value . . . I was born into a world with an ambition that can never be realized because of my deficient training [and] lack of ability, so why add to my sorrow by playing upon my vanity?"

False modesty? Perhaps. But Hunt was reared with a Calvinist work ethic that didn't allow for extraordinary attempts to pat himself on the back. He was born on a farm just outside of Columbia City in northeast Indiana. His Episcopalian father, Franklin Hunt, and Ohio-born mother, Martha Long, reared a dozen children—six sons and an equal number of daughters. Most of these offspring never escaped Indiana. But the oldest son, born on August 11, 1855, and christened Smith James Hunt (only later would he adopt the prefix "Leigh," believing he was a relative of the famous 19th-century British poet, Leigh Hunt), was in the business of escape at a tender age. He read voraciously and dreamed of great adventures, his imagination fueled by his own father's stories of gold seeking in California and Brazil.

Hunt loved learning, and by his high school years in Columbia City had decided to become a teacher. But he was far too impatient to confront the hoops of higher education. (The only varsity sheepskin he ever received was an honorary master's degree from Vermont's Middlebury College; this he won in 1884 apparently on the strength of an influential friend's recommendation.) That impatience, however, didn't hurt his career plans. Smith Hunt easily passed an Indiana teacher's license test in 1872 and, at the age of 17, accepted his first posting at a primary school in Larwill, Indiana, about six miles west of Columbia City.

His ascent through academia was meteoric. By 1874 he was principal of Columbia City High School, and just four years later he convinced the school board at Mount Pleasant, Iowa, to let him fill a higher-paying teacher's slot there, even though he lacked one crucial qualification for the job—he could neither speak nor write a foreign language. After six months, Hunt became principal of all Mount Pleasant schools and was developing a reputation for innovation. He created a quarterly newspaper for the town (edited by teachers and students) and arranged for each of his pupils to open an account with a local bank, a program that drew widespread support.

"Leigh" Hunt, as he had taken to signing his letters in Mount Pleasant, attracted as much attention from movers and shakers as he did among educators. The burghers of Columbia City had indoctrinated him into Republican politics (no easy task in the wake of Ulysses S. Grant's scandal-ravaged presidency), and it was also through them that he made his first investment, in a typewriter company. Unfortunately, that concern went belly up, sucking away all of Hunt's money, as well as $2,000 he had borrowed. This was a hard but valuable lesson. Hunt paid back all of his creditors when he took the Mount Pleasant position—but never again was he afraid to gamble with "other" people's money.

Perhaps Hunt's most significant and longest-lasting contact was with the powerful, Republican owner-editor of the *Des Moines Register*, James S. Clarkson. It was with Clarkson's muscle behind him that, in 1885, 29-year-old Leigh Hunt was named as president of Iowa Agricultural College (now Iowa State University), a promotion that ultimately would convince him that his future lay outside the orbit of education.

The college had been created in 1869 to provide instruction in botany, horticulture, and the veterinary arts. By the time Hunt arrived on the 900-acre campus in the tiny town of Ames, the college had already chewed up its first two presidents—victims of internal disagreements over whether the school should emphasize the pure as well as the practical sciences. Hunt tried quickly to mollify anxious students with concerts and improved meal services, and he won extraordinary powers from the Board of Trustees, which allowed him to issue strict new rules of student behavior without lengthy faculty debate. At least initially, these measures brought peace to the campus.

In the brief calm that followed, Hunt met a former Iowa Agricultural College student named Jessie Noble, the 24-year-old daughter of a leading Des Moines barbed-wire manufacturer, Henry Augustus Noble. Five feet tall, with long, dark locks and flashing brown eyes, "Jessie had all the attributes a young college president could wish for," historian Laurance Rand writes in *High Stakes: The Life and Times of Leigh S.J. Hunt.* "She was well-bred, well-read, intelligent, and exemplary in the social graces." The pair married on June 25, 1885.

Only weeks later, another storm hit the campus when a prankish break-in at a faculty member's quarters forced Hunt to expel the two students allegedly involved. This ignited protest and a flurry of petitions, insisting on the students' reinstatement. Hunt, brandishing his rules of conduct, would have none of it. But both professors and alumni had lost faith in their young administrator.

As Iowa State University records explain it today, Hunt's "lack of formal training and his dictatorial methods led to clashes with the faculty and students, and his resignation after 18 months in office." Leigh Hunt put a slightly gentler spin on his departure (he actually cited ill health as his reason for resigning), but he too looked forward to leaving the college— leaving it far behind, in fact. As he wrote to Clarkson, "We have decided to move to the Pacific slope as soon as I can honorably leave here."

In 1894, *Harper's Magazine* named the *Seattle Post-Intelligencer* "one of the four great newspapers on the West Coast." This was a significant leap from the *P-I*'s messy country journal days of only a dozen years before. To the surprise of nearly everybody conversant in the paper's transformation, much of the credit for its flowering lay with Leigh Hunt.

Not bad for a guy whose only previous practical links with newspapering had been the establishment of that quarterly digest back in Iowa.

Of course, when the former college president arrived in Seattle in November 1886—a full three years before Washington statehood—nobody knew the full extent of his background. And he wasn't fool enough to tip his hand. Brimming with hubris, Hunt made it clear that he had access to deep pockets in the Midwest and was prepared to funnel that money into a start-up daily if owners of the *P-I* wouldn't sell their own paper to him. The con worked, mostly because the syndicate that then owned the *P-I* didn't have much background in the business either.

Hunt reportedly paid $17,500 for the newspaper, and then set about remaking it as a major metropolitan tribune. He acquired an Associated Press franchise for better access to worldwide news; raised salaries to improve employee performance, and raided the more well-thought-of Portland *Oregonian* for men who could sharpen the *P-I*'s look and contents. Having watched James Clarkson as he wielded the might of the *Des Moines Register* to change history in Iowa's capital, Hunt made the *P-I* into his own bully pulpit. He championed Seattle as a railway terminus (after the Northern Pacific debacle, James J. Hill's Great Northern finally would be coaxed into the city in 1893). He encouraged development of Seattle's Volunteer Park. And, he set about shoring up the Republican faithful, who were discouraged by their party's recent association with anti-Chinese extremists and by the election, in 1884, of Democrat Grover Cleveland to the White House.

Hunt could be brutal in his editorial attacks, particularly against women's suffrage. The 1883 Washington Territorial Legislature actually had allowed women the right to vote, but Hunt believed, "the ideal woman is the woman whose first interest is her home and who, after that, devotes her time to the church and the amelioration of the condition of her brother man and sister woman." Hunt portrayed female enfranchisement as a Democratic plot endangering Washington's acceptance into the Union, and he cheered when the Territorial Supreme Court finally curtailed women's voting in 1888. It was thanks in part to Leigh Hunt that Washington women weren't allowed to cast ballots again until 1910.

But Hunt was a promoter at heart, not a newspaperman. He butted heads with recalcitrant editors and fired people who didn't want to toe his political line. Following a nervous breakdown brought on in 1887 by chronically poor health (he suffered particularly from kidney problems) as well as the pressures of recrafting the *P-I* as his media surrogate, Hunt finally decided to relinquish day-to-day management of the paper. He would concentrate instead on politics, real estate, the luring of industry to Seattle, and the building of a summer home on the then-remote Eastside, someplace where he could entertain the potentates who would help him realize his dreams.

Hunt lived in several homes during his Puget Sound years. These included a two-story townhouse at the corner of 4th Avenue and Columbia Street in Seattle, from which the *P-I* was published for a while after the 1889 Great Fire decimated Pioneer Square and consumed the newspaper's ornate headquarters.

But none of the other homes compared with the 14-room estate that he and Jessie built at the tip of Yarrow Point. It may have been the Eastside's loveliest home in its era, with almost-wraparound decks on two stories, a pair of chimneys, and plenty of windows to catch the evening light. Hoping not only to enhance his immediate surroundings, but also to interest other capitalists in Eastside retreats, Hunt planted cherry trees next to strawberry beds he found on the property. He added lawns, rare flowers, and bamboo, along with a fountain that lent his private Xanadu a Continental flair. He tapped a natural spring to the east at Houghton (still very much in use by Point residents). He cleared a park-like setting around the manse and stocked the grounds with deer—animals to delight his new son, Henry, born in October 1886.

The whole scene was bucolic, poetic. So it was fitting that Hunt, a lover of English verse, should have named this peninsula "Yarrow," in honor of two inspiring poems by William Wordsworth that dwell upon the wonders of Scotland's Yarrow River.

It's less appropriate that the peninsula immediately to the west of Yarrow—once known as Long Point—should today be called Hunts Point. After all, the entrepreneur's only connection to it is that he once bought 10 acres there and cleared evergreens, so that his view west from the mansion toward the Olympic Mountains would be unobstructed.

Hunt had his fingers in so many pies that it's difficult to follow the prints. With his Seattle attorneys and a pair of wealthy San Franciscans, he formed a company to buy, grade, and then sell land in suburban West Seattle. In 1890 he formed a syndicate to assume control of the Yesler Way cable car line, which ran eastward from Pioneer Square to Lake Washington and was a vital link in transportation to the Eastside. At the railway's ferry terminus, he created a park, which directors named in honor of a famous local Indian chief, Leschi.

Then there were Leigh Hunt's political manipulations. "Ward by ward," Rand writes, "Hunt and his partners built a powerful Republican machine in King County. Hunt used the pages of his newspaper to support Republicans and attack Democrats on local and national levels." In 1888 he went a step further, deliberately undermining one GOP congressional candidate from Washington in order to send someone he preferred to the nation's capital. Hunt's man won and reportedly was beholden to the *P-I* in the future, but some of Hunt's fellow Republicans worried that Hunt had finally become too independent and powerful for their own good. They were sure of it when, just after Washington won statehood in November 1889, Hunt stooped to mudslinging in hopes of defeating former Territorial Governor Elisha P. Ferry, another Republican, as the first state governor (the *P-I* hinted that Ferry had ducked service in the Civil War). When the *Seattle Press* complained of Hunt's czarlike tactics, Hunt and associate William E. Bailey (after whom Bailey Peninsula, now Seward Park, was named) bought the *Press*. Ferry won, anyway.

Much of Hunt's attention during the late 1880s and early 1890s, though, was directed at Kirkland. By 1891 the village had been platted, brick buildings were rising, and, as the *P-I* enthused, "a large foundry, machine shop, blacksmith shop, and pattern shop are in course of erection, and a sawmill is in operation."

Hunt had cast a wide net for project stockholders, reeling in $750,000 to $1 million from a who's who of the American rich that included Boston millionaire banker Joshua Sears, Senator Jacob Sloat Fassett of New York, former Michigan Governor Russell A. Alger, and Jacob Furth, the politically potent president of the local area's Puget Sound Bank. Hunt also incorporated a land-development business that controlled at least 2,000 acres in and around Kirkland. His father-in-law, Henry Noble, had forsaken his Midwest barbed-wire empire to come west as president of this new Kirkland Land & Improvement Company. "There are fortunes to be made here in real estate," Hunt wrote to his mentor, Clarkson—and Clarkson, too, bought into his dream.

But a dream is all it turned out to be.

The first trouble came in transporting Snoqualmie Pass iron ore to Kirkland. There was no railroad, and Hunt couldn't get one built fast enough to meet his ambitious timetable for the mill's opening. There also was the inconvenience of moving finished Kirkland steel over to Puget Sound ports. In the absence of a canal linking Lake Washington to the Sound—Congress wouldn't fund such a waterway until the 20th century—the cost of rail shipment west would increase the steel's expense and limit its salability.

Meanwhile, Leigh Hunt's imagination was stretching his pocketbook painfully thin. In 1891, together with Judge Hiram G. Bond, a national figure who'd made his money in Alabama coal and iron, Hunt bought a quarter share in the newly discovered Monte Cristo mines located northeast of Kirkland amidst the wild peaks of Snohomish County. They paid $25,000 and considered it a bargain. As the *Everett Herald* enthused, "Over in the Cascades, not more than fifty miles from Everett, are more minerals within a radius of ten miles than another place the world can show… The mines contain everything—gold, silver, copper, lead, iron, and in plenty."

After tapping no less than the sultan of Standard Oil, John D. Rockefeller, for money to build a rail line from Everett to Monte Cristo, Hunt—rosy-eyed as ever—predicted in the *P-I* that, by the start of 1894, "the surrounding cliffs will echo day and night with explosions in the deep tunnels on every side."

He just hadn't reckoned with the Panic of 1893. On May 4 of that year, about a month before the birth of Hunt's second child (a daughter named Helen), the National Cordage Company failed, setting off a Wall Street selling spree and bringing construction projects to a halt all across the country, and inciting Seattleites as well as other Americans to withdraw their savings from banks. Hunt, who had balanced so much of his duchy on credit, now found credit impossible to procure. Investment funds for the Monte Cristo project dried up and Hunt had no way to retrieve his money from the venture.

The depression had an equally disastrous effect on the Kirkland foundry. It never did receive the ore it needed. Furthermore, Russell Alger defaulted on his $20,000 subscription, inciting other shareholders to withhold payments. Even Jacob Furth, whom Hunt had considered a friend as well as a business associate, now turned on the publisher and demanded repayment of a $10,818 loan his bank had made to the project—"an act Hunt considered a 'betrayal' and for which he never forgave Furth," Rand explains.

Hunt tried desperately to shed his extensive real-estate holdings, but during the Panic they brought only cents on the dollar. In June 1894, he sold his interest in the *Post-Intelligencer* for $30,000, all of which went toward paying his debts—and he *still* owed money. Some of his other deep investments were a complete loss.

"A millionaire in February 1893," Rand concludes in *High Stakes*, "Hunt was a debtor one year later."

Imagine you're 39 years old. You've yanked some heavy-duty political strings in your time, run a daily newspaper, and toured with a U.S. president—Benjamin Harrison in 1891 as he visited the Pacific Northwest. But now you're flat broke and your father-in-law has to care for your young family while you hunt up your next million doing...*what?*

Leigh S.J. Hunt, however, wasted no time in getting started on the rest of his life. In December 1894, he set sail for Nagasaki, Japan, armed with venture capital that he'd managed to wring from his past supporters in New York, promising to return when he could settle up with his creditors. He was full of bright ideas...about maybe controlling West Coast flour distribution to Japan...about undercutting the trade in nails from Europe with shipments from Seattle instead...about creating a proper streetcar system for Shanghai, China. But none of these bore fruit.

It wasn't until 1896, when debts were again tightening their grip about his neck, that Hunt's self-confidence was rewarded. On April 12, he arrived in the Korean capital of Seoul intent on negotiating a 25-year operating lease on royal gold mines in northern Korea.

He couldn't have been on more unfamiliar ground than he was in Korea. This "Hermit Kingdom"—isolated for centuries, surrounded by hostile Chinese and rapacious Russians, and watched warily by the Japanese (who still hadn't forgotten Kublai Khan's 13th-century assault from Korea on their islands)—had been independent only since 1895 and the end of the Sino-Japanese War. But Korea's king, Kojong, the latest in a line of Yi Dynasty monarchs stretching back to the 14th century, was intent on modernizing his country and he saw foreign investment as an important means toward that end. Thanks to his contacts with American officials in Seoul, Hunt had the opportunity to secure management control over 600 acres of mines in Unsan Province. It was adventure and financial risk on a larger scale than anything he'd tried before. But it didn't seem to scare him. Neither, surprisingly, did it scare off some of the same people who'd previously lost money at Kirkland. Hunt had little difficulty in drumming up the $100,000 in collateral that Kojong requested.

There were greater challenges in inspecting his new holdings. Facing jungles filled with tigers, duplicitous engineers, and his own kidney ailments, Hunt admitted in a letter home that were it not for his pride and obstinacy he would, "give up the unequal fight, return to America, gather my loved ones…and in a humble way set about earning their bread." It would be years before Hunt felt conditions were safe enough to bring his wife, Jessie, and their children to Asia. Even then, on her first trip into the Korean mining country, Jessie had to dress up in male attire just to save herself from ambush.

But the results of Hunt's undertaking merited the risk. By 1901 his Oriental Consolidated Mining Company had found firm footing in Korea, and big wheels such as newspaper tycoon William Randolph Hearst were aching for a cut of the action. After a 10-day inspection of the gold works in 1901, an independent engineer estimated their worth at between $15 million and $30 million. "My only regret," wrote the engineer, "is that I am not a stockholder in this most successful and valuable mining company."

Hunt had other matters than just Southeast Asia on his mind. He hadn't been back to Puget Sound in seven years, and now that he'd built another fortune—proving that he had intelligence in addition to luck—it was high time to settle some old scores.

The Seattle financiers who received Hunt's invitation to dinner in March 1901 didn't know what to expect. All of them had loaned Hunt money or extended him credit before the Panic, and all had been left unpaid when Hunt lost his shirt. Thus, they knew what a salesman he could be. But what could he want from them now that his stature had risen again so greatly?

When they arrived at the five-story Butler Hotel, then the city's premier hostelry on the northeast corner of 2nd Avenue and James Street, they were escorted to a reserved room where they found assigned seats at a long table. The Kingpin of Korea, the former Count of Yarrow Point, was in a particularly convivial temper. With wine poured all around, he rose to thank his companions for their contributions to Seattle in his absence and to apologize to them for defaulting on their trust when he sailed off to the Orient. He hadn't forgotten their loyalty, he added. Then he asked them to look under their dinner plates where he had secreted personal checks, made out for whatever amount of money each guest had lost through his ventures or advice, plus 7 percent compound interest. Between the paybacks and the food, that night cost Leigh Hunt $200,000.

It seems that only one creditor conspicuously had *not* been invited to the Butler that evening—Jacob Furth. Hunt never did get over his grudge against the banker for calling in his Kirkland loan during the Panic.

The capitalist seemed at the top of his game. And yet, Hunt's health was failing—his kidney ailment now was compounded by a bladder infection. Doctors told him to slow down, maybe take two or three years off, go soak at the famous sulphur springs in Carlsbad, Germany. He had no time for such indulgences, however. His empire was threatened.

In 1896 Russia had negotiated rights to construct a branch line from the Trans-Siberian Railroad through Manchuria, a northeastern province of China bordering Korea at the Yalu River. As the years passed, though, and as St. Petersburg became interested not only in trains, but also in Korean timber, both China and Japan developed fears of Russian influence in the area. Diplomatic entreaties were made to Czar Nicholas II asking that Russian troops be withdrawn from Manchuria, and Nicholas had signaled his willingness to go along.

But then a Russian Secret Service officer met with Leigh Hunt in the fall of 1902, asking about timber speculations along the Yalu and suggesting that Hunt might like to be involved. The American bluntly refused, writes Rand, by saying "the timber was there, the river was there, but both were for the moment subject to no law." Therefore, business in the province was too risky, even for Leigh Hunt. He couldn't have foreseen the calamity to which his words contributed. By the end of the year, Russian troops had marched across the Yalu in hopes of finally bringing some law to the area—their own—and the Russo-Japanese War was in full steam by 1904.

Hunt had been smart enough to leave Asia by this time. He was in Africa chasing a new dream, this one based on a 1902 report by the British counsel general in Egypt, Lord Cromer, who had speculated that cotton might provide a fine investment opportunity in the still-undeveloped Sudan. Hunt agreed, but he was worried by one point—how would he find enough willing laborers to prepare the Nile's banks for cotton cultivation? His answer came from Booker T. Washington, founder of the Tuskegee Institute, an Alabama agricultural college for African Americans. Washington agreed to provide Hunt with some of his graduates as Sudanese colonists.

What Hunt envisioned was very different from the outlandish and offensive "repatriation" schemes that previously had been proposed by American racists. Hunt was looking for men who wanted to take a chance on a new life. He saw black Americans, still suffering from prejudice and inferior working conditions in their own country, as potentially eager to establish themselves in economic enterprises beyond U.S. borders. In the Sudan, Hunt explained to newspaper reporters, these African Americans would "serve as model farmers, to train the natives and teach them how to make the best use of these lands."

Some of his old supporters called the Sudan scheme "Hunt's Folly," yet the Tuskegee grads worked well with their Sudanese helpers on a new plantation and readied the first crop. Hunt was proud of these men and spoke highly of them to President Theodore Roosevelt, with whom he'd become friendly in 1901 and had provided advice regarding Korean hostilities. (Hunt also told stories about African wildlife; in 1910, after Roosevelt no longer was ensconced in the White House, the adventurous former president set off on an expedition to see the giraffes, lions, and waterbucks for himself.) Unfortunately, floods, locusts, and white ants quelled Hunt's enthusiasm for the Sudan project, and in 1907 the Tuskegee men packed up and left. Not many years after Hunt had abandoned these lands, however, the Nile became a major region for growing cotton and other crops.

Although his enthusiasm for adventure and business might never have been stronger, Hunt was growing weaker. A kidney had to be removed, reminding him of his own mortality, as did the loss of friends to age— James Clarkson in 1918, and Roosevelt a year later. By 1920, Hunt figured he had only "one good punch left." The question was where to focus his last energy.

This was when he and Jessie moved to Las Vegas, Nevada, partly for their health—the dry air would've gone for a pretty penny if only it could've been sold by prescription. But Hunt also was convinced that with a new dam being planned on the mighty Colorado River (today's Hoover Dam), local real-estate prices would skyrocket. Longtime Las Vegas residents called him "stark raving mad," according to *High Stakes*. Yet, more than two decades before Vegas was "discovered" by mobsters like Benjamin "Bugsy" Siegel and started to take off as a gambling mecca, Kirkland's father purchased hundreds of acres on the cheap and began raising funds to build a grand resort hotel about a mile southeast of downtown. Reviving his interest in gold mines, he also invested in new mineral claims at Eldorado Canyon, 30 miles south of Las Vegas.

Hunt turned 78 in 1933, a somewhat drawn, much grayer version of the man he'd once been. Four decades had passed since he'd first sought to prove himself as an entrepreneur in buying up the *Post-Intelligencer*. In the intervening years, he'd had more than his share of ups and downs, and now it looked as if he might be on his way up again. But then, on October 5, 1933, he began breathing heavily while climbing the stairs to his office. Shortly after reaching a hospital, Leigh Smith James Hunt was dead from a heart attack.

Almost nothing survives to remind us of the former Count of Yarrow Point. His ashes were cast into Lake Mead, that tremendous expanse of water created by Hoover Dam. His mansion still stands on Yarrow Point at 4654 95th Street, but it was remodeled in 1938 and is nearly unrecognizable. Kirkland remains, of course, but almost nobody acknowledges its true parentage. Of the Butler Hotel, setting of Hunt's score-settling dinner, only the ground floor remains—now the base of a modern parking garage. Hunt's wife and son are long gone, but his daughter, Helen, resided in a Massachusetts nursing home until 1996, when she died at the age of 102.

Leigh Hunt was the product of a unique time when America was still growing at a rapid clip and nothing seemed impossible. The men and women who make up today's roster of the fiscally powerful may be wealthier than Hunt ever imagined, but few equal his optimistic and wide-ranging entrepreneurial spirit, as well as his brash determination to succeed at any enterprise. Hunt could be foolish and mean-spirited, especially when it came to politics, but many of his ventures—whether creating Kirkland, building up Las Vegas, or establishing African-American agricultural enterprises in growing East Africa—seemed conceived not only to enrich himself personally, but also to pave the way to a brighter future for others.

You'd think after all of this that Kirkland would champion its former resident in some way. But there's not a statue, not a park, not a school, not even a plaque to acknowledge Hunt or his extraordinary vision when he looked out over that town site and saw more than just strawberry fields and tapering beaches. Leigh Hunt's wish was fulfilled—the book of his life has been closed.

Almost completely.

Citizen Blethen

Popular historian Murray Morgan, describing early *Seattle Times* editor and publisher Alden J. Blethen, said he "may have been the most brilliant newspaperman ever to operate in Seattle, and he certainly was the most controversial. Few Seattle citizens found it possible to be non-partisan about him; he himself was one of the least non-partisan men who ever lived. It is quite possible that, as his enemies claimed, people bought the *Times* because they wanted to see 'what the big-headed bastard is up to now'; but they bought more copies of his paper than they did of any other."

In our modern age, when editors rarely distinguish themselves from their publications, Blethen's celebrity seems peculiar. But this is hardly all that makes him memorable. He also was a politically ambitious, rabidly egotistical, and often choleric gent who tethered his fortune to young Seattle and wound up creating one of the West's foremost newspapers. More than a century after he assumed command of the *Times*, this daily continues to prosper under the control and majority ownership of Blethen's descendents. Not a bad legacy for a guy who once thought himself a failure at the newspaper game.

Alden Joseph Blethen was born into a family of six children in Waldo County, Maine, on December 27, 1845. His father, also named Alden, was a respected dairy farmer, carpenter, and justice of the peace who died before Alden Jr. could even celebrate his third birthday. The boy's mother, unable to run the family farm on her own, disappeared in 1850, leaving her children behind. Alden grew up a pauper. He was taken in by a farmer who worked him hard, and he finally ran away at age 13 or 14 to live with his mother, who had remarried.

Blethen figured on a career in education or, better yet, the law. "In the good old state of Maine," he would later reminisce, "the lawyer was the man who did things." So while other teenage males in the 1860s took up arms in America's Civil War, Blethen returned to school, subsequently clerked at a Portland, Maine, law office, married, and, after serving for a spell as a school principal, passed the bar in 1873. He moved back to Portland, hung out his attorney's shingle, and seemed bound for renown in law or politics or, perhaps, both. However, in 1880 Blethen was sidetracked. Packing his family off to Kansas City, Missouri, he became business manager of the *Kansas City Journal.*

The *Journal* revealed to Blethen the power of the press. With his encouragement, the newspaper launched a vendetta against outlaw Jesse James, which provoked James at one point to confront Blethen on a Kansas City street. This increased circulation substantially, helping the future editor to build his first fortune. That money quickly evaporated, though, after Blethen relocated to Minneapolis and made a series of losing investments in newspapers, banks, and real estate.

Dejected but still ambitious, Blethen moved to Seattle in 1896, just before the Klondike gold rush brought tremendous prosperity to the place. He used his remaining wealth to buy what his younger son, Clarance, described as "the decrepit little…(*Seattle*) *Times*," an evening paper —combining two older broadsheets, the *Press* and the *Times*—that was much over-shadowed by the morning Republican daily, the *Seattle Post-Intelligencer*. Within six months, Blethen had put his gazette on a firmer financial footing, with both its circulation and advertising sales on the upswing. Yet, he was not one to succeed quietly. A great admirer of outspoken *New York Journal* publisher William

Randolph Hearst, Blethen sought to make the *Seattle Times* his personal bully pulpit.

He carried on long-running feuds with other men who pro-posed to shape maturing Seattle to their own standards. He alleged in front-page "exposés" that Reginald H. Thomson, the city engineer who regraded Seattle for easier development, was arrogant and incompetent. Although he'd initially supported the civic-betterment crusades of Reverend Mark Matthews, a Tennesseean who had become pastor of the city's First Presbyterian Church in 1902, Blethen turned against Matthews after the minister tried to implicate the publisher in a conspiracy to protect illegal local gambling, prostitution, and liquor sales. In 1911, the *Times* devoted two full pages to portraying Matthews as a city "boss," denouncing him for his "over-weening political ambition—an ambition sure to lay him stark and cold and with all the stab wounds of popular disfavor."

The bombastic Blethen was especially vigorous in attacking rival newspapers and their editors. He derided Erastus Brainerd, who had edited the *Press-Times* before Blethen bought it and who then was the editor of the *Seattle Post-Intelligencer*, as a "crooked and crack-brained whelp." Returning the salvo, the more erudite Brainerd blistered his cross-town competitor as "dastardly and desperate...with only the rancid remains of a foul character,...a social pariah and outcast." This war of invective grew so heated that both editors eventually had to apologize to their readers.

Abandoning a youthful allegiance to the Republican Party, and hoping to further distinguish his paper from the *P-I*, Blethen gained a following for his crusades against Seattle's graft-ridden GOP establishment. He also was applauded for his civic boosterism, which the *Times* rarely failed to publicize. "If Alden Blethen ever does an action worthy of praise that he does not air in his paper," joked Harry Chadwick, editor of the *Seattle Argus*, "it must be when he is asleep."

But the lawyer-turned-editor "did not always use good judgment in the men and causes he chose to support or oppose," remarked Sharon A. Boswell and Lorraine McConaghy in their biography, *Raise Hell and Sell Newspapers: Alden J. Blethen & The Seattle Times*. "Colonel" Blethen, as he had taken to styling himself by the early 20th century (despite an obvious lack of military background), came under concerted assault for opposing anti-vice campaigns, cozying up too closely to James J. Hill and the powerful Great Northern Railway, and carrying on friendships with public figures who turned out to be thieves. More than once, the *Times* offices burned under suspicious circumstances.

Determined and opportunistic, daring yet practical, Alden Blethen wasn't so very different from the city he watched develop around him during his two decades as editor of the *Seattle Times*. By the time of his death in 1915 at age 69, Seattle had proved itself better than its failures and so had the Colonel. As a friend said by way of eulogy: "[Blethen's] life story might be used as a text for a sermon to the fainthearted of the world." The "big-headed bastard" may not always have been right, but he'd always been interesting.

(ITY OF GOLD

"Seemingly all men are liars in this town of Seattle."

THE WORDS ARE THOSE OF Alfred G. McMichael, a 40-year-old photographer from Detroit, Michigan. In the spring of 1898, he was trying to book passage by ship north from Puget Sound to Alaska and the trails leading from there to Canada's Klondike gold country—only to be frustrated and angered when vessels didn't leave Seattle according to schedule, or failed to depart at all.

But McMichael wasn't alone in his poor opinion of the town and its populace. In fact, he was downright generous compared to how some other visitors in the late 1890s viewed Seattle—the self-proclaimed "gateway to Alaska and the Klondike."

"During the gold rush [Seattle] was more wicked than Sodom; the devil reigned supreme," opined Arthur Arnold Dietz, an abstemious physical education instructor from New York City whose 1914 book, *Mad Rush for Gold in Frozen North*, recalled his 1897 swing through the Pacific Northwest:

It was a gigantic chaos of crime... [and] a maelstrom of raving humanity driven half insane by the desire for gold. Between 1,800 and 2,000 people from all over the world were there clamoring for transportation to Alaska when there was none. Money was plentiful and fabulous prices were asked for everything. Every scheme, legal and illegal, mostly illegal, ever devised by mortals to separate a man from his money was run "wide open." Unspeakable dives, houses of ill-fame existed on every block in the business section and women under the protection of the police solicited business everywhere. Gambling houses, saloons, and disorderly houses were run in notorious defiance of the law and under the same roof. Many pickpockets, professional gamblers, and gunmen collected about these places like flies about a cider jug, and would not stop at murder—to say nothing of lesser crimes.

As much as locals would've preferred to dismiss these criticisms out of hand, there was no denying they contained at least some nuggets of truth.

From the start of the Klondike gold rush in 1897, and until that great frontier adventure wound down two years later, Seattle acted every inch the boomtown, with all the pluses and problems that attended such swellings of success. Having recovered from the devastating 1889 fire, only to be brutalized by the Panic of 1893, Washington's most ambitious burg was more than ready to stage a comeback. And it saw its chance in the flood of men and money flowing to and from northwest Canada's legendarily remote Yukon region (then still part of the Northwest Territories). Being the closest American rail-port to Alaska, Seattle seemed a natural jumping-off point for gold seekers. But Seattle wasn't content just to wait for these hordes. It actively *invited* them, opening new hotels and ordering new ships to be built for northbound prospectors. The city even hired its own energetic promotion agent.

The result—tens of thousands of would-be Croesuses flushed through Seattle, all anxious to purchase boat fares along with veritable hillslopes of provisions they'd need to survive the Yukon's brutal winters. Yes, this gold rush also fetched to Elliott Bay unscrupulous confidence men, women of disputable virtue, and other slick sinners intent on "mining the miners." But then, a little crime seemed a paltry price to pay for the long-awaited news carried on the front page of the *Seattle Post-Intelligencer* at the height of the Klondike Stampede: "PROSPERITY IS HERE."

Rumors of vast mineral deposits in the Yukon had circulated ever since the early 1890s. But not until August 1896 did trail packer George Washington Carmack—together with his Tagish Indian brother-in-law Keish (familiar to whites as Skookum Jim), and another native man named Tagish (or Dawson) Charley—happen upon a significant bed of gold in Rabbit Creek, a tributary of the Yukon's Klondike River. Prospectors who were already working nearby quickly made their own claims along the waterway, which they renamed, appropriately, Bonanza Creek.

If not for inclement weather, the Klondike gold rush might have been in full roar by early 1897, but the cold and isolation of the Yukon's winter were dauntingly legendary. Waterways froze solid enough for dogsleds to use them as highways, and men stopped shaving after about October 15 because it was too much trouble to melt enough snow for grooming.

River traffic, which usually carried Yukon and Alaska news to the "outside world," was completely shut down by ice shortly after Carmack's discovery. However, the informal "moccasin telegraph" spread word throughout the surrounding region, and by January 1897 a few thousand veteran prospectors residing as far south as the Pacific Northwest had heard about the gold finds and were preparing to brave frigid temperatures for a crack at the riches. For the most part, though, this remained an "insiders' rush" until July 15, 1897, when the steamship *Excelsior* docked at San Francisco, finally bringing proof of the gold strike to "civilization" by disgorging the first load of successful Klondike miners. These grizzled, sunburned men probably would've been greeted with disgust had it not been for what they carried—saddlebags, carpet valises, and fruit jars cumbersome with gold dust and nuggets.

Among those miners was a former YMCA physical-training instructor, Thomas Lippy, of Seattle. The normally levelheaded Lippy had left the Pacific Northwest a year earlier with borrowed money and the vague hope of "making it" in the northland. Now, he'd returned to the States "a veritable Monte Cristo," as one account put it, sharing with his wife, Salome, a grip that contained more than 200 pounds of gold valued at over $51,000. Another Seattleite, laundryman Fred Price, stood nearby, but enjoyed considerably less attention. His $5,000 in gold made him a relatively "poor" Klondiker.

Word traveled fast—and far. Within hours of the *Excelsior*'s landing, there was hardly a corner of San Francisco where hyperbole about the subarctic mother lode wasn't being liberally exchanged. Before the day was finished, telegraph wires sped the prospectors' amazing tales clear across the continent. Suddenly, the slogan "Klondike or Bust!" rode everyone's lips, though few people knew where the Klondike was and fewer still were sure how to spell it—"Clondyke," "Klondyke," and "Klondike" were used interchangeably by the press in 1897.

Not since the 1849 California gold rush had the West Coast generated such widespread excitement. Demands for more and juicier news incited a feeding frenzy. Like their shipmates, the Lippys couldn't enjoy

Steamship *Portland*. UW Libraries, Hester 10609

their visit to the Golden Gate because whenever they tried to stroll out from their Palace Hotel suite, packs of ink-stained journalists descended upon them, determined to capture their every word. After a few days, the couple fled in disgust to Portland, Oregon.

Meanwhile, a second vessel from the north, the *Portland*, nosed into Puget Sound with 68 prospectors on board. So eager were *P-I* editors to scoop their competitors, that they chartered a tug at Port Townsend and sent reporters out to intercept the treasure ship as it swung abreast of Port Angeles at 2 a.m. on July 17. Six hours later, when the *Portland* finally reached Schwabacher's Wharf (in the vicinity of present-day Piers 57 and 58), its masts aflutter with banners and prospectors waving from the deck, the *P-I* already was peddling the first of three extra editions—to be snapped up by 5,000 envious Seattleites who'd come to watch from the waterfront.

"GOLD! GOLD! GOLD! GOLD!" screamed the headlines. "STACKS OF YELLOW METAL!" It all seemed too good to be true. But the 68 men who debarked from the *Portland* that day left little doubt that the Klondike provided what one Seattle editorialist termed, "'the open sesame' to a dreamland of wealth."

"They all have gold," enthused a reporter who had talked with prospectors on the *Portland*, "and it is piled about the staterooms like so much valueless hand baggage." When totaled up, the ship carried "a ton of gold" according to the *P-I*. Yet on this rare occasion the newspaper had *understated* reality. The *Portland* actually held closer to two tons of the precious metal. Regardless, "a ton of gold" was the catchphrase thereafter repeated in awe around the globe, enticing every thrill-seeker, avaricious soul, and ne'er-do-well hoping for a better life to join North America's last great frontier adventure—the Klondike Stampede.

Even before the *Portland* tied up at Seattle, she was booked solid for the return voyage to Alaska. Within another week, bank clerks, barbers, ferry pilots, and preachers from all over town had turned in their resignations and bought boat tickets to the raw southeast Alaskan hamlets of Skagway or Dyea, from which two parallel trails—respectively, the White Pass route and the more popular climb over Chilkoot Pass—led across the Coast Mountains separating Alaska from the Yukon and its Klondike Valley.

The *Seattle Times* lost most of its reporters to "Klondicitis," as the gold madness was being called, and the local police force ranks were equally decimated. Streetcars stopped running as drivers deserted their posts. Mayor William D. Wood, an attorney and real-estate speculator, was attending a convention in San Francisco when the rush began. Recognizing the wealth to be made in transporting would-be miners and freight from the West Coast to the Klondike gold fields, His Honor quickly went into partnership with Seattle investors, chartered a steamship in the Bay Area, and asked for a leave of absence from the mayor's job, telegraphing a resignation to the Seattle City Council that would go into effect if he didn't return from the north within 90 days. (He did not, and was replaced by fellow Republican Thomas D. Humes.) So excited was Wood about embarking for the Klondike that he neglected to load 50,000 pounds of his passengers' belongings and was nearly lynched at dockside.

As many as 1,500 people (mostly men, but also women and children) shipped north from Seattle by the end of July 1897, and nine more craft were waiting impatiently to leave. So great was demand for conveyance up British Columbia's Inside Passage to Alaska that pretty much anything capable of floating, no matter how long ago condemned, was called into service—from barges, to yachts, to rotten, rat-infested steamboats. Vessels often were dangerously overloaded. Sometimes they were double- and triple-booked at top dollar, propelling ticket holders to the brink of violence. The *Danube*, a boat that once had borne the lifeless body of Scottish explorer David Livingstone from Africa to Europe, "puffed out of Seattle so crowded that during one storm the captain was forced to lock forty-four men in the hatches among the horses," explained Canadian historian Pierre Berton in his extraordinary chronicle, *Klondike: The Last Great Gold Rush, 1896–1899*. Other vessels foundered with insufficient fuel or were dashed against rocks and sank. One, the *Clara Nevada*, sailed in defiance of laws that forbade the transport of passengers together with dynamite. Its explosion north of Juneau, Alaska, killed 65 people.

And still the rush charged on, powered not only by greed, but equally by optimism—the promise of more comfortable times ahead—and a craving for the sheer adventure of pursuing fantastic fortunes. "The man who had a family to support who could not go was looked on with a sort of pity," remembered J.E. Fraser, a "Klondiker" from San Francisco. "The man who didn't care to leave his business or for other trivial reasons, was looked on with contempt as a man without ambition who did not know enough to take advantage of a good thing when placed in his reach."

Capitalizing on a Canadian law that required prospectors entering the Yukon to pack in a year's worth of food and supplies—a burden that could weigh up to a ton—Seattle outfitters made out like bandits. Berton writes that local merchants "who before the rush had sold goods worth an annual three hundred thousand [dollars], now found that their direct interest in outfitting amounted to ten million." Anything a gold seeker thought he or she needed could be had on the streets of Seattle, from fur-seated trousers and "crystallized eggs," to milk tablets, canvas bathtubs, and huge "portable" stoves. Stores ordered so much provisions and equipment that piles of it created barriers 10 feet high along streets in what's now Pioneer Square. Shadier salesmen realized that some Klondikers would buy anything that promised to make them richer quicker. So they sold them "ice bicycles" with forward skis, "automatic" gold pans, x-ray machines that were supposed to pinpoint buried wealth, and even stock in a firm that was training gophers to find nuggets underground.

Horses that once had been mere steps from the glue factory commanded outlandish prices, and when they were in short supply, reindeer and Washington elk substituted. Told that dogsleds would help speed them to their pots of gold, fortune hunters fought over the malamutes and mutts being imported into the city on a weekly basis. After that, they shanghaied any household pets that were left outside. "Somebody stole our dog,"

Typical Klondike outfitting scene at Cooper & Levy's, 104–6 1st Avenue, in 1897. *UW Libraries, UW 4770*

whimpered young Mattie Harris, whose mother had refused to sell the family canine to a departing argonaut. "The man took him and went on. We couldn't go after him." So many dogs were sent north that the *Seattle Argus* proclaimed the city "a cat's paradise."

A reporter for the *New York Herald* summed up this frenzy quite nicely: "Seattle has gone stark, staring mad on gold."

"We had no doubt [Seattle] was in the pay-streak," remembered Illinois school teacher Robert Medill in *Klondike Diary: True Account of the Klondike Gold Rush of 1897–1898* (1949). "Great streamers were stretched across the streets, screaming in lurid colors, Klondike this, Klondike that. The town was full of strangers with the Klondike look in their faces."

As many as 48 different mining firms opened offices in the Pioneer Building alone, and new hotels were raised to catch the overflow from those that had existed before the rush began. Many stampeders passing through Seattle were too anxious to rest, however. Instead, they spent their money on entertainments, knowing they wouldn't see civilization again for a long while. Thus, billiard halls, saloons, and Turkish baths all did a boomtown trade. So did prominent local brothels, like those owned by Lou Graham and Rae Roberts, where virtue-challenged employees gave miners one last night of warmth to remember during the chilly days to come.

Reporting the Rush

Not since the Civil War had the American press thrown as many resources into reporting a single event as it did during the Klondike gold rush. And no wonder—this was a spectacle rampant with human optimism and daring, pathos and death, exactly the mix of material on which many newspapers then thrived.

Seattle dailies were as aggressive as any others in capitalizing on events up north. Shortly after the steamship *Portland* landed at Elliott Bay with its load of Klondike gold, Joseph A. Costello of the *Seattle Times* set off for Dawson City, promising that his dispatches would contain, "the earliest, most comprehensive, accurate, and uncolored reports from the new diggings." Costello had other goals as well. Like many Seattle journalists, he left town hoping to make a fortune in the Klondike.

Meanwhile, the *Seattle Post-Intelligencer* ticketed its own man onto the *Portland* as that ship departed Seattle for the return voyage to Alaska, only three days after its historic arrival. His name was Samuel P. Weston, and with him went a cage full of carrier pigeons. Since communications with Alaska and the Yukon were poor at best—there wasn't a telegraph line linking Skagway with cities to the south until 1898, and not until a year later was a line extended to Dawson—Weston intended to send accounts of the miners and their rapacious pursuits back to his newsroom tied to pigeon legs. What Weston hadn't figured on, though, was that carrier pigeons were accustomed to toting brief missives— they couldn't fly 1,000 miles or more lugging five-column reports that Seattle readers expected to digest with their morning coffee. Weston made it to Alaska, but his pigeons—and the articles they were carrying—apparently got lost on the way back.

Of course, Seattle wasn't the only West Coast city that envisioned its financial salvation in the Klondike Stampede. Tacoma and San Francisco, along with Vancouver and Victoria, British Columbia, wanted part of the gold rush action, too. But Seattle cinched main control of that commerce by hiring press agent Erastus Brainerd. A newspaperman by occupation (he'd briefly edited the *Seattle Press-Times*, precursor to the *Seattle Times*), the New England-born and Harvard-educated Brainerd was a huckster by inclination. Shortly after the *Portland*'s landing, he got busy blitzing news-papers and magazines with advertisements detailing Seattle's easy access to Alaska and the Klondike. He'd pen stories about the Seattle-Alaska connection for East Coast publications, then turn around and quote his hyperbolic phrases from those same stories in news releases. He assembled fat packets of photographs showing Alaska and Seattle, and dispatched them to European and South American rulers. (One such folder reached Germany's Kaiser Wilhelm II, who, convinced it contained a bomb, refused to crack the envelope.) So successful was Brainerd in retailing the connection between Seattle and the promise of Klondike wealth, that he, himself, set off north in the spring of 1898.

Estimates are that a million people seriously considered joining the Klondike gold rush in its initial days. About 100,000—mostly Americans, but also including British lords, Maori tribesmen, German crones in lace aprons, and others from all over the planet—eventually journeyed to Dawson City, the Yukon town adjacent to the gold fields. Some tried to cross Canada, a tortuous overland trek of almost 1,600 miles from Edmonton, Alberta, to Dawson. The well-to-do preferred a safer 4,722-mile voyage

First gold shipment to arrive in Seattle from Nome, Alaska, circa 1899. In addition to the Klondike rush in Canada's Yukon Territory, the mining excitement also spread to gold diggings in the Territory of Alaska. *UW Libraries, UW 2269*

by water—from Seattle to St. Michael on Alaska's west coast, and then up the mighty Yukon River. But the majority came first to Seattle, Vancouver, or San Francisco, many traveling on special "gold-rush cars," provided by America's transcontinental railroads. Then they boarded, bought, or did their best to hijack anything that might float them up the Inside Passage—more than 1,000 miles—to the southeast Alaskan mountain trails that would take them to the U.S.-Canadian border and beyond to the Yukon's headwaters. From there, they paddled small boats all the way to Dawson.

Scaling the Coast Mountains northeast from raucous Skagway or smaller Dyea proved a more daunting task than most Klondikers had bargained for. Blizzards and wily thieves waited to rob them of their energy and possessions, and frostbite and precipitous climbs reduced many hikers to tears. In 1898, as many as 70 people perished in an avalanche on the Chilkoot Trail—and that was considered the *safe* route. Regardless of youth or vitality, most gold seekers realized just how ill prepared they were to haul a ton of food and clothing—much less such extras as x-ray machines and stoves—over the 33-mile-long Chilkoot or the 45 mile White Pass Trail. But what choice did they have, after they had come so far?

Frank Thomas, an argonaut from Plymouth, Indiana, voiced a prevailing opinion in a letter home: "I am undoubtedly a crazy fool for being here in this God-forsaken country but I have the consolation of seeing thousands of other men in all stages of life, rich and poor, wise and foolish, here in the same plight as I."

A few wealthier prospectors hired members of local Tlingit tribes as packers. Others heaved their year's worth of supplies onto horseback (which proved disastrous when these steeds became stuck in mudholes or tumbled off narrow cliffside trails). However, the majority of gold seekers broke their loads into 50- or 60-pound portions, and then shuttled those loads along the paths by foot, cacheing each new installment while they backtracked to pick up the next one—eventually traveling up to 30 times over the same ground. Using this system, it could take three months or more to surmount Chilkoot Pass. And once over the mountains into Canada, the prospectors still had to build scows or rafts, and sail 550 miles through treacherous waters to reach Dawson City.

Even though Dawson was a wooden town of false fronts and muddy thoroughfares, by 1898 it was the largest city west of Winnipeg, Manitoba, and north of San Francisco, with a population of about 60,000. (Edwin) Tappan Adney, a gifted scrivener who joined the 1897 migration on behalf of *Harper's Weekly* and the *London Chronicle*—and eventually produced

Steamer *Humboldt* departing for Nome, June 2, 1901. *UW Libraries, UW 7807*

a book of his experiences, *The Klondike Stampede*, first published in 1900—
described the crowds reaching Dawson at the height of the gold rush:

It is a motley throng—every degree of person gathered from every corner of the earth,
from every State of the Union, and from every city—weather-beaten, sunburned, with
snow glasses over their hats, just as they came from the passes. Australians with upturned
sleeves and a swagger; young Englishmen in golf stockings and tweeds; would-be miners
in mackinaws and rubber boots, or heavy, highlaced shoes; Japanese, Negroes—and
women, too, everywhere.

Still, prospectors who found their footing on Dawson's wharves after months of traveling must've seen the place as a heavenly metropolis. It
certainly had its attractions, from hotels, saloons, and banks to gambling
dens, whorehouses, and opera stages. Dogsleds raced down the town's then-
flashy waterfront drive, and world-record breaking lines snaked to each
of Dawson's only *two* public outhouses. Members of Canada's North-West
Mounted Police were on guard against serious crimes like murder, but they
turned a benignly neglectful eye to saloons and gaming joints. Almost
anything a man desired was available in booming Dawson, be it beaded

moccasins, locally unearthed mammoth tusks, pink lemonade, Paris gowns, or champagne enough to bathe a hard-to-win lover. And everywhere, it seemed, some miner was celebrating his good fortune over a shot of whiskey, paying for the poison from a sack of gold dust. In fact, dust was so plentiful and traded so with such abandon in Dawson's heyday that boys hired to clean out one groggery made $20 a night merely by dissecting the sweepings.

Perhaps the only thing that couldn't easily be had was what these adventurers wanted most—gold. Newspaper accounts had lied when claiming that anyone who could reach the diggings would get rich. Paul T. Mizony, a 17-year-old from San Diego who landed at Dawson in 1898, noted, "hundreds…expected all they would have to do was to pick the nuggets above the ground and some even thought they grew on bushes." Only after the starry-eyed stampeders from Seattle and elsewhere finished their trip north did they realize that the best claims on the Klondike's tributaries already had been staked back in 1896, *a full year before the rush started!*

Notice to Newcomers

There are many men in Dawson at the present time who feel keenly disappointed. They have come thousands of miles on a perilous trip, risked life, health and property, spent months of the most arduous labor a man can perform, and with expectations raised to the highest pitch, have reached the coveted goal only to discover the fact that there is nothing here for them.

Any man of ordinary judgment might well have reached the conclusion long before he set out for Dawson that every creek and gulch adjacent to the city would be staked months before he could possibly reach it. The gold is here beyond question and should anyone have thoughts of becoming suddenly wealthy without any considerable exertion on his part he will fail nine times out of ten. On the other hand if he brings with him a due amount of pluck and every willingness to endure hardship and privation, in the long run the chances are favorable for his success.

—*Klondike Nugget*, Dawson City, June 23, 1898

Diminishing Returns

Of the 100,000 people who set off to the Klondike—

40,000 reached Dawson City

20,000 stayed to seek gold

4,000 discovered gold

300 found enough to be considered rich

50 managed to keep their wealth

Source: Klondike Gold Rush National Historical Park

By one reckoning, only about 4,000 people actually found significant amounts of gold during the epic stampede. Most, including veterans of other mining areas, didn't recoup so much as their travel costs.

"This is a country of contradictions," Jonas B. Houck, a resident of Detroit, wrote to his wife from Dawson in the summer of 1898. "It puzzles old miners to know anything about where to dig for gold. They will come here and dig where they think gold should be if it is anywhere in the country and not find anything and give it up in disgust; and some 'greenhorn' will dig where a person who knows anything about mining in other places would never think of looking and strike it rich."

Like Houck, many of the disillusioned no sooner arrived in Dawson than they turned on their heels and returned home. Others signed up to work for the "Klondike Kings," men who'd found fertile veins of gold, and they stayed to bleed the claims dry. Some, their passions not yet satisfied by chasing after chimerical fortunes, struck off for the next great adventure at Nome, a dinky outpost on Alaska's wind-scoured Bering Sea, where gold was discovered in 1898. Or they volunteered for service in the Spanish-American War, which erupted that same year. And, not a few came back to live in Seattle, helping to drive the city's population upward—from 55,752 in 1896, to 237,194 by 1910—and forcing a dramatic expansion in the housing market. In 1899 alone, 1,200 new houses were raised in Seattle.

The Emerald City's new blood and fame fueled an aggressive drive to transform the frontier burg into the Northwest's urban showcase. Money for such a makeover came from the gold rush itself. Congress had awarded Seattle a government assay office in 1898, ensuring that a large measure of the Klondike's $174 million in gold coming to the city between then and 1902 never left. Many who had chosen to stay on Elliott Bay and supply the prospectors made out better financially than the miners themselves.

The man who started this whole fevered rush for riches, George Carmack, tried to ride his celebrity beyond the north country. In 1898, and again the next year, he and his Tagish Indian wife, Kate (Shaaw Tláa), traveled to Seattle. But the local press treated them as curious savages, remarking on their disorientation among the city's tall buildings and fast-moving traffic, and made fun of the gold-nugget necklaces draped around Kate's neck. Her boisterous behavior under the influence of alcohol also was popular fodder for the press. "Mrs. George W. Carmack," the *P-I* reported in July 1899, "slept last night in the city jail, charged with being drunk and disorderly and disturbing the peace." The paper went on to say that she was arrested "while executing an aboriginal Yukon war dance in the second floor corridor of the Seattle Hotel." It wasn't long before Carmack disowned Kate (as well as their daughter, Graphie) and he also parted ways with Skookum Jim and Tagish Charley, never returning to the Yukon after 1900. Instead, he married an American businesswoman named Marguerite Laimee, whom he had met at a party in Dawson City, and he became a Seattle resident. Carmack spent the last dozen years of his life (he died in 1922) with Marguerite in a Colonial Revival house at the corner of East Jefferson Street and 16th Avenue, near present-day Providence Hospital.

Thomas Lippy, the YMCA instructor and star at the *Excelsior* landing, took some $2 million out of his claim on lower Eldorado Creek before selling it in 1903. He used the money to erect a grand home in Seattle, and contributed to various philanthropic enterprises. But he died bankrupt after a series of bad investments.

Rather than join the ranks of prospectors, Erastus Brainerd served in Alaska as a "mining consultant" before returning to Seattle in 1904, where, as the editor of the *Post-Intelligencer*, he railed against the profuse vices (gambling, prostitution, and drunkenness among them) that by then were part of the city's Klondike legacy. Whether the former civic publicist ever conceded that he might've been partly to blame for those increases in iniquity is not apparent from his writing. Amazingly, when Brainerd died in 1922, his obituaries failed to mention that he had made Seattle "the gateway to the Klondike."

THE WHEEL THING

T MUST HAVE BEEN AN ODD, even comic sight. Dozens of men and
women—the former in black suits, white shirts, and bow ties; the latter
wearing short skirts and those Turkish-style pantaloons named in honor
of feminist author Amelia Jenks Bloomer—all wobbling gleefully through
Seattle streets and woodlands of the late 1890s aboard what were then new-
style "safety bicycles."

Sunny days, especially, brought out a two-wheeling stampede. Their
preferred route was along a cinder path that began at 8th Avenue and Pine
Street, in what were still the far northern boondocks of downtown. From
there they headed northeast along Lake Union, then east for about 10 miles
to Lake Washington. They passed over what's now tree-shaded Interlaken
Boulevard at the north end of Capitol Hill, stopped for sandwiches, coffee, and gossip at a rustic Halfway House located between Roanoke Park
and 23rd Avenue, and crossed over marshes and cable car tracks to Leschi.
A bike route "more beautiful in any respect," remarked the *Seattle Post-
Intelligencer*, "would be hard to imagine."

Bicyclists of that era were generally white members of the rising middle
class, enjoying themselves aboard twin pneumatic tires when they couldn't
afford the gaudy four-wheeled horse carriages favored by Old Money
Seattleites. However, thanks to the popularity of songs such as Harry Dacre's
1892 "Daisy Bell" (better known as "A Bicycle Built for Two") and the subsequent, boastful "The Cycle Man," even silver-spoon-biting scions couldn't

Two women on a Lake Washington biking path, sometime between 1900 and 1903. This cindered trail began at 8th Avenue and Pine Street and continued through the woods by way of Lakeview to Lake Washington. As Seattle grew, many cycling paths were turned into streets. *MOHAI SHS2,968*

resist joining in, hoping to impress prospective partners with their pedaling prowess.

A Seattle-only sporting phenomenon? Hardly.

All over the country, "doctors pedaled to house calls, students peddled to school, salesmen cycled through their rounds," social historian Charles Panati wrote in *Panati's Parade of Fads, Follies, and Manias*. From 1894 to 1904—the height of America's bicycling craze—it was the abnormal household that didn't own or at least wasn't contemplating the purchase of one or more of the new recreational machines. Even corpulent New York multimillionaire Diamond Jim Brady could be seen riding pathways in Central Park with his celebrated companion, singer Lillian Russell—though, of course, their conveyances had to be both gold plated and diamond studded. Musing on what the nation would be like 100 years hence, artists of the Gay '90s showed cities bustling with happy, healthy pedalers. Pundits predicted that wars would soon be fought on bicycles. Some men bound for northwest Canada's Klondike region took along the most recent models, convinced that bikes would give them an advantage in scaling mountain passes (they didn't). Newspapers told of a woman who tracked down a philandering husband on her bicycle and only thus won a divorce.

Naturally, there were critics of this latest fitness fanaticism. Clergymen inveighed against bicycling as an invitation to sin, since it gave women freedom of travel they'd not previously enjoyed and let couples escape the vigilant gaze of their elders. Editorialists decried "blazing"—peddling along at pedestrian-endangering speeds. The *Georgia Journal of Medicine and Surgery* contended that bikes could cause unexpected gynecological side-effects in women, especially at high speeds when "the body is thrown forward, causing the clothing to press against the clitoris, thereby eliciting and arousing feelings hitherto unknown and unrealized by the young maiden." Booksellers worried over national illiteracy, warning that "people who are rushing about on wheels, days, nights, and Sunday, no longer read anything." In fact, the circulation of Sunday newspapers dipped significantly as more and more people spent the Sabbath frolicking on two wheels. Hat makers, concerned that cyclists were eschewing their products (chapeaux not being the most practical accessories for people careening around out of doors), won the attention of a Republican-led Congress with their proposal that every bicyclist be compelled by law to buy two hats each year. Fortunately, saner heads eventually killed the mad hatters' bill.

None of this, though, could deflate biking fever. According to Frank B. Cameron, author of *Bicycling in Seattle, 1879–1904*, U.S. production

The Century Turns

With fireworks and clanging bells, the dawning of the 20th century seemed especially hopeful in Seattle. Although not quite 50 years old, the city already had endured misfortune (the 1889 fire and 1890s depression), but it recently had benefited from gold flowing in from Canada and Alaska. Everywhere one went in Seattle in 1900 there were boomtown scenes.

True, this still was a place with more saloons than retail stores, and more prostitutes than professionals of any other variety. And, the University of Washington, relocated north of Lake Union in 1895 from its original location in the vicinity of today's Four Seasons Olympic Hotel, was a good half-day's streetcar ride from downtown and boasted only one significant structure—architect Charles W. Saunders' chateauesque Administration Building (now known as Denny Hall). However, hordes of passing-through miners had incited a proliferation of hotels, and the town's rapidly increasing residential population reached almost 81,000 in 1900—twice that of 1890, but only one third of what it would be 10 years hence—and was spreading out into new neighborhoods. The choicest residential addresses in 1900 were still on First Hill, but a new "counterbalance" electric trolley up Queen Anne Hill was encouraging the development of expensive "view" homes along Highland Drive.

Even at that time, Seattle was a hub of the Asian trade. Local commerce with Japan alone had grown dramatically during the mid-1890s and by 1900 exceeded $8 million a year. Eighteen new piers and waterfront warehouses were built in that year to handle goods transferred between railroads and steamships. Shipbuilding was a major local industry, with about 1,900 men employed in a dozen yards. The Moran Brothers yard, founded by three New Yorkers (one of whom, Robert Moran, had gained fame as the take-charge mayor during Seattle's Great Fire), was the busiest and most successful, scoring a coup in 1900 by winning the contract to construct the battleship *Nebraska* for the U.S. Navy.

Nowadays, we complain about the tens of thousands of cars clogging downtown streets and we grumble when traffic comes to a halt on Lake

Washington's floating bridges. But in 1900, there was only a single automobile on Seattle's roads. It was a three-horsepower Woods Electric model owned by one Ralph S. Hopkins, described in reports as a "capitalist." He'd purchased the vehicle in Chicago and driven it west—much to the amazement of rubberneckers along the way. It was considered a mere novelty in Seattle, where most folks still got around by carriage, streetcar, or foot, with sportier types buying bicycles for weekend leisure riding. If one needed to cross Puget Sound, there were myriad small craft—the storied "Mosquito Fleet"—to transport people. Ferry service across Lake Washington was spottier, but there weren't many takers, anyway. Only 400 residents were living on the present site of Bellevue, and Kirkland's dreams of becoming an industrial mecca, or "the Pittsburgh of the West," had been shattered by the Panic of 1893.

Much more has changed since the 19th century gave way to the 20th. In 1900, for instance, the evening *Seattle Times* was the more progressive local daily newspaper, but it didn't have the clout or following of the conserva-tive morning daily, the *Seattle Post-Intelligencer*. Staid Republicans, rather than today's activist Democrats, dominated the city's elected offices. There were only a few high-end restaurants in Seattle (mostly in hotels), and almost no recognizable celebrities on the sidewalks (although former frontier marshal Wyatt Earp allegedly operated a 2nd Avenue gambling house in 1900, before moving on to the gold rush town of Nome, Alaska). A man could buy a new suit in those days for $12.50 or a 20-pound bucket of lard for $1.70. Georgetown, Ravenna, and West Seattle were still separate towns, waiting to be annexed to Seattle over the next decade. And Woodland Park, formerly land baron Guy Phinney's "country estate"—complete with extensive flower gardens and a menagerie—had only recently been sold to the city. It would take another 10 years for the menagerie to start expanding into what's now Woodland Park Zoo.

Judged by modern standards, the Emerald City of 1900 seems downright quaint. Which is probably exactly how city residents in the year 2100 will look back at what we now think is cutting edge, boomtown Seattle.

jumped "from 200,000 bicycles in 1889 to over a million in 1899." Cameron adds that, until 1893, "there were perhaps less than two dozen bicycles in Seattle." Seven years later, as many as 10,000 bicyclists could be found in the city.

Those were times starved for fun. The financial depression following the notorious Panic of 1893 had closed banks, mines, and many other businesses across the land. Unemployment was up from 3 percent to 18.4 percent, and land values had plummeted as much as 80 percent. Any distraction was welcomed, be it Thomas Edison's phonographs, or increasingly popular dog shows, or the most recent fad— keeping goldfish in home aquariums.

Bicycles had been around since 1839 when blacksmith Kirkpatrick MacMillan of Courthill, Scotland, built the first one in order to more easily visit his sister in Glasgow, 40 miles away. By the 1860s, the wide boulevards of Paris were aswarm with what were then called "pedal velocipes," or more colloquially, "boneshakers," thanks to metal-rimmed tires that let their riders feel every road imperfection.

But another 20 years of evolution were required before bike sales would take off worldwide. The spoked tension wheel, invented in London in 1876, led to creation of the "ordinary" model, with its large front wheel that lengthened the distance a rider could go with each turn of the pedals. After that, bicycles adopted diamond-shaped frames, a chain-linkage drive, medium-size wheels of equal diameter, coaster brakes, and a comfortable padded seat. Perhaps the most important change came in 1888 when a Scottish veterinarian in Belfast, John Boyd Dunlop, perfected his air-filled pneumatic tire. In the 1890s, most bikes looked similar to those we buy today. They were referred to as "safeties," being so much more stable and controllable than their high-wheeled predecessors.

Seattle's first bicycle supposedly came from San Francisco in 1879, ordered for the son of a bookkeeper named Lipsky. There were only 3,000 people in town back then—and very few flat, smooth places on which to ride. Seattle was crowded with precipitous hills—regrading wouldn't be taken up seriously until the late '90s. In 1895, George F. Cotterill, a civil engineer (who'd be elected as mayor in 1912), described most downtown Seattle streets as "strewn with wrecks of old planking which had survived from five to 10 years of traffic. Spikes, splinters, and holes were the principle [sic] features which distinguished the remains."

Yet by 1896, when the town could still boast of only one mile of paved thoroughfare, there were already 300 bike riders here. Many of them held membership in one or more wheeling associations, such as the Seattle Bicycle Club founded in 1894, or the Triangle Bicycle Club formed a year later. To make up for the lack of decent city roads, both of those clubs constructed special quarter-mile tracks for their riders and racers—one at Woodland Park, the other on the YMCA grounds between Cherry and Jefferson streets and 12th and 14th avenues. Between 1894 and 1904, more than a dozen tracks—most surfaced with packed sand or cinder, some made of boards—were erected in the Puget Sound area, including four in Seattle and others in Tacoma, Everett, Olympia, and Port Townsend. Racing reached its high point here in about 1901, when 1,000 or more spectators might show up at a track on Sunday to watch racers who'd come from all over the Northwest and had probably competed the previous season in Europe.

The expanding ranks of bicyclists earned political clout. Their clubs agitated for the use of convict labor to improve King County roads. They pushed even more fervently for construction of public bike paths throughout the city. The aforementioned long route from downtown to Lake Washington was opened in 1897. Other courses fingered north to Green Lake, west to Fort Lawton and Magnolia Bluff, and from Ballard to Fremont. More energetic riders ferried across Lake Washington and rode east to Snoqualmie Falls or south for a Sunday dinner in Kent.

Maintaining city paths could be expensive and difficult, what with washouts, horses and cattle tearing up surfaces, and gophers tunneling underneath. The city council eventually was persuaded to license bikes at $1.25 a year. Enforcing law and order among cyclists proved no less challenging. Ordinances were passed to prohibit bike travel on some sidewalks and restrict speeds. Seattle's first "bike cop" was hired in the 1890s to chase and apprehend speeders, fill holes in paths, and shoo away wandering cows or bears. Stolen machines were a significant problem, too. *Bicycling in Seattle* reports that in 1897, 183 bikes went missing. Few were ever recovered. Most were taken to nearby towns and sold for as little as 75 cents—a tremendous markdown from their original $50 to $150 price.

At the peak of Seattle's bicycling vogue, 23 bike shops lined the six blocks of 2nd Avenue between Marion and Pike streets, according to writer Frank

Cameron. And, another 17 firms—including the Bon Marché—sold the machines elsewhere in the city. More than 100 bike brands were available, from the imported "Cleveland Special" and "Halladay Temple Scorcher," to locally made models such as the "Rainier" and the "Seattle." On weekends, the city's more than 25 miles of bike paths hosted not only two-wheeled safeties, but also tandems and triplets. Women were so ubiquitous on these courses that some men actually complained of the racket raised by bloomers billowing in high winds.

Analysts often blame the demise of the turn-of-the-century bicycle craze on the coming of the automobile. However, cars were only partly to blame. Bikes, after all, had been used more for entertainment and exercise than for serious transportation. So it was other developing diversions—among them golf, crew races, football, and mountaineering—that may have detracted most from bicycling's continued following. By 1903, Seattle bike clubs were closing, tracks had gone out of business, and paths were being covered over by new residential tracts and road-builders. Only two local bicycle shops remained open in 1907.

Not until the 1970s did biking see a resurgence, both as a sport and the basis for a new messenger business. Fortunately, by then dress styles had changed. Can you imagine modern bicycle messengers zipping around in bloomers or bow ties?

ANGEL OF THE TRAIL

W
AS THAT THE MUFFLED REPORT OF A GUNSHOT? Patrolman Claude G.
Bannick reined his horse up on Seattle's Pike Street between 6th and
7th avenues, and cocked a more attentive ear on the moonless night
of October 27, 1902.

As he did so, another blast rang from a nearby alleyway linking Pike
with Union Street. Bannick wheeled his mount about and spurred down
the house-lined passage. Immediately, he heard scuffling, and a woman
in a billowing white nightdress burst from a doorway and ran screaming
through the alley toward him. Close on her heels was a tall mustachioed
man, a smoking Colt revolver raised in a meaty fist. Before the cop could
intervene, the pistol flashed again and the fleeing woman stopped abruptly,
turned slightly, then crumpled into the lane's deep mud.

Bannick's momentum carried him past the stilled and bleeding figure, and on toward the assailant standing beneath a building window. He
heard a fourth shot as he went, but in the dark the patrolman couldn't
determine the bullet's target—he was just glad it wasn't *him*. Finally, about
four feet from the man, Bannick leaped from his saddle, anxious to take
control of the situation. But he was too late. The gunman lifted his weapon
one more time—*and fired at his own head*.

No matter how many times this scene was recounted later in Seattle
courtrooms, it never grew any less grisly. Or less shocking. Mollie Walsh
Bartlett—once the beloved operator of a Yukon rest stop servicing

prospectors during the Klondike gold rush—had been murdered in a filthy alley by her own husband, Mike Bartlett, former co-owner of a Yukon packing service. His motive was said to be jealousy. But, as newspapers made clear through the dribble of new information and innuendo over the 13 months following the slaying, nothing about the case was quite that simple. Tangled up in it were not only allegations of a wife's infidelity, but fears of a husband's drunkenness, rumors of inherited insanity, and a generation-changing event, the Klondike Stampede, that couldn't soon be forgotten by those people who'd ventured to the cold north in hot pursuit of fortune.

She stepped off the S.S. *Quadra* at Skagway, Alaska, on October 9, 1897. Slender, 5-feet-6-inches in height, with long dark hair (usually worn up), Mollie Walsh was attractive and vivacious enough that men would one day duel for her affections. But in the capitalistic chaos of early Skagway, chances are they were too distracted to pay her much attention at first.

Only four months before, ships from Alaska had docked at San Francisco and Seattle bearing men rich with gold nuggets sifted from Yukon tributaries in northwest Canada. Quickly, any man in the contiguous United States who'd ever dreamed of easy money planned sea passage to Skagway or nearby Dyea, from which mountain trails led to the Yukon. Tens of thousands made the trip, many of them so keen to reach the gold fields that they abandoned their craft in Skagway's long bay. By the time of Mollie's arrival, the glacier-shaded harbor was so congested

Mollie Walsh Bartlett. *UW Libraries, UW 3934*

with vessels that new ones had to anchor up to a mile offshore. Overloaded scows then shuttled passengers and cargo to the beach, "picking their way between the thrashing forms of goats, dogs, mules, and oxen left to fend for themselves in the cold waters," as Pierre Berton casts the scene in *Klondike: The Last Great Gold Rush, 1896–1899.*

Skagway rose from a forested flatland above the beach. It was a farrago of tree stumps and tents and hastily rendered wooden structures, a place attuned to the discordant rhythms of saws, neighing horses, creaking wagons, and men bargaining for goods to see them through a months-long journey north. John Muir, the California naturalist, compared Skagway to "a nest of ants taken into a strange country and stirred up by a stick."

This hardly seemed the place for a respectable woman. But Mollie Walsh was as uncommon as the town itself.

In their book *Murder, Madness, and Mystery,* authors Art Petersen and D. Scott Williams say that *Mary* Walsh, as she was known originally, was born in either Wisconsin or Iowa in 1872. Nine years later, she moved with her immigrant Irish clan—father Patrick, mother Susan, and two brothers—to St. Paul, Minnesota.

As the state capital, St. Paul was a thriving commercial center and in those days a Midwest rival to Chicago. By 1890, its population exceeded 100,000 and there was plenty of work to go around—including a job for Mary at a laundry. She was "one of the prettiest and brightest girls in the east part of the city," according to a St. Paul newspaper story of 1903, "industrious…and always on the lookout to better her condition." Seeing few opportunities for betterment in Minnesota, on Thanksgiving Day in 1890, 18-year-old Mary with an English girlfriend quit St. Paul without even saying good-bye to her family.

A note left behind said she was bound for Butte, Montana, a copper boomtown on the Northern Pacific rail line. However, her path may not have been direct. Thora McIlroy Mills, a Canadian researcher with access to a diary kept by Skagway's first Presbyterian preacher, Reverend Robert M. Dickey, wrote in the early 1980s that Mary "was one of the 'Irish colleens' recruited…for the Irish Industries Village at the Chicago World's Fair in 1893." Although most of that exposition closed within the year, a store did remain open to peddle Irish linens and lace, and Mills suggests that Mary worked there for a time.

Two years after the fair, she appeared in the *Butte City Directory* on the payroll of another laundry—now listed as *Mollie* Walsh, the name by which she become renowned after sailing from Seattle to Skagway in 1897.

Her entry into Alaska could have been rough, even disastrous (many females were swept right off boats into a life of mercantile venery). Mollie, though, had the advantage of encountering Reverend Dickey on board the *Quadra* and being taken under his wing.

A clean-shaven, rather meek-looking fellow, to judge from photographs, Dickey had come north convinced that anywhere greedy men and licentious ladies were headed, a man of the cloth would be wise to follow. Skagway seemed ripe for moral cleansing. In addition to petty larceny and public intoxication, it suffered the criminal predations of one Jefferson Randolph Smith, more familiarly known as "Soapy" Smith—thanks to his earlier fondness for a Denver con game involving the selling of soap bars with paper money wrapped around them as prizes. Smith, a mustachioed former Georgian, was a politically savvy crook, mounting a reputable front while at the same time controlling an extensive network of card sharps, grifters, harlots, spies, and murderers. From his 1897 arrival in Alaska until a vigilante gunned him down a year later, Soapy was "the Uncrowned King of Skagway."

Smith probably cheered as Dickey built his Union Church in town, figuring it would draw more "suckers" up the Inside Passage. Mollie Walsh was pleased as well, but for different reasons. The church provided a rare retreat from Skagway's rowdiness, a place for "informal conversation, stories, and repartée," as author Thora Mills described it. Employed during the daytime at one of 19 busy local eateries, Mollie could spend her evenings at church with Dickey and the town's married women. The reverend approved. "Miss Walsh is a pretty Irish girl," he remarked in his diary, "full of fun and not averse to making fun of herself in a crowd." On one occasion, she told of turning down *three* marriage proposals. The first proved the most comical. Apparently her suitor wasn't satisfied when Mollie insisted she had no qualifications to recommend her as a wife.

"Oh, yes!" said the man. "You're not crabby!"

"But," argued shy Mollie, "I'm not good-looking."

"Oh, that's all right," the man stated. "I never had much use for good-looking girls anyway."

However, Mollie didn't have much time to enjoy this camaraderie. By the end of March 1898, Dickey—his mission at Skagway firmly established—prepared to seek new congregates inland. Mollie thought she'd be safer moving on, too. Seems she'd gotten on Soapy Smith's bad side recently. In the course of nursing a dying prostitute, Mollie and Dickey had convinced the poor woman's friends to give up whoring—a blow to Soapy's bottom line. So now, with the reverend leaving, Mollie decided to take her saved wages and follow the miners up the tortuous White Pass Trail.

More than 30 miles she went, across the Alaska-Yukon border as far as Shallow Lake to a settlement known as Log Cabin. There, Mollie opened a grub tent. It was a prime location—every hungry stampeder and pack train boss trudging over White Pass passed right by her front door. "She had only a small sheet-iron stove with a narrow lunch counter in front of it," as packer Jim Pitcher depicted the roadhouse. "The eats as I recall weren't anything special, but the girl's hearty enthusiasm, quick wit, and a dusting of freckles over her nose made her a favorite with all who stopped there. All simply loved diminutive Mollie Walsh."

One who was particularly taken with this angel of the trail was Jack Newman, a "big-fisted, big-hearted" roughneck and one of the region's best-liked cargo movers. Mollie had helped Newman heal a frostbitten hand, and melted his heart in the bargain. He was so smitten that he fended off other swains. Violently, when necessary. As the tale goes, Packer Jack once told a faro dealer to steer clear of Mollie. The gambler demurred, calling Newman "a low-down shaggy wolf and a ring-tailed wampus-cat." In response, Newman caught his rival out in the middle of Broadway, Skagway's main street, and before a large, betting audience, shot the dealer in the legs "to keep him from running to Log Cabin anymore."

He did less well at discouraging handsome 32-year-old Mike Bartlett, who'd met Mollie at a restaurant in Skagway, then visited her rest stop regularly. Jack tried everything he could to keep this pair apart, even ordering Mollie to bar Bartlett from her tent—but that just made her angry. "She said I wasn't her master, not being married to her, and this was a public eating-place, so anyone in the whole northland was welcome," Jack Newman told the *Seattle Star* long afterwards. "One thing led to another. Trifle piled on trifle. Neither of us would weaken. Then Mollie up and married the skunk."

Others had a higher opinion of Mike Bartlett. After he shot Mollie to death in Seattle, acquaintances would describe him as "a sober, industrious, and law-abiding citizen." The *Seattle Times* added that, as a freight transporter,

Bartlett "had made a name for himself—a name that was known and respected by the various communities in which he lived."

According to *Murder, Madness, and Mystery*, Amasa "Mike" Bartlett
was born in 1865 into a south Texas ranching family. He had two older
brothers, Al and Ed, as well as a sister, Josephine. The boys grew up han-
dling horses and mules, and after their father died in 1881, they used those
talents to keep food on the family table, moving wherever work took them.
By about 1885, the Bartlett brothers were in Washington state, teamstering
at mines and logging camps.

The Klondike Stampede brought them new opportunities. Men who
could efficiently haul great loads of goods over the 600 miles of trails and
rivers between Skagway-Dyea and the Yukon claims near Dawson received
a pretty penny for their services—one big operation collected as much as
$5,000 a day. Mike, Ed, and Al wanted a cut of the action, and by late 1897
they had it. Bartlett Bros. Packers and Forwarders was one of eight large-
scale packing enterprises in the area. They had an office in Skagway, a hotel
at Lake Bennett (where hikers from Chilkoot Pass boarded boats to continue their trek north down the Yukon River), and another office in Dawson
City at the confluence of the Yukon and Klondike rivers.

Not even a year had passed, though, before they were forced to re-
consider this venture. A narrow-gauge railroad was being laid from Skagway
to Whitehorse, an upper Yukon River town. From this transfer point, it took
freight-hauling boats just a few days to reach Dawson. Rather than fight a
losing battle to keep their long-distance trail trade profitable against cheaper
rail rates, in June 1898 the brothers hied their 75 to 100 mules off to Dawson
and concentrated on packing in and around the adjacent gold fields.

This move at first seemed propitious. Dawson had thrived during the
rush for riches. Yet, by the time Mike Bartlett and Mollie Walsh were wed
at Dawson's St. Mary's parsonage on December 11, 1898, the town's decline already was in the wind.

The Bartlett boys hoped to cover themselves by expanding their business. After gold was discovered at Nome on the Bering Sea, they shipped
toward that area in hopes of capturing the freight trade there. Demands
for their services proved minimal, however. The animals had to be returned,
further draining the Bartletts' resources, which already were at risk due to
their speculative ventures, such as the building of a hotel in Dawson, and
the steep cost of maintaining a "high life" style in the Klondike.

Mike, for one, liked to gamble—and he knew how to party. When
Mollie gave birth to a son in August 1900 aboard the sternwheeler *Seattle*

Bartlett Brothers pack train en route to mines in Yukon Territory, circa 1899. *UW Libraries, Hegg 3010*

No. 3, returning from Nome, Mike bought dinner for all 65 passengers (at a total cost of about $2,000) in exchange for their help in naming the child. The result—*Leon Edward Seattle No. 3 Yukon Woodpile Bartlett. Leon* by his mother's choice; *Edward* for his Uncle Ed; the names of the boat and river on which the infant took his first breath; and *Woodpile* because the ship's crew was loading fuel at the riverside when he was born.

Mike couldn't keep this pace up much longer—as Ed Bartlett testified in 1903, his youngest brother had been worth $100,000 in 1900, but "before the beginning of the next year, the fortune had decreased to about $16,000." Al was reportedly already broke and had wandered off into central Alaska. By 1901, levelheaded Ed, too, had given up and left for Eagle City, farther down the Yukon River.

All these pressures didn't help Mike and Mollie's marriage. Neither did her relationship with another Dawson businessman, John F. Lynch. As the *Dawson Sun* later gossiped, Lynch's "fascination for Mrs. Bartlett was apparent to everyone"—everyone, it seems, except for Mike, who said he trusted Mollie and his friend Lynch.

That trust was finally violated in the autumn of 1901. Mike had asked Ed to return north and straighten out the business. Meanwhile, he'd gone off to the gold fields, leaving behind a blank power of attorney for Ed to pick up on his arrival in Dawson. With both brothers absent, Lynch—either acting on his own or with Mollie's encouragement—filled out the power of attorney form himself, liquidated the Bartletts' holdings, and in company with Mollie and her 13-month-old son headed south.

"Crazed with grief," Mike Bartlett sped after them. What followed was something of a wild chase, from Alaska to as far south as Mexico, with stops in San Francisco and Portland. Bartlett's recklessness in asking everybody he encountered whether they'd seen his wife made his progress easy to follow, thus his quarry remained one giant step ahead of the packer-turned-tracker. But Bartlett finally caught up with Lynch in Seattle and got back what remained of his Dawson property deeds. Mollie was in Seattle, as well, though not with Lynch. She was staying at a Washington Street lodging house. Confronting Mollie with a pistol and threatening to shoot either himself or her (newspaper accounts differ), Mike convinced his wife to accompany him back to the Klondike.

The reconciliation was short lived, however. "After his trouble," the *Seattle Times* explained, "he drank continuously and became a physical wreck." Before long, Mike was "the tyrant of his family," added the *Seattle Post-Intelligencer*. Mollie needed to get away, and in August 1902 returned with little Leon to Seattle. Mike joined her there a month later—much to her dismay, for his carousing and continuing suicide attempts brought about Mollie's eviction. She moved instead to the cheap backroom of a family home off Pike Street. It was there, on October 13, 1902, that she had Mike Bartlett arrested, telling police officers he'd "abused her in all ways which he could devise, called her all the names nature could suggest, and had often threatened to make away with her very existence." Yet Mollie—the "soul of honor," as Reverend Dickey had once labeled her—subsequently pleaded for her husband's release, insisting that jail time might make him even more dangerous. Mike swore in the presence of a *P-I* reporter that he "would not harm a hair on the little woman's head." The judge reluctantly suspended his sentence.

Only two weeks later, Mollie was dead in an alley, shot twice in the back by the man she'd sworn to love and cherish, one bullet passing through her heart. Mike evidently had thought to kill himself, too. As policeman Claude Bannick (later Seattle's chief of police) approached him, he fired twice at his own head—and suffered no worse than a scalp wound, "more painful than dangerous."

Amazingly, on December 2, 1903, Mike Bartlett was found not guilty of murder by reason of insanity. His derangement perhaps was inherited, but it certainly was brought on by jealousy and drink. With young Leon sitting in court drumming up sympathy for his dad, defense witnesses were paraded by the jury to testify that Mike's mother had been demented, and that his brother Al, after vanishing into the Alaskan wilds, had been relegated to an insane asylum at Salem, Oregon.

After his release, Mike Bartlett proclaimed that he would remain in Seattle "for a time" working with his brother Ed, who had a part in the city's extensive regrading project. Later, Mike is supposed to have tried gold mining in Tibet and lumberjacking in the Northwest, before doing time in an asylum. He hanged himself in 1905.

Leon reportedly was left in the care of his Aunt Josephine in Los Angeles. He served as a soldier in World War I, and died in a Washington, D.C., soldier's home in the 1950s.

Meanwhile, Mollie Walsh Bartlett had been buried at her parents' gravesite in St. Paul, and nobody thought much about her after that—with the exception of Mollie's original paramour, Jack Newman, who had become a Seattle resident. On July 21, 1930, this old White Pass packer had erected at Skagway a bronze-and-granite bust of Mollie, the "angel" he'd never forgotten. It stands there still in a small park on 6th Avenue, an obscure vestige of Alaska's gold rush heritage, telling briefly about the "courageous girl" who "fed and lodged the wildest gold crazed men."

And dangling from the bust's neck is a medallion engraved with a face that looks suspiciously like Packer Jack when he was young. Mike Bartlett may have won Mollie's hand, but it seems Jack Newman is the one who'll remain with her forever.

The Great Chase

Unlike San Francisco or Denver, Seattle can't claim much of a "Wild West" history. Yet in 1902, it hosted what the *New York Times* called "the most remarkable manhunt in the annals of crime." The quarry—a "cold-blooded," rifle-packing desperado known as Harry Tracy.

Born Harry Severns (or Severynns) in Wisconsin in 1875, he left home in his late teens to work on railroads and in logging camps across the northern United States. But he didn't confine himself to lawful employment. In 1897 the man now styling himself as "Harry Tracy" was tossed into the Utah State Penitentiary for having burglarized a house, but escaped within four months, making his way to the Hole-in-the-Wall outlaw refuge near Thermopolis, Wyoming. There, he reportedly fell in with members of Butch Cassidy's Wild Bunch, robbing banks and raiding ranches, though he evidently wasn't a member of the Cassidy gang. Tracy subsequently was arrested for murdering a Colorado rancher, but escaped before trial, and in 1898 headed west to Portland, Oregon. He took up with a gambler and thief named David Merrill, and for several months this pair terrorized the bustling river town with daylight holdups of trains, streetcars, and saloons. But, in February 1899, both men were captured and imprisoned in the Oregon State Penitentiary at Salem.

This story might have ended there, except that Harry Tracy despised confinement. On June 9, 1902, he and Merrill, armed with Winchester rifles smuggled to them by a former convict, blasted a bloody path into the prison's main yard and, after grabbing a ladder, fled over a wall and into the surrounding woods. While lawmen organized a chase, the desperadoes pushed north, reaching the area around Chehalis, Washington. That turned out to be the end of the line for Merrill, because during the course of their escape, Tracy had learned from a newspaper report how his partner had helped Portland police capture him three years earlier. A "fair fight" over the matter led to Merrill being shot in the back, after which Tracy continued on to Olympia, where he hijacked a gasoline launch and ordered its captain to take him to Seattle.

Dropped off at Meadow Point on Shilshole Bay on the evening of July 2, Tracy started walking toward Ballard, then a separate small town known for its shingle production. (Ballard was annexed to Seattle in 1907.) Early the next day, a watchman spotted Tracy crossing the University of Washington campus, following the Seattle, Lake Shore & Eastern Railroad tracks (since supplanted by the Burke-Gilman Trail), and called the King County Sheriff's Office. Knowing that the rails led to the suburb of Bothell at the north end of Lake Washington, deputies and a couple of newspaper reporters set off in a downpour to ambush Tracy, only he got the upper hand instead, killing two of the pursuers. County Sheriff Edward Cudihee wasn't amused. A former marshal in Leadville, Colorado, Cudihee vowed to "run the killer to his death."

Tracy was a moving target. Returning to Seattle, he held up in a family home near Woodland Park just long enough to enjoy a homemade meal before Cudihee tracked him down. In the resulting melee, two possemen were killed. Later, the bandit forced a fisherman to row him across Puget Sound to Port Madison on Bainbridge Island, where Tracy ordered another frightened family to feed him, then set off across the Sound once more, bound for West Seattle. On July 7, the outlaw turned up in Renton and apparently charmed a mother and her daughters (one of whom remembered Tracy as "a gallant, tenderhearted man, a brilliant conversationalist") before slipping out the back door in time to avoid Sheriff Cudihee at the front entrance.

"How long can flesh and blood withstand the fatigue of constant movement and exposure to the elements?" asked the *Seattle Post-Intelligencer* as Tracy remained at large. "Even for a semi-human, the end must be at hand." However, the fugitive defied expectations. After holding up a family in Kent on July 9, and dodging what had looked like certain capture on the 11th, Tracy sets his sights eastward, possibly toward Hole-in-the Wall. Almost three more weeks passed with no reliable news of his whereabouts, until it was reported that he'd stolen a horse near Ellensburg on July 30. By this time, the outlaw had been fighting and running for almost two months, often without knowing precisely where he was going. Any hope he might've had that regular folk would let him pass unmolested was foiled by the rising price put on his head—$4,100 for bringing him in, dead or alive.

On August 3 when Harry Tracy reached the ranch of Eugene and Lucius Eddy near the eastern Washington town of

Creston, about 50 miles west of Spokane, he decided to rest. After taking the brothers hostage, he stayed with them for three days, even helping to repair their barn. Meanwhile, word of Tracy's whereabouts had leaked to Creston, where a citizen posse took shape. On August 5, five armed riders thundered out of town on their way to the Eddy ranch. Tracy saw them coming and, after grabbing up his rifle, sought protection behind a boulder in the middle of a wheat field. A lucky shot hit the outlaw's right leg, but he refused to give up. For hours Tracy held his pursuers at bay. Finally, as the loss of blood sapped his strength and with evening approaching, he tried to crawl off into the high grain, only to be shot again, this time in the right thigh. As more possemen gathered on the scene, Tracy realized he was trapped. But he wasn't going back to prison. He pulled a revolver from his shirt and stuck the muzzle to his head. Hearing a muffled shot, the posse ducked for cover. It wasn't until the next morning that they worked up the courage to discover that Harry Tracy, "the terror of the Northwest," had found his final escape.

GOING FOR THE GREEN

O N THURSDAY, APRIL 30, 1903, a slight, bearded gentleman with a receding hairline stepped off the morning train from Portland. The hem of his dark suit jacket was lifted slightly by a combination of breezes and residual steam belching from the locomotive. His eyes cast about intently for a contingent of local officials, who he'd understood would be meeting him and his associate upon their arrival in Seattle. He trusted that they wouldn't be late, for he had much work to do—an entire city to transform and make beautiful with new public parks—and he was most anxious to get started.

Not until later that night, after a tour of Seattle's existing commons and some of its viewpoints, did John Charles Olmsted feel free to relax and share with a *Post-Intelligencer* reporter his initial impressions. "I think the landscape conditions in Seattle are remarkably fine," enthused the designer from Brookline, Massachusetts. "On one side you have the Sound and on the other you have Lake Washington. Beside these fine bodies of water there are Green Lake and Lake Union… I do not know of any place where the natural advantages for parks are better than here. They can be made very attractive and will be, in time, one of the things that will make Seattle known all over the world."

Olmsted was being generous, for he knew as well as anybody that northwest Washington's principal municipality was then almost completely *un*known. It had only two real claims to fame—it had burned to the ground in 1889, and it became rich as the jumping-off point for the Yukon and Alaska gold rushes. Neither of these events, of course, had helped Seattle cultivate any air of refinement. This was still a boomtown shedding the raw wooliness of its frontier roots. Sure, there was some nationally acclaimed architecture standing here, and there were some pleasant areas for outdoor recreation—including Woodland Park that extended over the former estate of Guy Phinney, the flamboyant Englishman who'd made his fortune in Canadian real estate; Madison Park, which originally was an amusement enclave on the shores of Lake Washington; and Alki Beach, which until 1902 had been accessible only by ferry.

But what Seattle lacked, its civic leaders concluded, was an elegant, comprehensive plan, including a unified strategy for the propagation of urban greenswards. So, with the help of master landscaper Olmsted—and the enthusiastic support of taxpayers—they set about to create one.

Theirs was a courageous and foresightful campaign blocking thousands of acres of land against future urban and suburban development. And its timing could hardly have been more propitious. If such a far-reaching and aggressive project had been suggested many years earlier, locals might've dismissed it because they weren't yet worried about the city growing uncontrollably. Had the plan been set aside until many years afterward, chances are that business lobbies and the fretting over the scheme's expenses would've conspired to prevent its realization. Either way, this place would have been worse off. "In the absence of the Olmsted plan," charges historian Richard C. Berner in *Seattle, 1900–1920: From Boomtown, Urban Turbulence, to Restoration*, "the city would have had no coherent blueprint for the future at all. Its growth would have been dictated entirely by commercial considerations."

It was hardly surprising that Seattle park commissioners should have appealed to John Olmsted for direction. After all, he was the nephew, stepson, and inheritor of the creative flame of Frederick Law Olmsted Sr., a former journalist and farmer who eventually had become 19th-century America's most renowned landscape designer.

Olmsted *père* was born in 1822 and grew up in an America where towns were still mostly small, with nature reigning close at hand and the nearest thing to a formal park likely being the local cemetery to which regular folk often retired for picnics. But as the republic became increasingly urbanized, Olmsted recognized the need for natural areas for escape amid city settings. He, along with British architect Calvert Vaux, was chosen through a competition to design and supervise construction of Manhattan's Central Park. Olmsted went on to mastermind or influence leafy retreats in Brooklyn, Detroit, and Baltimore, to plan the United States Capitol grounds and lay out entire parks systems for Boston and Buffalo, and to produce the site layout for Chicago's classically conceived World's Columbian Exposition of 1893. His work at the Chicago fair helped inspire the so-called City Beautiful movement. Over the following decade, City Beautiful forces took hold in many of America's ambitious metropolises, preaching the design orthodoxy of building impressive, often white buildings surrounded by ample complements of open parklands. "Openness is the one thing you cannot get in buildings," Olmsted Sr. had once counseled his followers. "Picturesqueness you can get. Let your buildings be as picturesque as your artists can make them. This is the beauty of a town. Consequently, the beauty of the park should be the other. It should be the beauty of the fields, the meadow, the prairie, of the green pastures, and the still waters. What we want to gain is tranquility and rest to the mind."

Olmsted Sr., however, wasn't always faultless in judging where some of these natural wonders should and shouldn't be located. Visiting San Francisco in the 1870s, for instance, he was asked by the board of supervisors to rule on the wisdom of building a giant new park in that city's sandy western reaches. Olmsted walked over the property, listening to the proposals for its edenic rebirth, and then recommended that a completely different site be selected. There was no way, he declared, that such a "great sand bank" could be made hospitable to a complexity of flora. Today, that "great sand bank" is magnificent Golden Gate Park.

Not everybody, too, was easily swayed by his passion for relieving the monotonous uniformity of urban tracts with natural havens. Indeed, one of Frederick Law Olmsted's most spectacular failures in this regard occurred in Tacoma. In 1873 the City of Destiny had hired him to develop its comprehensive plan. But councilmen there quickly rejected the exquisite gridless, park-lined, and contoured street arrangements he offered. One critic expressed astonishment at "blocks [that] were shaped like melons, pears, and sweet potatoes." Historian Murray Morgan writing in *Puget's Sound* explained, "Speculators who wanted to buy corner lots saw no merit in a downtown deliberately left deficient in four-way intersections. Olmsted's dream of a business district without bottlenecks was to them a nightmare."

Improbable Dream

Even before Seattle's original downtown had risen completely from the ashes of the 1889 conflagration, business was outgrowing the Pioneer Square district. Regrading of the city's often steep slopes—a task consuming public energy from the 1890s through the 1920s—opened up new commercial real estate to the north, which renewed debate about just what Seattle should look like in the future. After approving the Olmsted plan to propagate new parklands across the town's face, in 1910 local voters also established a 21-member Municipal Plans Commission, charged with creating a comprehensive program for the town's growth. It, in turn, hired a director of planning, Virgil G. Bogue.

A 64-year-old New Yorker, Bogue claimed ample experience as an engineer. He'd worked with Frederick Law Olmsted Sr. on the design of Brooklyn's Prospect Park, supervised railroad laying in Peru, built train terminals in San Francisco and Baltimore, and constructed significant portions of the Northern Pacific. Like Reginald H. Thomson, who headed the Municipal Plans Commission, Bogue refused to respect or be limited by the capriciousness of topography. He had big ideas, much in line with that era's City Beautiful movement. And, he seemed possessed of the persuasive powers necessary to turn dreams into reality.

The cornerstone of Bogue's grand scheme for Seattle was a

Nonetheless, Olmsted Sr. never wavered from his belief that the best cities integrated sylvan tracts among commercial and residential ones. To him, as to other opinionmakers of his time, parks provided even more than physical and spiritual medicine—they also were a means of "social control," as Olmsted defined it, tending to "weaken the dangerous inclinations" of the citizenry by removing them from the "bustle and jar of the streets" where tension and violence so often reigned.

All of this he drilled into his son, Frederick Law Olmsted Jr., as well as his older stepson John (whose mother had married Olmsted Sr. after the death of her first husband, his brother). By the time Frederick Law Olmsted Sr. retired in 1895 (he passed away in 1903), the two stepbrothers were well equipped to carry on their progenitor's Massachusetts-based practice.

new Beaux-Arts civic center complex in the Denny regrade area, comprising a courthouse, federal building, art museum, library, and city hall topped with a 15-story tower. These would all face a European-style plaza at 4th Avenue and Blanchard Street, and be connected via a broad tree-shaded boulevard to a railroad station at the southwest corner of Lake Union. There was much else to commend about Bogue's vision, including an intricate rapid-transit system with 33 miles of electric-powered subways and 27 miles of elevated trains, a five-mile commuter transit tunnel burrowed beneath Lake Washington, and still more new parks, with all of Mercer Island set aside as "a people's playground." The Bogue Plan encompassed an area of more than 150 square miles.

When first unveiled in September 1911, Bogue's designs were heartily endorsed. They quickly lost support, however, as naysayers complained of the expense (Bogue figured that the civic center alone would cost $3.5 million to build), and wealthy businessmen rallied against a project that would shift government offices out of the downtown's south end, where these entrepreneurs had so many of their principal real-estate investments. Within five months, negative press coverage convinced Seattle voters to reject the Bogue Plan by an almost two-to-one margin, though some elements of it were later built in piecemeal fashion around the city.

John Olmsted, who had become a full partner in his stepfather's firm in 1884, was quick to prove himself in Seattle. By October 1903, he'd already surveyed the town and submitted to the parks board a plan outlining what the *P-I* called "a complete chain of parks and parkways, with playgrounds located at suitable points throughout the city." One of Olmsted's foremost ideas was to provide a park or playground within one mile of every home. Unfortunately, since business and industry already had scooped up much of the best land hereabouts, the city had to exercise its broad powers of condemnation in order to acquire whatever barely developed or undevelopable land was available. Seattleites cheered Olmsted's progress. In 1906, 1908, and 1910, they passed the bond issues necessary to implement his plans.

Under John Olmsted's patient supervision, a 20-mile belt of parklands and boulevards took shape, eventually reaching north and west from the Bailey Peninsula (rechristened Seward Park) on Lake Washington to Fort Lawton (today's Discovery Park) in Magnolia. Beacon Hill, Green Lake, Woodland, and Volunteer parks, as well as the Mount Baker neighborhood, were all eventually influenced by Olmsted's City Beautiful vision. So were Seattle's far northern reaches where the Olmsted firm designed the lush Highlands subdivision in 1909 for local business barons, such as airplane manufacturer William E. Boeing and mill owner Charles D. Stimson. Arguably, the 200-acre Washington Park Arboretum, planned in 1936 and stretching south from Lake Washington's Union Bay, was the final jewel in Olmsted's necklace of parks. It was set aside as urban wilderness in 1904, but wasn't developed into a park until the University of Washington agreed to manage it jointly with the city.

There were only a few occasions when Olmsted found his beautification proposals snubbed. The city was obdurate, for example, against constructing a "crest drive" from the Mount Baker district north to the Denny-Blaine area, where majestic alcazars of the wealthy might sprout. The expense of acquiring this property was simply deemed too dear. However, the city fathers did give their go-ahead for establishing Lake Washington Boulevard, which meanders pleasantly north along the lakeshore from Seward Park through the Washington Park Arboretum, and fingers off west into sinuous Interlaken Boulevard. In 1908 they also turned thumbs up on lowering Green Lake—which proved to be a mistake. Olmsted wanted to reduce the water level so that he could create an encircling boulevard. This was accomplished in 1911, and the seven-foot drop exposed hundreds of acres of land. But lowering Green Lake had a most undesirable side effect—the elimination of creeks and springs in the natural drainage basin created stagnant waters. By 1921, the lake had become a smelly, algae-infested swamp famous for causing an annoying ailment known as "Green Lake Itch." The Health Department was forced to close the lake to swimmers, but a massive cleanup in 1961–62 and more recent algae treatment programs have supposedly made it safe.

Interestingly, and in spite of the fact that they courted work in the Northwest, the Olmsted Brothers firm demonstrated a marked antipathy toward this area's native flora. Olmsted Sr. had drawn inspiration from 18th-century English landscapers, endorsing a micro-managed, formal, almost painterly approach to arboreal design that didn't take into account regional diversity. John C. and Frederick Jr. thought Seattle's ubiquitous fir trees looked fine from a distance, but were "mean and crowded at close quarters." They also believed firs would fail in the onslaught of factory smoke, thus they recommended that "fir trees, in fact all conifers, and evergreens would better be removed at once." At Volunteer Park (named in 1901 to honor Spanish-American War veterans), the Olmsteds replaced all of the natural shrubbery with imported exotica. They did the same on the grounds of the former Hollywood Farm, now the Chateau Ste. Michelle Winery, in the Eastside suburb of Woodinville.

It was primarily in peripheral greenswards, such as Seward Park, where they did permit the hegemony of some "wild" vegetation. They made excellent use of Northwest shrubbery, too, at the Alaska-Yukon-Pacific Exposition, held on the University of Washington grounds in 1909. Their site plan called for a variety of bedding plants, but at the focal point of the fair—the grand Arctic Circle—rhododendrons predominated, "selected for their rich evergreen texture and dark color, which handsomely set off

The Olmsted Brothers landscaped the Alaska-Yukon-Pacific Exposition grounds. The fair's official photographer, Frank H. Nowell, shot this view toward Lake Washington. *UW Libraries, Nowell x1040a*

Cause for Celebration

At noon on June 1, 1909, President William Howard Taft, seated at the other end of the country in the cavernous East Room of the White House, lowered a finger upon a telegraph key decorated with Klondike gold, causing a gong to resound at the University of Washington. Thus began the Alaska-Yukon-Pacific Exposition (AYP), Seattle's first world's fair and its unofficial "coming out party." Previous American fairs had commemorated the anniversaries of discovery or original settlement. But this one, as historian Norman H. Clark once contended, celebrated only the fact that "in the story of civilization there is probably no record of more astonishing growth than occurred in the region around Puget Sound."

During its 138-day run, the AYP was attended by 3,740,551 patrons from all over the globe, among them New York Governor Charles Evans Hughes and silver-tongued orator William Jennings Bryan, whose address at the fair evidently was so stimulating that listeners rushed the stage and plucked silver buttons from the Great Commoner's coat. Even the adipose Taft couldn't stay away. He seemed impressed, not only by Seattle in general, which he declared to be "one of the most magnificent combinations of modern city and medieval forest, of formal gardening and Nature's handiwork...that has ever delighted the eye of men in this or any other country," but also by the AYP's gold-panning exhibit that produced for the rotund president a small nugget that he promptly pocketed.

Visitors stood in awe of the fair's main neoclassical temples. Some had been designed by local architects, such as John Graham Sr., though the overall planning was done by a San Francisco firm, Howard and Galloway, and its chief designer, the French-born Édouard Frère Champney (who later moved to Seattle). The Olmsted Brothers, of course, were responsible for the landscaping. Fairgoers toured state pavilions (including New York's, a replica of the mansion owned by William H. Seward who had negotiated the U.S. purchase of Alaska from Russia in 1867). They also crowded into the Pay Streak carnival center, where dancing girls performed and scale models of the vessels *Merrimac* and *Monitor* re-created the famous Civil War duel. By the time the AYP closed, Seattle not only had permanently enhanced the elegance of its university grounds, but also had confirmed the city's rise to prosperity and final emergence from abject bumpkinhood.

the light cream of the buildings," as later reported in a *Pacific Northwest Quarterly* article. The Seattle Chamber of Commerce was so pleased with the Olmsteds' work that efforts were made to preserve the fairgrounds as a public park. The university eventually reasserted its control, but maintained some elements of the Olmsted plan, especially its orientation providing for the best views of Mount Rainier.

The Evergreen State was about as far as the Olmsteds could travel from their home in Massachusetts and still be in the contiguous United States. However, they seemed to have showered Washington with their talents.

Not wanting to be shown up by Seattle, its "wetside" rival, Spokane formed a park board in 1907 and promptly hired John Olmsted to begin planning its own park system. Over several visits, and after touring existing and potential park sites, he submitted his preliminary recommendations and report in May 1908. The plan called for the creation of four large parks, or "reservations of country scenery," including substantial acreage along the Spokane River. It also endorsed the development of five medium-sized parks, a number of parkways and boulevards "specially fitted for pleasure driving and walking," and several smaller parks and playfields. Much of the plan was implemented, though it sometimes took a while. For instance, Olmsted had suggested turning as much riverfront property as possible into parkland. Yet, not until construction began on the Spokane World's Fair of 1974 were railyards that stood between downtown and the Spokane River removed. The area now is part of Riverfront Park.

In addition to citywide beautification projects, the Olmsted firm took on a variety of smaller public and private commissions. Its designers directed landscaping at the capitol campus in Olympia, they planned sections of Rosario Resort (the former estate of Seattle shipbuilder-turned-mayor, Robert Moran) on Orcas Island in the San Juans, and they were consulted in regard to park plans for Sedro Woolley, Bellingham, and Walla Walla. They also collaborated with such renowned architects as Spokane's Kirtland Cutter in landscaping residential grounds across the state. Catherine Joy Johnson, who has spent years studying and photographing Olmsted works throughout Washington, particularly residential ones, says she has counted almost 200 residential spaces on which the Olmsted firm worked, "though many of them weren't completed." Most are not now open for public viewing.

Still, it's in Seattle where the Olmsteds' influence seems most keenly felt. As John Olmsted predicted, his extensive parks plan was one of the things that made Seattle famous.

GOD'S OWN SINNER

O N THE MORNING OF MAY 7, 1906, Mr. and Mrs. Edmond Creffield were walking through downtown Seattle on their way to purchase a dress for Mrs. Creffield. They strolled along Pike Street and turned south on 1st Avenue. When they reached Cherry Street on the edge of Pioneer Square, George Mitchell suddenly appeared out of nowhere, raised a pistol, and put a bullet in the back of Edmond Creffield's head—killing him instantly.

It certainly was premeditated murder most foul, and probably warranted the death penalty. Yet most people seemed to agree with Seattle District Attorney John Manning, who said Mitchell "did a very laudable act in eliminating that miserable animal Creffield from the face of the earth." The citizens of Corvallis, Oregon, where Creffield had earlier made his mark, even tried to award Mitchell a gold medal.

Edmond Creffield was not a popular person—with good reason. During an era that continued to be influenced by the restrictive parameters of Victorian morality, Creffield had been an unabashed debaucher. From 1903 through 1906, he led the Northwest's most outrageous cult, preaching free love to any woman who would listen. He and his followers held services during which they rolled around deliriously on the floor. Stories circulated about religious proselytes standing naked in fields at night and howling at the moon. At one point, Creffield even claimed to have precipitated the great San Francisco earthquake. Although this region has hosted other holy (con)men in the decades since, Edmond Creffield, with his synthesis of sex and sermonizing, was in a class all his own. And amen to that.

Franz Edmond (sometimes recorded as "Edwin") Creffield wasn't always such a notorious character. Born in Germany, he began his adult life as a righteous sort of man who would volunteer eagerly to ring bells outside department store windows at Christmastime. He'd been a deserter from the German army, and was trained in Europe for the priesthood. Soon after he arrived in Portland in 1903, Creffield joined the Salvation Army and was dispatched to do good deeds in the southern Oregon town of Corvallis.

But at some point during his trip south, the insulation of Creffield's moral wiring wore through and he short-circuited badly. His first unusual deed was to establish the "Bride of Christ Church" and promote himself as the second Jesus Christ. He began calling himself "Joshua," and immediately enlisted a hundred fanatic ladies who were convinced that being the bride of Christ or the mother of His child was a quick way to garner some nifty perks in Heaven.

These ladies' disgruntled husbands, fathers, and brothers were much less enthusiastic over the behavior of the appropriately nicknamed Holy Rollers. Corvallis resident Charles Mitchell, for instance, watched his 16-year-old daughter, Esther, become one of Creffield's most devout followers. Mitchell bitterly described a typical prayer service of the Bride of Christ Church to a Seattle reporter: "Creffield was accustomed to get women and girls into his rooms, put them under hypnotic influence and have them strip off their clothing, roll on the floor and become defiled. He was not satisfied with ruining young girls, but caused them to utterly debase themselves."

"God only knows the days and nights of anxiety and mental agony that have been suffered because of the work of that man Creffield," griped Victor Hurt, a Corvallis businessman. "Peaceful, happy families have been broken up, virtuous women have been led astray, children have been turned against parents and wives against husbands, through some strange, unaccountable power this man Creffield exerted."

Hurt knew well what Creffield could do. Before the apostle's arrival in Corvallis, Hurt had lived with his devoted wife, two daughters, and a son in a home where it was said, "happiness reigned unbroken." Soon the bizarre Holy Rollers had every Hurt but Victor under their spell. With Mrs. Hurt's sanction, the Creffielders took over the Hurt residence. They torched the furniture. They left dead cats and dogs scattered about the house, presumably in the aftermath of some frenzied ceremony. They wore peculiar clothes and performed "unnatural rites" that made them "conspicuous all over Christendom." It was reported that "for days at a time," the Hurt family "lay prostate upon the floor of their own home, refusing all food and joining [Creffield] in continuous prayer."

Finally, as Hurt was preparing for a business trip to the East Coast, Creffield mentioned he was planning to enlarge the Hurt abode to "accommodate a larger number of Rollers." The citizenry of Corvallis "warmly congratulated" Victor Hurt when he finally threw the prophet out.

Corvallis didn't find it that easy to get rid of Creffield, however. Together with Charles Brooks, another former Salvation Army worker, Creffield reorganized his efforts in another house. There they continued services with the help of 10 young female followers, still including Mrs. Hurt and her two daughters. This continued until January 4, 1904, when a group of men who claimed to have "suffered more or less in the family circle on account of the effect the new faith has had on members of the household," kicked in the door of Creffield's new headquarters and dragged both the Christ-pretender and Brooks outside. There they were commanded to strip. As Joshua removed his last article of attire, he spied a pile of feathers next to a bucket of tar.

"Let us pray," Creffield said to Brooks.

A gruff voice responded: "We have had too much of your kind of prayers already."

Tar and feathers were applied liberally, and the men were told never to darken another Corvallis doorstep—on threat of death. So without delay, the two fluffy fanatics scurried north to the small town of Albany, Oregon. The next day brought "a sensational sequel to the affair," as one Corvallis newspaperman reported. "Giving off strongly from his person the odor of tar, and with his face and neck red from excessive scouring, Apostle Creffield…was in Albany today for the purpose of getting married." No one blamed Victor Hurt for not attending his daughter Maud's wedding.

It was a peculiar honeymoon. Creffield and his blushing bride traveled to Portland for the purpose of visiting Mrs. Burgess Starr and her sister, Esther Mitchell, who had strayed from the cult's Corvallis flock. Actually, Burgess Starr had moved his family to Portland just to escape Creffield's vile influence. Mrs. Starr was so eager to rejoin the Rollers that her husband had to slap an adultery suit on Reverend Joshua before he could quell her enthusiasm.

News of Edmond Creffield had spread quickly throughout the region, so Portlanders were not thrilled to see him in their growing river town. Newspapers condemned his actions and his very presence. Parents kept close rein on their female offspring while Creffield was about. Residents of the town didn't breathe easier until it was announced that the promiscuous prophet and his new spouse were once again moving on—heading back to Corvallis, of all places.

Not until a month later, though, did anybody see the "bogus saint" again. He had decided to hide out for a while, in a trench beneath Victor Hurt's house. It wasn't a bad hiding place, though the only comforts available to Creffield were a filthy pillowcase and blanket. Loyal followers smuggled food in to him. Through a crack in the foundation, the apostle continued to instruct the faithful. He existed nicely under those conditions for some months, though he suffered from the awkward fact that as more and more of the congregation were committed to the state insane asylum, his food supply dwindled.

The dirty, starving, and very nude Joshua Creffield wasn't a pretty prophet when authorities finally dragged him into the daylight. With a long beard and dark, baggy eyes that stood out against his pale skin, he looked much older than his 31 years. However, his religious fervency was in no way dimmed. "The Lord commanded me to hide. So I hid," he explained to his captors. "I am not crazy. I am Elijah."

Some preferred the non-Elijah interpretation of his state. Creffield was hustled back to Portland to face charges of violating Mrs. Burgess Starr, and sentenced to two years in the Oregon State Penitentiary. Rather than plead for judicial leniency, Creffield noted that Christ had had his ups and downs, too. Once the guru was behind bars, most of his followers came to disavow and even ridicule the Bride of Christ Church. Maud Hurt Creffield filed for divorce.

Things remained quiet on this front until February 1906, when Creffield was released from prison and made his way to California, just in time to take credit for the ruinous San Francisco earthquake in May, which he alleged was the result of a three-way curse that also doomed Portland and Corvallis. The sullied saint tried to boost his spiritual stock still further with an announcement that he was "the risen Christ, his rising being his emergence from prison, and his death being his captivity there."

The resurrected Creffield returned to Oregon, where his troops—despite their previous repudiations of his "mission"—immediately gathered to his side once again. Maud Hurt remarried the old reprobate, and Esther Mitchell was overjoyed to learn that she had been chosen to give birth to "Christ's child." "A Babe born of a Virgin," Maud Creffield called it.

The Creffielders re-established their cult in the Oregon coast town of Waldport, but the cult's rebirth soon was aborted. The husband of one of Creffield's feminine followers tried to shoot the guru and recapture his loved one. Joshua escaped this time because the husband had purchased the wrong cartridges for his pistol. Though he survived, Creffield viewed the attempted assassination as a bad omen. He fled to Seattle with his wife and Esther Mitchell, only to have George Mitchell—who had followed his sister, Esther—put an end to the licentious pastor of the Bride of Christ Church with a closely aimed bullet. Portland's *Oregonian* delicately headlined the event, "HOLY ROLLER SHOT DOWN LIKE A DOG."

Responding to a telegram for help from Mitchell, Victor Hurt left Corvallis immediately for Seattle, to "secure the aid of the best lawyers in that city to defend Mitchell against whatever charges may be brought against him." The help wasn't needed. The *Seattle Times* editorialized that murderer Mitchell deserved "immediate freedom," and he received it, returning to local streets a hero.

Shortly after his release, however, Mitchell's sister said good-bye to him as he was preparing to board a train at King Street Station. As George turned to leave, Esther drew a gun and executed him in the same manner he had done in her beloved Creffield. Frank Hurt, Victor's son and a longtime member of the cult, reportedly furnished money for the weapon.

The bodies kept piling up. Maud Hurt Creffield was soon after found dead at the age of 26 in her Seattle jail cell. She was buried next to her infamous hubby in Seattle's Lake View Cemetery, beneath small gravestones that have been either severely weather-beaten or abused over the last century.

Esther Mitchell was committed to the Washington State Insane Asylum. In 1909 she was released and for unrecorded reasons was placed in the custody of Victor Hurt. Rather than return with her to the Hurt home in southern Oregon, Victor left instead to join the ragged remnants of Creffield's Holy Rollers in Waldport.

That seems the final ironic twist in this tale, for Victor Hurt to become a convert. History isn't clear whether he did. All we know is that it was he who'd said from the start that Creffield and his church had a "strange, unaccountable power."

Class Act

"Historically what's the first sign of a real community developing? The construction of a school building," contends Katheryn Hills Krafft, a coordinator with the King County Landmarks and Heritage Program. "Schools are only put up in places where people intend to stay, to raise their families. They are signs of permanence and promises of longevity. The history of a place can be read, in part, through its schools."

That is certainly true in Seattle. Although this burg's first privately funded school was established in 1854, and its earliest public educational facility opened 16 years later, it wasn't until after the Great Fire of 1889 that school construction here really took off. Locals wanted both to alleviate the congestion that had plagued classrooms, and to prepare for an influx of new students brought to the Puget Sound area by parents hoping to cash in on the timber trade and long-promised cross-country rail connections. Eighteen new schools were erected within the city limits between 1889 and 1899, as Seattle's population doubled, and another 28 rose over the succeeding 10 years as the number of residents almost tripled again.

While the Seattle School District employed a number of architects to help fulfill its infrastructural needs—some of whose names remain familiar a century later—the greatest burden fell on a less well remembered cabinetmaker-turned-designer, James Stephen. During his eight years as the district's first architect, Stephen was responsible for the planning and building supervision of more than 50 new institutions of learning or additions to existing edifices. The "look" he created in wood and, later, brick architecture remains familiar in schools all over town—such as John Hay Elementary (1905; currently housing the Bilingual Orientation Center) on Capitol Hill; north Seattle's renovated Greenwood Elementary (1909); the Summit School (1904–5; now the private Northwest School) on First Hill; the Wallingford area's Latona Elementary (1909; refurbished as the John Stanford International School); and what today is the shop-filled Wallingford Center (1904; formerly the Interlake School). His influence extends across the state, too, in landmarks stretching from Everett to Pullman.

But the January 2001 fire that destroyed Queen Anne's Frantz Coe Elementary, a fine 1907 example of Stephen's work, demonstrates the fragility of this legacy, as well as the need to mindfully protect it. If, as Krafft suggests, our past can be told by our classroom structures, then every chapter counts.

James Stephen's own story begins in the mid-1850s when his parents emigrated from Scotland to Canada. James was born in Woodstock, Ontario, on March 29, 1858, and by age 16 he and his family had relocated to Detroit, Michigan, where James—presumably trained in woodworking by his cabinetmaker father—took a job building organs. But he wasn't satisfied, so after the clan moved to Chicago around 1880 (where his father went to work for the Pullman Car Company), James enrolled in a correspondence-school architecture course, and after two more years, he established his own practice in Hyde Park, Illinois (later incorporated into the Windy City), where he married a former Missourian, Ida Mary Rowan, and started his own family.

However, the flames that flattened 30 blocks of downtown Seattle in June 1889 convinced Stephen—along with many other architects and builders—that he could do better by moving to Puget Sound. Though most of the plum rebuilding contracts went to Elmer Fisher, another designer with Scottish roots who had progressed from crafting furniture to drafting buildings, there were ample commissions left over for firms like Saunders & Houghton, which hired Stephen "while the town was still smoking," as he later told his children. Over the next few years, partners Edwin W. Houghton and Charles W. Saunders created multiple commercial blocks and several schools. It was good training for Stephen, who in 1894 finally broke away to enter his own partnership with German-born Timotheus Josenhans. During their three-year association, this pair executed a number of noteworthy projects, including three buildings at the new Washington Agricultural College, Experiment Station, and School of Science (now Washington State University), one of which is present-day Thompson Hall (1894–95). However, the steep drop in construction projects following the 1893 Panic sent Stephen off for a year, to construct prefabricated sternwheelers for use in Alaska, before he could return to architecture.

In the spring of 1901, the Seattle School Board decided to raise a series of wood-frame grammar schools with identical floor plans. Their exemplar was Green Lake School, which Stephen had recently designed for a lot on North 65th Street. Colonial Revival in style, with a pedimented gable roof, central pillared portico, and two stories (plus a raised brick basement), the structure proved to be an ideal model for the young city. It allowed schools to be built in phases, beginning with central sections that contained eight classrooms, and then adding wings to increase the number of rooms to 12 or 20, as needed. New schools were distinguished, as well, by variations in their elevations and embellishments. For instance, Interlake School and unexpanded John Hay Elementary both followed this model plan— however, the Hay school is set apart by octagonal towers flanking its main entrance. Nineteen schoolhouses across Seattle were erected using this model plan, many of them designed by Stephen, with others farmed out to architects such as Charles H. Bebb and Louis L. Mendel (1902; University Heights School) or Charles W. Saunders and George W. Lawton (1902; Horace Mann Elementary).

No doubt, due to his crafts-man background, "Stephen understood how to build buildings

Studying Stephen

For a better feel regarding James Stephen's architectural vision, just visit a few of Seattle's school buildings—
- **Greenwood Elementary School**
  144 Northwest 80th Street
- **Queen Anne High School** (Queen Anne High School Apartments)
  201 Galer Street
- **Latona Elementary School** (John Stanford International School)
  401 Northeast 42nd Street
- **Interlake School** (Wallingford Center)
  4400 Wallingford Avenue North
- **Summit School** (The Northwest School)
  1415 Summit Avenue

in wood like no one else," says landmarks authority Krafft, whose interest in Stephen dates back to the late 1970s when she worked to win Summit School a spot on the National Register of Historic Places. Stephen's genuine love of wood is obvious if you wander through his schools, paying particular attention to their intricately detailed staircases.

After a 1907 trip to study educational facilities in the Midwest and New York, however, the architect developed a second model for Seattle's grade schools, using fireproof materials—brick, terra cotta, and concrete—in place of wood. This plan called for nine classrooms on two floors. Roofs were steeply pitched and facades were executed in Jacobean style, an amalgam of Tudor and Elizabethan styles, which then was much in vogue. Seven of these more costly edifices ($60,000 apiece) were constructed in 1908–9, including Greenwood Elementary and Emerson Elementary. During that same period, Stephen labored on Seattle's two oldest extant high schools—Lincoln (in Wallingford, 1907) and Queen Anne (1909; later converted to housing).

Amid all of this, Stephen somehow found time for projects that had absolutely nothing to do with education. He designed homes, commercial piles, and even the original, northernmost section of Seattle's downtown YMCA (1905; demolished in 1999). Yet even after he quit as district architect in 1909, he continued working on schools around the state (including Everett High School, 1908–10) in partnership with his oldest son, Frederick. James Stephen retired in 1928 and died a decade later.

"It's impossible to live in Seattle and not notice Stephen's work," enthuses Krafft. "The fact that he isn't better known is because he was not a self-promoter."

Fortunately, the last six decades have seen others champion his creations. Several of Stephen's local schools have been designated landmarks. While a few, such as the original Green Lake Elementary, are gone, neighborhood activists have fought to save others—either to have the structures continue serving their original purpose, or to be adapted to non-educational uses. Built to educate children, they now teach adults some lessons about Seattle's heritage.

Luna Park. *UW Libraries, UW 321*

END OF INNOCENCE

S WITH SO MANY OTHER AMUSEMENT PARKS of its time, it sat on the water, bordered by the beach—actually and symbolically on the very edge of things. It was a great fake of pasteboard, nuts, and bolts and 11,000 electric lights that forced back the night, a permanent carnival reclining on pilings driven into Puget Sound. It was the realized unconscious of its supposedly innocent age—thrilling and just a little frightening at the same time.

Because it was always intended to be a magical place, as well as a successful business, the builder called it Luna Park after one of the gaudiest but most prosperous components of New York's Coney Island. For eight summers from 1907 to 1913, it drew a democracy of locals to Duwamish Head in West Seattle. People came to ride the Great Figure-Eight roller coaster, the giant Circle Swing, the Canals of Venice, the Cave of Mystery, and the Shoot-the-Chutes (with a lagoon built right atop the pilings). They gawked at an "Original Human Ostrich," high divers, and daredevil riders on their loop-the-loop runs. They sat raptly before The Great Davenports, who performed "mid-air extravaganzas on the high wire," and the marching 17 Fremont Zouaves, who gave "an exhibition of fancy and lightning drilling seldom if ever equaled." They sipped red lemonade, rode in hot-air balloons, tried their luck at shooting galleries, and remained ever vigilant for pickpockets, who found amusement park goers easy marks. They watched crude motion pictures and comely Egyptian actresses, and their own images distorted to every extreme in a hall of mirrors. And they couldn't help but wonder at an exhibition called The Infant Electrobator. What other oddities might be found in this place?

"Play is not a luxury," one social reformer contended at the turn of the last century, "but an absolute necessity to the working world of today." Luna Park, then, was filling a social need. It provided an escape valve for summer energies, a place where Seattleites could be entertained not only by acrobats and sideshow acts, but by each other. It was the apotheosis of the ridiculous and the profane, yet it was no more predictable or less confusing than life itself.

Duwamish Head was a natural location for an amusement center. Summertime revelers and campers long had frequented the broad shoulders of Alki Beach, and speculators considered it several times as the ideal site for a major resort. Presaging the construction of Luna Park, a former Klondike gold miner in 1901 had built something there called the Coney Island Baths, which offered "a good bath and swim and use of fresh running water." Suits could be rented if you failed to pack your own.

In early 1907, Charles I.D. Looff quickly realized Seattle's potential when he visited the Puget Sound area. After all, he was no neophyte to the amusement park industry. A furniture carver-turned-carousel artist from Schleswig-Holstein (in what is now part of northwest Germany), Looff had installed the first carousel at Coney Island in 1876, the year of America's centennial celebration. It was a polychromatic marvel of camels, zebras, and ostriches, as well as standard horse figures, some of them decorated with lighted jewels. He went on to create a number of machines for that Brooklyn enterprise, gaining fame and setting the highest standard for carousel carvers of his day. In 1890 he opened his own factory nearby, selling carousels and other funhouse rides to institutions around the country.

Fifteen years later, after a dispute over the land on which his factory sat (the City of New York condemned it in order to build a park), Looff relocated from Brooklyn to Rhode Island and began planning a national amusement park empire. Within another decade, he was a multimillionaire, had his entire operation based in Long Beach, California, and was the proud proprietor of entertainment facilities in Santa Cruz and Santa Monica, California, in addition to Luna Park on Puget Sound.

The *West Seattle Enterprise* declared in the spring of 1907 that Looff's $200,000 complex at Duwamish Head would supply "about every modern appliance and equipment possessed by an up-to-date seaside pleasure resort." This included not only a roller coaster and "Wonders of the Ocean" (an early aquarium), but also a large saltwater natatorium (a swimming center where bathers enjoyed separate-sex tanks), band shell, skating rink, and dance pavilion. Not to neglect his roots, Looff installed one of his prized carousels—complete with prancing horses and "sneaky tigers"—in a round, cavernous, onion-domed edifice that was encircled by windows and resounded with what the *Seattle Times* termed "an immense orchestration, the music of which equals that of many bands." Attractions such as the bear pit and billiards parlor earned slightly less press attention, though they certainly had their patrons.

A *Times* reporter, touring the 10 to 14 acres of Luna Park only days before it was completed, positively gushed over its modernity—a garage had even been built to accommodate "automobile loving patrons"—as well as its declarations of decorum. "It will be the policy of the management," explained the *Times*man, "to conduct the park on strictly legitimate and moral lines, and nothing will be permitted which will offend anyone. Women are perfectly free to visit Luna Park unattended, and it will be a paradise for children."

Indeed, to entertainment-starved Seattleites this place offered a distinctly paradisiacal atmosphere on opening day, June 27, 1907. "There was an unusually large attendance, the management estimating the number at from four to five thousand," observed the *Seattle Post-Intelligencer*. Young ladies in frilly bonnets and tight-waisted dresses, men in dark suits and derbies, and parents with children anxious for a crack at the rides reached the amusement park easily by crossing Elliott Bay aboard the ferry *West Seattle*, or they hopped a new streetcar, which only that afternoon had begun running from downtown Seattle. "From 7 o'clock in the evening until the last boats left at night," the paper continued, "the new resort was ablaze with light, and was gay with the hum of the visitors. The eleven concessions, including side shows, theater, cafes, fortune tellers, illusions and similar attractions, were crowded to capacity."

This was well before movie theaters became ubiquitous, of course, and decades in advance of the popularity of radio and television. Circuses and amusement parks were the ultimate diversion until well after the Great Depression. Following Coney Island's example, similar facilities had sprung

Balance of Power

Don't antagonize the press. At least not too much. That's a caution politicians come to understand well, and a lesson that George F. Cotterill learned the hard way during his turbulent two years in city hall (1912–14).

A British-born Republican-turned-Democrat, the mustachioed Cotterill first ran for public office in 1900 when he sought the mayor's office in Seattle. He lost that race, but six years later tried for a seat in the state senate, and won. While in Olympia, Cotterill backed construction of the Lake Washington Ship Canal, helped to preserve Seattle's city parks shorelines, and endorsed a constitutional amendment, passed in 1910, that granted voting rights to women. But it was his support for the municipal ownership of utilities, his opposition to vice of all varieties, and his permissive attitudes toward "socialist" demonstrations that made him a target of Alden J. Blethen, the pugilistic editor and publisher of the *Seattle Times*.

When, on his second try, Cotterill was elected as Seattle's mayor in 1912, Blethen viewed it as a "calamity" and set out to make the new chief executive's life hell. His best opportunity came in July 1913 during the city's annual Potlatch celebration, when a street fight erupted between some U.S. servicemen and a soapbox speaker from the Industrial Workers of the World (IWW), who had allegedly promoted anarchism and insulted the

up in virtually every major U.S. city. By 1919 there were 1,500 of them, each trying to outdo the others with exotic spectacles—freak shows, re-creations of wars, and acts that involved large animals leaping from great heights into tubs of water.

Looff and his employees, too, did their best to portray Luna Park as larger than life. Its architecture was an imposing amalgam of Atlantic City kitsch, Spanish Mission, and carnival gothic. A double-spired entrance gate was hung with banners and, again in imitation of the playland's Coney Island namesake, crowned with an imposing heart and crescent moon insignia. Looff apparently didn't know or didn't care that the original Luna Park was actually named after the sister of its co-owner, *not* the Roman moon goddess.

Unfortunately, Luna Park wanted to be all things to all people and that's what finally got it into trouble. Along with the arcades and thrill rides,

American flag. Blethen was a rabid supporter of the military (though he'd never done a turn in any of the services himself) and the *Times* reflexively took sides against the IWW. The report grossly inflated the fight, making it sound like a riot, and further inflamed passions by suggesting that IWW members were thumbing their noses at law and order.

After a *real* riot broke out in Pioneer Square the next day, resulting in the destruction of IWW offices and the Socialist Party headquarters, Cotterill declared a state of emergency. He had saloons closed down, outlawed street speaking, and even prohibited publication of the *Times* to stop further "incitement to disorder." Incensed, Blethen found a sympathetic judge who would restrain the Seattle police from enforcing "czar" Cotterill's order against the *Times*, and who also issued arrest warrants against the mayor and his chief of police. The paper followed up with editorials decrying that the 47-year-old "foreign-born American Mayor"—quite a stretch of insult, given that Cotterill had moved with his family to the United States when he was only 6—was a socialist sympathizer. The *Times* demanded that the voters recall him. Blethen's campaign failed, but it did drive Cotterill out of city politics. He went on to run unsuccessfully for the U.S. Senate, and finished out his career as an employee of the King County Assessor's Office.

it boasted "the longest bar on the bay." This was an inauspicious time to be promoting the consumption of spirits. With the local area's annexation to the rest of the city—approved by voters only days after the park first opened in 1907—West Seattle adopted the vice-fighting stance of Seattle's latest mayor, former judge William Hickman Moore, and commenced a campaign to eradicate saloons from within its borders. Charles Looff's fantasyland on the Duwamish tideflats was an easy target.

"Many Drunken Girls and Boys at Luna Park," the *P-I* would later headline, and an accompanying story detailed events at a park dance:

Girls hardly more than 14 years old, with their youthful escorts, mere children in appearance, mingled with the older and more dissipated patrons or sat in the dark corners, drinking beer and smoking cigarettes. One young man, whose appearance indicated that he was less than 11 years old, left the dance hall so hopelessly drunk that he fell on the sidewalk in front of a policeman.

By 1910, however, Moore's reform efforts had fallen out of style, and city councilman Hiram C. Gill soon supplanted him in the mayor's seat. Gill favored a wide-open town. *McClure's* magazine reported that "thirty or forty gambling-places opened up under the administration of Hi Gill." His handpicked police chief, Charles W. Wappenstein, was found to be taking kickbacks from prostitution—$10 per harlot per month, which amounted to a healthy income based on estimates that at least 500 women were then working the bawdy trade in Seattle's tenderloin. If there was carousing going on at Duwamish Head, it was just sinning as usual.

But West Siders were incensed. They hadn't voted for annexation in order to be overrun by libertines and vagrants. It finally was more than they could bear when two of the police chief's cronies erected a 500-room brothel on Beacon Hill. Decent-minded folk screamed for Gill's head. Luna Park was implicated when the *P-I* reported that its then-manager, W.W. Powers, also owned 50 shares of stock in the overgrown whorehouse.

Luna Park, tarnished by this debacle, nonetheless survived, but apparently without Charles Looff (who would die in 1918). When it opened for the 1913 summer season, control was wielded by one William H. Labb, who claimed to have built the White City amusement center in South Chicago in 1905 and operated other parks in Indianapolis, Los Angeles, and San Francisco. Labb promised he would expand and improve West Seattle's entertainment complex, but to do so required selling "a small portion of stock" in Luna Park at $1,000 a share. "We make this offer," Labb said, "to get others interested with us in the park and so push it on to quick success."

No such luck. Luna Park didn't enjoy so much as one more season's operation, though the natatorium—with its huge billboard exhorting, "Let's Swim!"—remained in business until a serial arsonist set flame to that one-story frame building in April 1931.

Apartment and condominium complexes now shoulder up to Alki Avenue where Luna Park once stood. However, when Puget Sound is low, you might still spot some of the old pier pilings. Try to imagine how this place looked when it hosted women in full-length swimming gowns rather than bikinis, and children were entranced by acrobats rather than GameBoys, back when it was the bright, raucous "Coney Island of the West."

Mayor of Wappyville

Hiram C. Gill believed that folks should be left pretty much alone, whether they were good, bad, or indecent. So he saw no problem in his acting as the attorney for most of the town's brothelkeepers—even after he was chosen in 1907 to become president of the Seattle City Council. Nor did he see any reason why local police should spend all their time trying to purge prostitution and gambling from this port town. Instead, he advocated confining vice to the district south of Yesler Way, where it could be regulated, but still was available to satisfy "natural" urges.

The idea had its critics, certainly among the churchgoing and prohibitionist set. Yet when "Hi" Gill joined the mayoral race in 1910, he decided to make that proposed restricted district part of his platform, along with his opposition to labor unions and the municipal ownership of utilities. "What Seattle needs," declared Republican Gill, "is a mayor who will get a chief of police to handle the restricted district, who will back the chief up when the delegations of citizens call and protest—one who will stand by the chief of police. And I'm the bird." Voters agreed, electing the Wisconsin-born lawyer over Democrat William Hickman

Moore, who'd already served one term as mayor and was associated with anti-vice zealots. During his swearing-in, Gill tried to assure Seattleites that they had acted wisely. "I don't pretend to be a very good man," he conceded, "but I know the law and will enforce it." That was one more promise, though, than he could keep.

Mayor Hiram C. Gill, circa 1911. *Webster & Stevens MOHAI 83.10.8,878*

The new mayor's most crucial error was his appointment of Charles W. Wappenstein as the chief of police. A soft-spoken former Cincinnati cop, Wappenstein had joined Seattle's police department in the 1890s and weathered at least one official attempt to dismiss him for corrupt practices. Even his detractors agreed that the familiarly known "Wappy" could be an able lawman, when he put his mind to it; however, he also abused his office in order to fatten his wallet. Putting him in charge of the city's official red-light district was like assigning a thirsty man to guard a beer keg. At the same time as Gill assured constituents that his police chief had cracked down on the spread of licentiousness beyond "Wappyville," as the restricted area came to be called, Wappy himself was busy keeping tabs on the hundreds of trollops and dozens of all-hours gambling dens that paid him "kickbacks" each month in order to operate, and he encouraged the proliferation of vice in every corner of town.

Gill only had been in office a few months when word of Wappy's misdeeds started to leak out. Reformers demanded that the mayor fire his top cop and aggressively begin cleaning up Seattle again. His refusal led to denunciations of Gill as "a menace to the business enterprises and moral welfare" of Seattle. In addition, it started the circulation of petitions to schedule a recall vote that would remove the mayor from office. This momentum was impossible to stop. By February 1911, Gill was out, replaced by the "clean living" real-estate man George W. Gilling. Chief Wappenstein was convicted later that same year of corruption, and sent to prison.

Amazingly, Hi Gill staged a comeback in 1914, returning to the mayor's office—this time as an anti-vice reformer. But after his re-election in 1916, when Seattle's criminal venues started to boom once more and the mayor was put on trial for accepting protection money from bootleggers, voters had had enough. Hi Gill didn't even survive the 1918 primary election. He died a few months later, in January 1919.

Opposite: On February 2, 1911, thousands gather to hear Mayor Gill defend himself against accusations of not enforcing Seattle's anti-vice laws. Gill spoke to packed seats at the Grand Opera House and the Seattle Theatre, both located on Cherry Street. An additional 8,000 onlookers standing outside couldn't get into either auditorium. *Webster & Stevens MOHAI 83.10.9,222.2*

Seattle elevator girl wearing a flu mask, 1918. *Webster & Stevens MOHAI 83.10.10,779*

16

DANGER IN THE AIR

NOBODY WHO LIVED THROUGH THE AUTUMN of 1918 could ever forget how nature declared war on humanity, just as humans were ending the First World War against themselves.

The firestorm of battle that had engulfed Europe for four years was then dwindling to coals. Germany, in full retreat on the Western Front, would be granted an armistice on November 11, 1918, effectively ending the conflict—though a formal treaty wasn't inked until 1919. At the same time, however, the United States was under attack by a particularly virulent form of influenza—the Spanish flu—that seemed to rise out of nowhere and was spread merely by *breathing*.

Some claimed the disease had been deliberately created and covertly circulated by German spies. Others posited that it had incubated accidentally in Europe through the mixing of poisonous gases with vapors given off by rotting corpses. There was even one theory, advanced through the press by the wife of an American official living in France, that the Spanish flu was some form of mesmeric warfare engineered by the German army— a "malicious suggestion on the world…frightening unto death thousands of our people."

But no psychic "suggestion" could have killed as many humans as this pandemic did in 1918 and 1919. Twenty to 40 million people perished around the world, and 675,000 of them were Americans—more Americans than those who died in combat during all of the wars fought in the

20th century. Most bewilderingly, casualties weren't just the aged or the infirm, the common victims of flu. They primarily were men and women in the prime of their lives, from about 21 to 40 years of age. Regardless of whether rich or poor, obscure or renown, everyone appeared susceptible. Among the flu's victims were Irma Cody Garlow, Buffalo Bill Cody's daughter, and Leopold Kahn (a.k.a. "Admiral Dot, the El Dorado Elf"), one of showman P.T. Barnum's first dwarfs. President Woodrow Wilson, actress Mary Pickford, and General John Pershing all contracted the disease, but survived.

Like other U.S. cities, Seattle suffered. Public gatherings were prohibited in order to stem the spread of the disease by personal contact. Residents took to wearing gauze masks, hoping to protect their lungs. Yet few families in the city escaped without at least one of their number being struck down by the Spanish flu, and it wasn't unusual for whole clans to succumb at once. On October 18, 1918, the *Seattle Union Record* headlined a grim fact—Seattle's morgue was "jammed with dead bodies." And the news was destined to get much worse.

It's hard now to imagine in our era of rabid health consciousness and frequent medical breakthroughs, but during that postwar autumn fear held Washington's largest city tightly in its grip. No one knew for sure whether he or she, or the people they cared most about, would wake up one morning full of vigor and optimism—and then be dead by nightfall.

History knows it as the Spanish flu. However, that's a misnomer, for while Spain was particularly hard hit by this long-ago contagion, the epidemic apparently started in the United States. In March 1918, ill soldiers at Fort Riley, Kansas, began filling the camp hospital. Before spring was out, 48 of them were fitted for caskets. Cause of death was listed as pneumonia.

From there, the silent killer traveled rapidly and extensively. Almost two million soldiers, many of them from Kansas, unknowingly carried the flu with them to Europe that summer. By the end of August 1918, another military hospital, this one in Boston, Massachusetts, was overwhelmed by men complaining about hacking coughs, muscle aches, fevers as high as 105 degrees, wild bouts of delirium, and a bluish complexion with purple blisters—not at all the kinds of minor ailments normally associated with the flu. This version hit its victims within one to three days of exposure, could overcome even a hardy man within an hour, and often progressed into severe bronchial pneumonia. Odder still, when doctors autopsied the casualties, they found lungs filled with a bloody, foamy fluid. The victims quite literally had drowned.

Not surprisingly, the disease couldn't be contained to the ranks of the military. Patriotic gatherings heralding America's participation in what was then known as the Great War were popular all over the nation. Every time civilians crowded into streets with army or navy inductees to sing songs and boost public morale, it threatened to escalate the epidemic. As September wound to a close, Boston counted 1,000 of its citizens dead from influenza. By the third week of October, Philadelphia had lost 4,500 and the city had to appeal to the federal government for funds just to bury the decaying dead before they caused a secondary epidemic. As the airborne slayer wound west, Chicago's death toll rose to 8,500. By mid-October San Francisco reported another 4,000 cases of influenza—one doctor claimed to have seen 525 new patients in a single day.

Seattle Mayor Ole Hanson must have cringed when, in the midst of this mounting crisis, he was told by the city's health commissioner, Dr. J.S. McBride, "the circumstances for an uncontrollable epidemic hardly could be worse."

The big problem, of course, was that Seattle was surrounded by military facilities—a naval training station at the University of Washington, the army's Camp Lewis 35 miles to the south, and Bremerton's Puget Sound Navy Yard. The transfer of sick men from Philadelphia to Bremerton in September 1918 imported influenza into the area. Within weeks, Camp Lewis was hit too, and the *Seattle Post-Intelligencer* reported in early October that 700 instances of "flu-like" illnesses had been recorded at the UW naval station.

McBride had downplayed this news from the military bases. But after the first two *civilians* died in Seattle, Mayor Hanson—a former real-estate agent and ex-state legislator who was more than aware of how his response to the crisis might affect his political ambitions—decided to make the fight against influenza his greatest campaign yet. He told McBride to do whatever was necessary to protect Seattleites from contagion. The health commissioner responded on October 5 by forbidding dancing in the city (then a favorite evening amusement), closing pool halls and the public library, prohibiting "all entertainments in cafes, restaurants and hotels," and ordering businesses to "prevent the gathering of crowds." Later, theaters and schools were shut down. So were churches, with McBride telling any ministers who protested, "religion that won't keep for two weeks is not

Although Seattleites generally appreciated the restrictions under which they had to live during the influenza scare, they didn't have to *like* their state. A bit of doggerel from the October 8, 1918, *Seattle Post-Intelligencer* captured the spirit of those days:

Too Much Precaution

By Carlton Fitchett

At home we're trying mighty hard to follow the directions. To fight the "flu" we stand on guard, with fear in our complexions. With windows open to the breeze we wait with breath abated, and every time the children sneeze the house is fumigated.

The doctor says, "Take lots of air, if you'd escape contagion; rub antiseptics in your hair while Spanish 'flu' is ragin.'" So on the porch I moved my bed, a process quite exciting, and rubbed some ratbane on my head to keep the germs from biting.

That night it rained and also blew; the rain fell helter-skelter, and though the sheets were soaked clean through, I scorned to flee to shelter. I figured this was but a ruse, a sortie to upset me, and if I waved the flag of truce the germs would up and get me. All night I fought temptation off to seek my bedroom stuffy, and in the morning had a cold and eyelids red and puffy.

A doleful life I led that day and not a bit decorous; the street cars running out our way were open-faced and porous, and when I took a seat inside the drafts were far from pleasing, and so I oped my features wide and started in a-sneezing.

The boss, a man of little shame and much inclined to scoffing, he dubbed me a Castilian name when I came in a-coughing. They wouldn't let me in at home, they shunned me as a leper. The shows were closed, I couldn't roam to view some vodvil stepper. With rancor I did cogitate while through the rain a-sloshin'; the reason for my sorry fate was too darned much precaution!

worth having." Most of the press endorsed McBride's drastic regulations. The *Seattle Times* told residents that it was their "patriotic duty to . . . check the spread of the disease."

Linking the civilian battle against influenza with the U.S. military's titanic struggle with Germany proved highly effective not only here, but across the country. It made it easier to convince citizens that they should stay in their residences, give their homes a "thorough cleaning," and, when in public, wear six-layer gauze masks that authorities said would curb the airborne transmission of influenza—though such porous masks couldn't possibly have restrained the microbes that caused the disease.

Across the United States, a sense of community solidarity kept people's spirits up while they pulled together to defeat the dreaded flu, even as worries abounded that no cure would be found. One national health official lamented to local authorities that the best thing they could do was "hunt up your wood-workers and cabinet-makers and set them to making coffins. Then take your street laborers and set them to digging graves." The use of folk remedies was rampant. Some mothers told their children to stuff salt up their noses, wear goose grease poultices, or eat inordinate amounts of onions. Patent medicine companies capitalized on people's fears by pushing bogus panaceas. Seattle came up with its own vaccine and began inoculating residents, but like similar cures developed back east, this was never more than experimental.

By mid-October, reports in the newspapers of Seattle's fight against the influenza were competing with dispatches from the war front. The numbers of sick and dead were growing, with 1,368 cases reported locally by October 11. Emergency hospital services were stretched to the limit, especially since so many doctors had left to help in Europe. Downtown stores, wanting to maintain their business activities but at the same time wishing to endorse public safety, urged Seattleites to, "shop by telephone. It is not unpatriotic."

As the weeks wore on, stories appeared about undertakers garnering unfair profits, as well as landlords who hoped to protect themselves by evicting from their rental properties sick tenants and nurses who'd been exposed to flu patients. A phony policeman levied $5 fines against people he met on downtown streets who weren't wearing masks—he made a tidy bundle before being caught. Worse happened in San Francisco where an actual health inspector shot a man who refused to don his mask.

On November 11, 1918, news of victory in Europe finally forced Seattleites out of their doldrums—and a little out of their minds. The

P-I reported that the streets were filled with celebrants and "not a gauze mask was visible." Mayor Hanson and Dr. McBride reiterated that continued vigilance against the disease was essential, but it was a losing cause. Seattle wanted to celebrate the victory over the Germans, and also victory over influenza—the number of new cases, in fact, had dropped since October. The health department reluctantly lifted the rule about wearing gauze masks. Business activity started to pick up again. Theaters reopened and immediately were filled—with the *P-I* joking in a headline, "'Flu' May Be Followed by Film Epidemic."

A second wave of influenza struck Seattle in December 1918, causing commissioner McBride to order a 10-day quarantine for the newly sick, but the city no longer took the peril so seriously. The worst of the epidemic was over—at least in the United States. It continued to rage for a few more months in the South Pacific and Europe, and killed 60 percent of the Eskimo population in Nome, Alaska. Records show that at least 1,372 Seattleites perished from the Spanish flu.

No cure for the contagion had been found. It appeared simply to have run out of people who were susceptible to its dire affects. However, that was blessing enough, for when the body counts were done, they showed something nobody could have expected—more civilians were dying at home than soldiers on European battlefields in the autumn of 1918.

LADY IN RED

VEN AT THE END OF HER LONG LIFE in 1970—when gravely ill in a Chinese hospital and proudly refusing to accept intravenous nourishment while surrounded by doctors and nurses whose language she couldn't understand—Anna Louise Strong remained a mystery to many. She had been reared in privileged circumstances, but was familiar to Seattleites for her spirited condemnation of capitalism. She had reported on Seattle's famous workers' strike of 1919, befriended Eleanor Roosevelt, taught English to Soviet leader Leon Trotsky, and once flirted with Chinese Premier Chou En-lai, who would visit her on her deathbed. This woman, journalist, and revolutionary would be characterized in a *New York Times* obituary as "an ardent apologist" for Communists, but others would praise her for "clarity of vision and enduring commitment."

A mystery? Certainly she must have bewildered some less impassioned or adventuresome observers, who considered her outspoken devotion to social progress to be unladylike and her interest in Communism naïve. Yet she provided an easy explanation for the perfervid curiosity that propelled her from one cause, one country, and one ally to the next. In her 1935 autobiography, *I Change Worlds: The Remaking of an American*, Strong described herself as "motor-minded," meaning that she tended—just like "most Americans," she wrote—to act first and think later. Without that self-confident drive, Strong might never have exceeded the limits that were placed upon other women of her era, or made the mark that she did in Seattle and the rest of the world.

Anna Louise Strong's roots were deep-sunk in America, with both sides of her family tracing their genealogy back to colonial times. Her parents, Ruth Tracy and Sydney Strong, had met in 1880 while students at Ohio's Oberlin College. Ruth was gregarious and ambitious—unusual in those days because women weren't encouraged to go on to higher education. Sydney studied for the ministry, though he also embraced Charles Darwin's evolutionary dogma. The pair married after Ruth finished her degree, and they moved to the pocket-edition prairie town of Friend, Nebraska, where Sydney began preaching to Congregationalists. Anna Louise, the first of three children, was born on November 24, 1885.

Anna Louise Strong in 1913. *UW Libraries, UW 340*

A familiar anecdote recalls Anna Louise, not yet two years old, being swept from the front yard of their home by a small cyclone—like Dorothy in *The Wizard of Oz*—and deposited in a cow pasture some distance away. "When they found me," she claimed in *I Change Worlds*, "I was somewhat worried by the cows but not at all by the cyclone." This was only the start of her stormy life.

Socially awkward but intellectually precocious, Anna Louise finished high school at age 15, studied for a year in Germany, and then at 19—not long after the demise of her influential mother—graduated summa cum laude from Oberlin. Anna Louise was already writing. Her first volume of poetry, *Storm Songs*, went to print shortly before she left college and helped secure her a position as an associate editor at the *Advance*, a fundamentalist Protestant weekly in Chicago. She produced copy "tirelessly" for the newspaper under four pseudonyms, churning out children's stories, book reviews, church news, and what she would later describe as a column "expressing an ironic, feminist viewpoint." Which doesn't mean that Anna Louise identified closely with the vote-seeking suffragists of her youth—like her mother, she believed that intelligence and courage would win her respect in the world, even if she was unjustly denied the ballot box.

This conviction was seriously challenged when, after only half a year's work at the *Advance*, she suddenly was fired because the editor had determined to take on and train a new young associate. To "save face," Anna Louise enrolled in graduate school at the University of Chicago, earning a Ph.D. in philosophy at the extraordinary age of 22. She went on to organize exhibits around the country that spotlighted the needs of children reared in America's cities. Eventually, in 1916, weary of exhibition work and abandoning a disappointing relationship with an older widower, she came to Puget Sound, where her father had been living for the last decade and leading the Queen Anne Congregational Church.

In that year immediately preceding America's entry into World War I, Seattle was numbered among the nation's most progressive cities, brimming with political idealists and labor organizers. These leaders recognized that there was a substantial potential for growth of their radical organizations among workers in the West's newly developing industries. Anna Louise hadn't chosen Seattle for its politics, but had hoped to enjoy her father's company and indulge her "love of the western mountains." (An enthusiastic climber, she would lead the first winter ascent of Oregon's Mount Hood and guide parties on Mount Rainier's glaciers.) However, the Reverend Strong's prestige among liberal and pro-labor forces, combined with Anna Louise's own well-publicized efforts on behalf of child welfare, made her an appealing candidate for public office. She considered running for the state legislature, but was eventually convinced to campaign for an unpaid seat on the Seattle School Board. Championed by labor unions, women's groups, and locally federated ministers, "I easily captured the election," she remembered years afterward, becoming the board's first female member.

Then 31, she was a commanding figure at 5 feet 9 inches tall, 150 pounds, with bobbed dark blonde hair and wide-set almond-shaped blue eyes. But the conservative bankers and businessmen who'd long controlled the school board weren't about to let a woman significantly sway policymaking. "The machine rolled over me weekly," Strong wrote, "voting appropriations for matters about which I understood little." Frustrated, she turned her attention to larger, more controversial matters, such as labor issues.

In mid-August 1916, thugs working for the owners of a mill in nearby Everett had beaten 18 striking members of the International Shingle Weavers Union. The Everett police promptly prohibited speechmaking downtown, riling workmen who wished to publicly air their grievances. This in turn attracted the attention of the Industrial Workers of the World, or "Wobblies," a growing radical union that openly disdained industrialists. On November 5, two boatloads of IWW protesters sailed north from Seattle in support of the shingle makers, only to be met at the Everett docks by a sheriff and 200 hastily deputized and armed local men. Shots ripped the air, and by the time the "Everett Massacre" ceased, at least seven men (including two deputies) were dead and another 31 lay wounded. Seventy-four Wobblies were arrested for conspiracy and murder.

Strong arranged to report on the protesters' trial for the *New York Evening Post.* "I was not consciously taking sides in any struggle," she noted in *I Change Worlds,* yet she quickly came to admire the Wobblies as "direct inheritors of the fighting pioneer." After the trial ended in an acquittal for one defendant and the summary release of the rest, Strong spent more time with IWW leaders, and she began writing for the *Seattle Daily Call,* an IWW-owned paper. None of this helped her standing among the right-leaning school board. Neither did her subsequent opposition to U.S. involvement in World War I. President Woodrow Wilson's declaration of war on April 16, 1917, was a blow to her confidence in the American political system. "Nothing in my whole life, not even my mother's death, so shook the foundations of my soul," Strong wrote. "'Our America' was dead! ... The people wanted peace; the profiteers wanted war—and got it!"

However, it was only after a woman friend of hers was jailed for distributing anti-military-draft circulars that Strong suffered from the full wrath of her political opponents. Other school board members, backed by Seattle's mainstream press, proclaimed her a criminal by association. They ridiculed her pacifism and impugned her patriotism, dubbing her "the lady in red" for her "Bolshevik sympathies." Finally, in early 1918, they demanded her public recall from the school board. She lost the vote—25,000 to 21,000—causing *Seattle Times* editor Clarance B. Blethen to crow, "The sound of the door locking behind [Strong] will be music in the ears of the Seattle boys who have already reached the trenches in France."

Once again, a storm had disrupted Strong's life. Rather than being disappointed, though, she was relieved to end her school board responsibilities. And, the closer-than-expected recall vote convinced her that she could build an audience sympathetic to her opinions. She returned to journalism as a feature editor for the *Seattle Union Record,* another union-friendly newspaper, and set about sharpening her perspective on the failures of capitalism and the future of labor politics worldwide. This perspective would prove invaluable to her when she set out to report on the most important story of her career up to that time—the Seattle General Strike of 1919.

Trouble had begun three months after the Armistice ended hostilities in Europe. At that time, Seattle shipyard workers, whose wages had been controlled during the war, sought to renegotiate their contracts, but a national supplier of steel threatened to cut off allocations unless employers resisted. Angry, the workers voted to strike and other unions joined them in a show of solidarity. At 10 a.m. on February 6, 1919, whistles rang out from local mills and ships, and Seattle's industrial exertions grounded to a halt.

The sudden quiet was unnerving. People imagined the outbreak of riots or revolution. Strong's editorial of two days before had only inflamed fears. With this strike, she had remarked in the *Union Record*, "we are starting on a road that leads—NO ONE KNOWS WHERE!"

Businessmen considered this a summons to adopt socialism. Mayor Ole Hanson had a different take—he saw the strike as a direct test of his leadership. A red-haired man with an energetic speaking style that

A group of men and a boy carrying groceries during the Seattle General Strike, February 7, 1919. Though businesses, stores, and streetcars were shut down, union members set up food lines, delivered milk to babies and drugs to hospitals, and maintained the city's electrical system and ambulance service. *Webster & Stevens MOHAI 83.10.10,698.2*

Taking Wing

William E. Boeing, an engineer and son of a Michigan timber baron, first became fascinated with flying when he attended a California air meet in 1910. Five years later, in his seventh year as a Seattle resident, he bought his first aircraft, a floatplane, but quickly damaged its pontoons when touching down on Puget Sound waters. Realizing there wasn't a local source for spare parts, he decided to construct his own pontoons—and designed a superior version of the aircraft itself. In 1916, with the help of a navy officer and friend, G. Conrad Westervelt, Boeing built the first "B & W Seaplane." A year later, the Boeing Airplane Company was established next to the Duwamish River in the now-storied "Red Barn," which Bill Boeing originally had intended as a place where he might build a yacht. (The Red Barn currently is part of the Museum of Flight, located on East Marginal Way, 10 miles south of Seattle.)

World War I sent the company's coffers soaring with military contracts, but a decline after

compensated for his short stature and high voice, he had been elected mayor (replacing roguish Hiram C. Gill) on the same day that Anna Louise Strong was recalled from the school board. Hanson had been a grocer and realtor before entering politics as a vice and ethics reformer. His first campaign, on a platform for ending racetrack betting, had earned him a seat in the Washington Legislature and the nickname "Holy Ole." Though he switched party allegiances with an opportunist's abandon—he started out as a Republican like his hero Theodore Roosevelt, then later supported Democrat Woodrow Wilson "because he kept us out of the war," but by now was a Republican again—he had always styled himself a friend of labor. Yet, the 1919 strike now found him promising to call in soldiers "to protect life, business and property" if necessary. It wasn't. As Murray Morgan observed in *Skid Road*, the strike's "very success worked against it: the town was so quiet, there was so little activity, that the strikers lost their feeling of unity... There were no martyrs. No pickets had been beaten up. Nobody had been arrested. It was hard to stay angry." By day three men were drifting back to their jobs, and after six days America's first general strike was over.

After being considered a rather lackluster leader during his first year in office, Hanson's response to the strike raised his stock, and his political the war's end nearly convinced Bill Boeing to abandon aircraft development in favor of something steadier—maybe the manufacturing of furniture or boats. Instead, he helped start the international airmail business and by 1920 Boeing again was receiving military contracts. In 1927 the company began carrying the U.S. mail between San Francisco and Chicago, then the longest such route in the world. A year later, the firm inaugurated commercial passenger flights under the corporate flag, United Air Lines. (United later was split off by a government antitrust decree.) Boeing already had the country's largest aircraft plant when World War II called for the firm to fill European and Pacific skies with warplanes, particularly the B-17 "Flying Fortress" and the equally famous B-29 "Superfortress." In the mid-1950s, the company introduced America's first commercial passenger jet, the Boeing 707.

sights. Boasting that he'd "stopped revolution," he resigned as mayor a month later and rode the national lecture circuit all the way to the 1920 Republican National Convention, where he sought the presidential nomination, but lost to Ohio Senator Warren G. Harding. Embarrassed, Hanson subsequently moved to California.

Anna Strong, meanwhile, wound up in jail accused of sedition. Although the charge soon was dropped, the affair soured her on Seattle and increased her interest in the Soviet Union, which she believed could be a model of social progress for the world.

For the rest of her days, Strong traveled around the world observing how people lived, worked, and were governed, and she reported her findings to American readers.

She went to Moscow in 1921 as a publicist for a Quaker relief society and as a magazine correspondent. She soon founded the *Moscow Daily News*, an English-language paper for foreigners living in the Soviet Union, but clashed with censors who didn't approve of her humor. She met and grew to admire Trotsky, only to denounce him later. She married a Russian-Jewish editor five years her junior (he died a decade later). She investigated revolutionary movements in Mexico and became acquainted with the painter/rebel Diego Rivera. She traveled to Spain during the 1930s Spanish Civil War, and then carried on a long correspondence with first lady Eleanor Roosevelt, lobbying (unsuccessfully) to win American aid for the Loyalists opposing Francisco Franco's fascist takeover. She wrote books extolling Soviet virtues and defending its leaders—yet friends said she would break into tears at hearing how Premier Joseph Stalin had treated people who drew his ire. In 1949 Strong was expelled from the USSR as a traitor and likely American spy. At the same time, the FBI suspected she was a Soviet spy.

She retreated to the United States, to be feted by literary clubs and invited to lecture in Seattle and elsewhere on the international spread of Communism. With the Cold War just beginning and anti-Communist "witch hunts" in full cry across the country, she was now "a pariah among the American left," states Seattle author Barbara Wilson in her introduction to a 1979 reprint of *I Change Worlds*. Yet Strong refused to join the chorus of former Communists and leftist sympathizers who exercised their disillusionment in anti-Soviet screeds. When Stalin died in 1953, Moscow invited her to return, claiming that her earlier expulsion from the Soviet Union was the result of a frame-up. She went back.

Anna Louise Strong spent the last dozen years of her life in Beijing, China. She'd had an interest in China since at least 1946, when she conducted an interview with Mao Tse-tung in which he had first said, "all reactionaries are 'paper tigers.'" Now in her 70s, she composed a monthly four-page newsletter chronicling the Cultural Revolution for China-watchers all over the globe. While she'd been largely forgotten in America and even the USSR, in China "she was not only respected but admired," according to *Right in Her Soul: The Life of Anna Louise Strong*, written by her great-nephew Tracy B. Strong and his wife, Helene Keyssar. "China was one of the few countries that still treated her as a special person; she did not need to remind the Chinese leaders that she had been first in more places and at more world-shaking events than anyone could remember." Indeed, when Anna Louise died in Beijing at the age of 84, it spurred public mourning in that city.

Most Seattleites weren't so moved by this event. Yet, those who'd studied Strong might've appreciated knowing that her last words, spoken clearly before she collapsed in a hospital bed, were: "Is it possible?" They must surely have asked themselves that very same question when considering the decades-long rise to prominence of this motor-minded woman.

WARREN'S PEACE

N OTHING SEEMED TO BE GOING RIGHT. First of all, the president was late. His ship, the *Henderson*, had been expected to steam into Seattle at 9 A.M., but was delayed leaving a previous stop at Vancouver, B.C. Then, in a dense morning fog off Port Townsend, the *Henderson* rammed one of its two escort vessels, the U.S. Navy destroyer *Zeilin*. This only briefly disturbed the president's party, but sent the *Zeilin* limping toward Bremerton for structural repairs. By the time the *Henderson* finally rounded Magnolia Bluff on its way south, cueing a welcoming fusillade from the big gray guns of the Pacific Fleet anchored in Puget Sound for official review, it was 1 P.M. on Friday, July 27, 1923.

Fifteen minutes later, the transport docked at the old Bell Street Terminal, greeted by about 10,000 folks who'd been willing to wait on the pier—along with Washington Governor Louis E. Hart and Mayor Edwin J. "Doc" Brown—for President Warren G. Harding's tardy arrival. A grand waterfront reception had been planned, and Harding was supposed to lunch and give a little speech at the Seattle Press Club, but the itinerary now needed to be condensed. The reception was cancelled. Instead, a parade immediately swept the chief executive and his wife, plus some Cabinet members and a blaring naval band, off through the gaily-festooned city streets up to Volunteer Park. There, 15,000 girls waited to present the Hardings with blue delphinium boutonnieres and handkerchiefs, which had been decorated by Camp Fire Girls attending Vashon Island's Camp Sealth. From here, the presidential motorcade sped to Woodland Park where thousands of picnicking boys, guests of the local Elks' Lodge, tried to catch the president's glance during a mass pledge-of-allegiance ceremony.

Although still behind schedule, the president's attendants sighed with relief when Harding's cream-colored automobile rolled into the University of Washington Stadium later that afternoon. The rest of the day should be smooth sailing, they figured. An estimated 30,000 people filled the stadium to hear Harding declaim on the subject of Alaska, from where he had just returned. After that, aides banked on time enough for a drop-in at Seattle's Orthopedic Hospital and a swing by the Press Club before heading to King Street Station, where the presidential entourage was to board a train for California's Yosemite National Park.

Harding's speech got off to a roaring start. Cheers echoed through the arena's vast bowl as he recommended governmental assistance for Alaskan farmers, endorsed regulation of the territory's canneries and careful conservation of its forests, and predicted that the Last Frontier—an American territory since 1867, and a particular focus of Seattle's interest since the Klondike gold rush—would be split in two, and "in a very few years" southeastern Alaska would become a new U.S. state.

Yet in the midst of his address, Harding was suddenly struck dumb and grabbed onto the lectern to keep from falling, the pages of his address slipping from his fingers. Commerce Secretary Herbert Hoover, who was seated behind the president, steadied him and retrieved the manuscript, but Harding clearly was shaken. He went on to complete the day's program; however, his retinue thought he acted "unusually tired." When Harding boarded the train at 7:30 P.M., he went straight to bed, his personal physician announcing that the president was suffering from ptomaine poisoning probably brought on by some "rotten crabs" he'd eaten the night before.

Only later was the optimism of that diagnosis obvious—and by then, Seattle had become part of the final act in a presidential disgrace that went unrivaled for half a century.

Seattle is now a familiar destination for White House occupants and aspirants, but the city didn't begin hosting presidents until 1880, when Rutherford B. Hayes shook some 2,000 hands during a reception at Squire's Opera House on 1st Avenue. He was followed in 1891 by Benjamin Harrison (whose outdoor oration was cut short by rain), and later by Theodore

Roosevelt, who enjoyed his Seattle visit (his ship was greeted by what's been called the "greatest naval parade in the history of Puget Sound"—30 steamships), and William Howard Taft, who wasn't so pleased (a bee stung him badly during his stay).

Harding's whistle-stop tour of the West, though, wasn't so much for pleasure as it was motivated by self-preservation. The president's men hoped that by liberating Harding from a spreading viper's nest of scandals back in Washington, D.C., and reconnecting him with voters, he could somehow quiet the growing number of critics who believed his administration was, well, *incompetent*.

Frankly, Harding never had been an ideal choice for the highest office in the land. His nomination at the 1920 Republican National Convention in Chicago was an 11th-hour compromise struck among delegates deadlocked over the party's two frontrunners, General Leonard Wood and Illinois Governor Frank Lowden. A "dark horse" like U.S. Senator Harding seemed to be just the anodyne that the convention needed. A fellow Republican solon called Harding "the best of the second-raters." The *New York Times* was somewhat less generous. "We must go back to Franklin Pierce," it opined, "if we would seek a president who measures down to his political stature."

Warren Gamaliel Harding—55 years old when elected, affable, handsome in a grandfatherly sort of way—was a fervently patriotic, Baptist churchgoing newspaper publisher from Marion, Ohio, who'd first been elected to Capitol Hill in 1915. He quickly grew notorious for being more interested in golf and scented women than roll calls. Harding gave stemwinding speeches profuse with platitudes and pieties, but hated to utter definitive opinions about anything. His grasp of economic matters was feeble, at best, and he lacked faith in politics or much interest in international affairs. In the wake of World War I and President Woodrow Wilson's ill-fated crusade for a League of Nations (the precursor to today's United Nations), Harding's vision for his country was frightfully isolationist, and would lead him to craft a foreign policy of retreat cloaked as the protection of democracy.

For all of this, there was something oddly endearing about the man. While his Democratic opponent, Ohio Governor James M. Cox, barnstormed the United States with sage and considered pronouncements, Harding conducted his campaign primarily from the creaky front porch of his Buckeye State abode. The Republican standard-bearer presented himself as every inch the down-home Midwesterner, with his tobacco chewing, backroom pokerfests, and not-overly-discreet affection for whiskey—right in the middle of Prohibition. Harding was congenitally loquacious, and his full, plangent voice resonated authority. He thought he could turn a good phrase, yet his orations were typically filled with platitudes, embarrassing mispronunciations, clumsy neologisms ("re-revealment"), and puzzling sentence constructions ("We must prosper America first"). Even so, people paid attention to his prattlings about how the nation should somehow turn its clocks back to an earlier, Arcadian era. And they forgave him when he blundered through speeches ghost-written by his GOP handlers. Partway into one such diatribe, Harding admitted, "Well, I never saw this before. I didn't write this speech and don't believe what I just read."

When voters went to the polls in November 1920, they handed Harding the largest popular majority yet recorded in a presidential contest (including victories in all 39 Washington counties).

The new president-elect made some significant Cabinet choices, including Charles Evans Hughes, a onetime New York governor and ex-U.S. Supreme Court justice to serve as Secretary of State, and former mining engineer Herbert Hoover was chosen to head the Commerce Department. However, Harding was a weak administrator. He mostly left the heavy lifting of policymaking to his appointees (a mistake, as it turned out) while he took long horse rides on Sundays and found time to answer the White House front door himself. It wasn't long before Harding realized what a mistake he'd made in accepting the presidency. "I'm in jail," he told a friend, "and I can't get out. I've got to stay."

His wife, for one, wasn't about to let him get out. Florence Kling Harding (he called her the "Duchess") was a chilly, ardently ambitious first lady. A divorcee five years older than her husband, she rewrote the president's opinions and (like Nancy Reagan 60 years later) consulted astrologers in hopes of protecting his future. Her worries were reflected by one seer, who warned that Harding "might not live through his term… I see the sun and Mars in conjunction on the fifth house of the zodiac, and this is the house of death; sudden, violent, or peculiar death."

Dangers to Harding's reputation were at least as much of a concern as an astrologer's prediction of his demise. Asked on the eve of his presidential nomination "whether there is anything that might be brought up against you that would embarrass the party," the Ohioan had told GOP bigwigs that there was "nothing, no obstacle." Somehow, though, he neglected to mention his mistresses. Harding had at least *two*—the young

Nan Britton who allegedly bore him a child in 1919, and Carrie Phillips, a longtime "friend of the family," who'd threatened to be in evidence during the 1920 campaign, until the Republican National Committee paid her and her husband "$20,000 plus a monthly stipend and got them out of the country for the duration," explains Paul F. Boller Jr. in an anecdotal history, *Presidential Wives*. Soon afterward, rumors circulated that one of Harding's ancestors was "a West Indian Negro of French stock," and it took all of the Duchess' persuasive craft to convince "Wurr'n," as she always slurred her husband's name, that silence could bury the accusations faster than a landslide of public denials.

By his second year in office, the 29th president was suffering from depression. He was once retrieved, crying, from the White House lawn. (Only later would news of Harding's mental disorders leak out. He had been hospitalized at age 24 for a nervous breakdown, and after that was a periodic guest of private sanatoria.)

And it didn't help his mood to see his administration rocked by charges of graft, bribery, and other gross misconduct.

The first embarrassment was Charles R. Forbes, an old poker buddy Harding had named as director of the Veterans Bureau. Not only was Forbes spending his department's budget flagrantly, but he also was skimming profits from war surplus goods and bootlegging hospital narcotics to drug dealers. After Harding confronted him, shouting that he was a "double-crossing bastard," Forbes fled to Europe. An assistant left behind to take the heat shot himself. Then a personal aide to the U.S. Attorney General was implicated in a bribery scheme, and he too committed suicide.

"This is a hell of a job," Harding groused to William Allen White, a Kansas Republican and influential newspaper editor. "I have no trouble with my enemies. I can take care of my enemies all right. But my damn friends, my God-damn friends, White, they're the ones that keep me walking the floors nights!"

Dr. Charles Sawyer, an old Marion crony and Harding's personal physician, recognized the strain and despair that washed over the president with each new imputation of corruption. Sawyer suggested that an extended foray beyond the Beltway might have recuperative affects. Thus, on June 23, 1923, while a major U.S. Senate investigation of the Harding White House was gathering steam, the president and first lady, together with Sawyer and members of the executive staff, boarded Harding's private railway car, the *Superb*, and sped west on an excursion taking them as far as Alaska.

Harding, who once had hoped to become America's "best-loved president," realized a bit of that dream during this trip. At a time when presidential visits to the hinterlands were rare, he was lionized at every stop along the route, given souvenirs and keys to cities as his train meandered through the country. In Alaska, he drove a spike to officially complete the Alaska Railroad, was sworn in as a member of the fraternal Arctic Brotherhood, and his name was given to several landmarks. But this acclaim was faint medicine against his funk. As the journey continued, it became increasingly common for the president to accost staffers or reporters and ask them what they would do if they'd learned that their trusted friends were crooks. Nobody knew quite how to reassure the most powerful man in the land, when he was cracking up before their very eyes.

The final blow to Harding came after he left Alaska and was cruising by boat south through the Inside Passage. The *Henderson* received a coded communiqué that was rushed to the president. Although the missive subsequently was destroyed, Harding's reaction to it—he turned positively white—has led to conjecture that it carried word of further scandals being uncovered. He was still gray and fatigued when he debarked at Seattle. His faltering at the UW Stadium only confirmed the toll that stress had taken on his health.

Was Dr. Sawyer merely allaying public fears when he announced that tainted crabmeat and, perhaps, a mild case of bronchial pneumonia had sickened the president? Maybe. He, of course, knew of Harding's depression and his previous heart trouble. Certainly, the decision to clear the president's immediate schedule and rush him out of Seattle to San Francisco, where he might find superior medical facilities, demonstrated the staff's magnitude of concern.

Rest seemed to do him good. Ensconced in Suite 8064 of San Francisco's illustrious Palace Hotel, the "Man from Marion" was sitting up after a few days, his high fever broken. Aides looked forward to completion of an itinerary taking him through the Panama Canal to Puerto Rico and the Virgin Islands.

But on Thursday, August 2, after the president and first lady had poured through an article in the *Saturday Evening Post*, one that encouraged Harding's enemies to withhold judgment of him until inquiries into his administration's rumored malfeasances were complete, the Duchess went to get something in her room across the hall. During her absence, a nurse fetched Harding a glass of water, but stopped when she saw his face suddenly twitch, his mouth drop open, and his head flop to one side. The first lady, returning at that very moment, started screaming for help. But it was too late. Harding had died of a cerebral hemorrhage. Just as the psychic predicted, he hadn't survived his first term in office.

The *Seattle Times*, which only days before had chided Harding for his too-brief visit to Puget Sound, now stated, "Seattle will have cherished memories of President Harding." A memorial was held at UW Stadium, site of his last address, and a motorcade retraced its path through Seattle, this time with the president's car empty. Some proposed renaming Mount Rainier in Harding's honor, and the Elks raised money for a stone monument at Woodland Park.

Within months of Harding's demise, however, scandals broke that forever tainted his legacy. First came the Teapot Dome affair, showing that Harding's flamboyant secretary of the interior, Albert Fall, had taken money from oil companies desiring preferential access to a former naval oil reserve in Wyoming. Then, Secret Service agents disclosed how they'd helped the president arrange trysts with Nan Britton in the closet of his White House office. Rumors also circulated that Florence Harding (who burned many of her husband's papers before she left the Executive Mansion, and died not long after that) had poisoned "Wurr'n" to spare him the pain of impeachment. The capper came in 1927, when Britton published her tell-all chronicle, *The President's Daughter*. After that, Seattleites weren't so anxious to tout their Harding ties.

The last "cherished memory" of his visit disappeared in the 1970s, when an expansion of Woodland Park Zoo forced the removal of Harding's monument—"the only 'permanent' memorial sculpture erected in Seattle," according to James M. Rupp's *Art in Seattle's Public Places*, "that no longer exists."

Body in the Steamer Trunk

Wealthy but eccentric Kate Mooers was such a tight-wad, even her murder had to be done on a shoestring.

In February 1921, this 72-year-old woman, who sported furs and claimed bank deposits enough to keep her comfortable for life (the spoils from three previous marriages), made the mistake of wedding a 38-year-old, recently paroled, highway robber named James E. Mahoney. It was just 10 weeks later that Mahoney—angry that Kate had severed him from her will and put him on an abstemious allow-ance—poisoned his wife and stuffed her into a steamer trunk. He then went looking for a skiff and, finding that boat rentals on deep Lake Washington cost more than the cash he had in his pocket (thanks to dear Kate), he decided to rent a cheaper craft on shal-lower Lake Union and dump her there. His first try was a horror—*the trunk floated.* So Mahoney loaded it full of concrete chunks and tried again.

With the luggage and its incriminating contents successfully sunk, Mahoney forged a power of attorney to enter his wife's vault and cash out some of her bonds, and then he boarded a train bound for St. Paul, Minnesota. His plan was to falsify letters from Kate to her family, then return west alone, claiming they'd had a lover's spat and that his wife had sailed away to Europe. But Mooers' relatives were suspicious of the handwriting on the letters from "Kate," and they raised doubts at the bank that held her savings. Soon after he reached Puget Sound again, Seattle detectives arrested Mahoney for having forged the power of attorney. Then, connecting his Lake Union boat rental with his spouse's disappearance, they dragged the lake bottom inch by inch until August 1921, when the trunk containing Kate Mooers suddenly bobbed to the surface, apparently buoyed by gases released during bodily decompo-sition. Wags called it a case of posthumous revenge.

Although Mahoney was indicted for first-degree murder and given the death penalty in September 1921, not until November 31—the night before his hanging—did he confess to his crimes.

HIS BRILLIANT CAREER

H
E LIVED TO BE 81, and in the last years of his life—after Seattle had out-grown its fascination with his bootlegging escapades, after the big wheels who'd once sought his ear and his liquor were pushing up tomb-stones, after most of the world had forgotten he even existed—he'd occa-sionally discuss with interviewers his early wild, lawbreaking days.

He had a "soft-spoken way of talking," recalled newspaper columnist Emmett Watson, and an "easy assurance." He was still "big, cheerful, square-faced," as one magazine described him in 1964. It wasn't hard to picture him organizing midnight speedboat deliveries of Canadian liquor from across stormy Puget Sound, and then chatting it up later with friends, such as Mayor Edwin J. "Doc" Brown or airplane giant William E. Boeing. In his younger days, he walked Seattle streets in tailor-made suits and dia-mond cufflinks, with a broad, confident smile and pockets full of imported cigars and wads of cash. For several years, he grossed more than $200,000 a month from his illegal activities.

He was the most audacious, successful, and colorful of the bootleg-gers to work Seattle during America's brief and disastrous flirtation with Prohibition in the 1920s. He was, as the press labeled him with unguarded respect, "King of the Northwest Rumrunners."

Yet after being released from prison, he sought redemption in reli-gious labors and the readings of Christian Science founder Mary Baker Eddy. When people asked him whether he really was the same guy they'd read about during Prohibition, he'd answer firmly: "No, not anymore."

And, at some point in those last interviews of his life, he'd always urge special consideration for the young men and women who, like himself, were drawn into criminal careers. "They need compassion," he'd say. "Just because a man makes a mistake, why should we condemn him?"

Roy Olmstead knew what it meant to be condemned.

Prohibition against the manufacture, sale, and distribution of intoxicating beverages had been hotly debated in Washington since even before the 1889 statehood convention. The early years of the 20th century saw a number of counties, especially in eastern Washington and in areas without major urban centers, go completely or partially dry. Although Walla Walla rejected an anti-saloon campaign in 1909—despite support from Governor Marion Hay, who condemned taverns as a "cancer in the body politic"—a year later Bellingham voted to go dry, as did the millworkers' town of Everett. In the run-up to the election, Everett played host to both evangelist Billy Sunday and famed criminal-defense attorney Clarence Darrow, who argued for the merits of shutting down local watering holes. However, Everett reversed itself in 1912 with residents, deciding by a margin of about 1,000 votes, to go "wet" once more.

Although Seattleites in 1911 had recalled pro-saloon Mayor Hiram C. Gill and replaced him a year later with former state senator George F. Cotterill—"probably the most widely known prohibitionist in the West," as Norman H. Clark wrote in his wonderful history, *The Dry Years: Prohibition and Social Change in Washington*—they hadn't yet been treated to aggressive campaigning regarding liquor control. But the statewide adoption in 1912 of direct voter participation through the initiative and referendum would embolden anti-saloon forces. Two years later, Washingtonians were asked to approve an initiative taking effect on January 1, 1916, that would forbid the "manufacture and sale" (though, notably, not the consumption) of alcohol statewide.

Seattle newspapers and the chamber of commerce adamantly opposed the measure, calling it unenforceable and an effort by small-town moralists to dictate metropolitan behavior. *Seattle Times* editor Alden J. Blethen assailed the initiative's authors for leaving open the loophole permitting the copious consumption of spirits in private living rooms, but forbidding it in public barrooms. "Instead of destroying the saloon," Blethen predicted, the initiative would "establish a saloon in every household."

Nonetheless, the measure passed. As the year 1915 gasped its last, Washington went dry, closing down groggeries as well as Seattle's nascent liquor industry. This was four years before the U.S. Constitution's Eighteenth Amendment, the so-called Volstead Act, became law.

Roy Olmstead turned 31 that year. A native of Beaver, Nebraska, he had a wife and two daughters, and had been with the Seattle Police Department since 1906. Described by his onetime chief of police as "quick and responsive...upright...bright and competent," he'd sailed up through the ranks. By 1910 he was a sergeant, and by 1916 a lieutenant—"the baby lieutenant" with the "brilliant career," as the press described him.

Historian Clark recalled Olmstead's competence and honesty. He "made frequent appearances in court to recommend probation for certain prisoners, and because he reasoned well and spoke with authority, the court was pleased to accept his judgment." Olmstead learned an unexpected lesson from this—his clout in the courts was worth a great deal to some defendants. "He soon began to sell his authority," Clark explained, "and in keeping with his character and the times, he sought high-risk investments for his money." From observing the 1920s scene, he knew that rumrunning was the highest-risk, highest-payoff enterprise around.

At 2 A.M. on March 22, 1920, lights and gunshots suddenly flashed across the nighttime beach at Brown's Bay near Edmonds. A tugboat, from which men had begun unloading cases of liquor, was caught in the crossfire. As Prohibition agents blasted away from the surrounding woods, an automobile leaped to life and careened around a roadblock, disappearing in a roostertail of dust. The agents, however, were able to identify the man behind the wheel—it was Roy Olmstead.

The "baby lieutenant" was nabbed at his home that afternoon and immediately dismissed from the police department. He pled guilty to a federal charge of violating the new Volstead Act, paid $500 in fines—and discovered he was famous. By playing the Brown's Bay incident to the best dramatic effect, the press made Olmstead a household name. When he decided to get into bootlegging full-time, he had little trouble finding 11 venture capitalists who'd stake him with $1,000 apiece.

Olmstead's second career was, if anything, more brilliant than his first. At its height, he employed about 90 people, from pilots and navigators to bookkeepers and salesmen. He utilized several boats that could outrun Coast Guard craft as well as various pirates plying Puget Sound during Prohibition, and made business connections up and down the West Coast. He befriended the keeper at a D'Arcy Island leprosy station, northeast of

Victoria, B.C., where he'd cache shipments until it was safe to bring them south through the Sound. Olmstead even averted an export duty of $20 per case, which the Canadians slapped onto any booze bought for export to the United States, by claiming that his delivery boats were bound, instead, for Mexico. He plowed the money saved into buying larger shipments than his competitors could afford, and passed the savings (up to 30 percent) along to his clientele.

By 1924 Olmstead conducted what the *New York Times* described as "one of the most gigantic rumrunning operations in the country." He did so well that he got out of retailing and went into the wholesale business. He'd deliver not only to the many Seattle-area "speakeasies" (especially in Belltown), but right to the homes of Seattle rainmakers, as well as to exclusive venues such as the Arctic Club and to the policemen who kept his business wheels greased. He seemed unconcerned about federal agents—"Those sons of bitches," he said once, "are too slow to catch cold"—or about Seattle's finest. On occasion, he'd send shipments right up to the city's main docks, off-loading booze into trucks marked "Meat," "Fresh Fish," or "Occidental Bread"—and laugh heartily as "bought" cops conveniently turned their heads.

He even expanded into legitimate businesses, just in case rumrunning took a nosedive. Using some of the money that he might otherwise have socked away in his big safe, which was secreted behind a sliding wall in a nondescript house on Beacon Hill, Olmstead developed KFQX, the city's first radio station (now KOMO). KFQX operated out of the top floor of Olmstead's grand white home in the Mount Baker neighborhood at 3757 South Ridgeway Place. (This mini-mansion still stands, though it no longer has the prominent backyard pond from the Olmsteads' period of occupancy.) The radio station's principal driving force and star was Elsie Olmstead, née Elise Campbell, an Englishwoman from Liverpool whom Roy had met in Vancouver and taken as his second wife. (He divorced his first wife in 1924 after she'd allegedly assisted federal agents against her husband.) As "Aunt Vivian," Elsie read bedtime stories to children over the air.

So "civilized" did bootlegging become under Olmstead—no corrupted merchandise, no violence, no spin-off gambling or prostitution rackets—that Seattleites began to think of him as an asset. He was invited to the best soirées, and hobnobbed with bankers and politicos. By one newspaper report, "it made a man feel important to casually remark, 'As Roy Olmstead was telling me today…'"

But it was all too good to last.

Roy Olmstead and second wife Elsie, in 1928. *MOHAI 86.5G.2261.1*

With shotguns raised, Prohibition agents stormed into the Mount Baker house after dinner on November 24, 1924, right in the middle of the Aunt Vivian show. Herding the Olmsteads and their few guests into the living room, the agents started looking for liquor. No luck—Roy wasn't stupid enough to keep intoxicants around. So William Whitney, an assistant Prohibition advisor, began calling the Olmsteads' friends, telling them—in a passable imitation of Roy's voice—to come over for a party and to bring booze. Whitney's wife was along to impersonate Elsie. By midnight, 15 people had been suckered in and arrested.

Two months later, a federal grand jury returned an indictment against Roy Olmstead and 90 other defendants for conspiring to violate the Volstead Act. Prominent evidence in the case had come from taps on some of the telephones used by the Olmstead "gang."

Roy Olmstead had known people were listening to his calls for some time, but he hadn't worried about the taps so much as he'd had fun with them, deliberately salting erroneous information about liquor drops into his conversations. Now those taps were coming back to haunt him. His attorney, George Francis Vanderveer, Seattle's storied "Counsel for the Damned," pointed out in court that the tapping of phone wires was prohibited by the state, and contended there was no excuse for trying to enforce the law by deliberately breaking it. But the judge overruled him. (Vanderveer later would take this defense against "whispering wires" all the way to the U.S. Supreme Court, which decided in 1928 that wire-tapping was used legally against Olmstead.) It was the biggest liquor trial in the Prohibition history of the United States.

On March 9, 1926, Roy Olmstead was fined $8,000 and sentenced to four years at Washington's McNeil Island Penitentiary. Twenty-two others (but not Elsie) also were convicted.

The King of the Rumrunners served his full term, with the customary time off for good behavior, and was released on May 12, 1931. Life on the outside wasn't so easy as he'd known it before. He took work in a credit bureau—tame duty after his smuggling days, but something he stuck with even after Prohibition was repealed in 1933 and he was offered jobs managing a liquor distributorship and a nightclub. With Elsie's help, he won a full pardon from President Franklin D. Roosevelt in 1935, but then eight years later, after Roy had gone into real estate sales and finally become a foundry molder, Elsie divorced him, saying he'd "deserted her without cause" in 1940.

Shortly after his release from the penitentiary, Olmstead had told newsmen, "I won't go back on that island—ever." As it turned out, though, he did. Not as a prisoner, but as a Christian Science practitioner, taking his religion to inmates at McNeil Island as well as at the King County Jail. He'd keep up that practice from the 1940s until his death in 1966.

Another thing Roy kept up was his wit. When former *Seattle Times* writer Don Duncan asked 81-year-old Olmstead whether he'd ever carried a gun in the course of his bootlegging adventures, Olmstead just smiled and shook his head. "I figured if old Roy couldn't talk himself out of trouble, it was a lost cause."

NIGHT OF THE KLAN

OOKING BACK NOW, it seems a most chilling sight—a wooden cross, 40 feet tall and 20 feet wide, lighted by hundreds of electric bulbs. On July 26, 1924, men and (reportedly) a few women milled about the cross at the Pickering field, one mile west of Issaquah. Their heads were exposed, but their bodies were attired in flowing white robes that glowed smartly in the artificial illumination. As that evening wound on, the Ku Klux Klan hosts exchanged smiles, shook hands, distributed pamphlets, and approached any adult within speaking distance.

Are you enjoying the festivities? Would you like to join the Klan, too?

A 32-piece brass band drew visitors from all over town—in fact, from all over the valley since in 1924 there were few obstructions to prevent the music's spread. Issaquah schoolchildren presented a patriotic play. Mayor David Leppert from Kent sat behind a typical wooden school desk of the time, lecturing all comers on the values and ramifications of a Klan-supported education bill that would go before the voters in that fall's general election. Three Klansmen re-created the Bunker Hill monument's famous "Spirit of '76" tableau of haggard Revolutionary War soldiers marching and playing instruments in support of their country. This was the introduction to a speech by Klan elder Walter McDonald on the heady subject of "Americanism."

Stewart Holbrook, an ex-lumberjack from New England, was a new arrival in the Northwest that year and would go on to become one of the region's premier historians. In *Far Corner: A Personal View of the Pacific Northwest*, Holbrook recalled how he came upon the Issaquah rally unexpectedly and was amazed. "An immense field was swarming with white-robed figures," he wrote, "while over them played floodlights. Loudspeakers gave forth commands and requests. Highway traffic was being directed by robed Klansmen. I was more than two hours getting through the jam."

The so-called Invisible Empire had promised to "put Issaquah on the map" with this rally and, at least to historians and secret-society watchers, it did just that. No other KKK-sponsored convocation (or "konklovation" as Klansmen preferred to call them) in the state ever exceeded this one in size. In fact, authorities called the Issaquah rally one of the biggest public events ever mounted by the KKK in the greater Pacific Northwest region. Attendance estimates that night vary widely—the lowest being just a few thousand, including a good number of reporters sent to cover the affair. Sheriff deputies and highway patrolmen, on the other hand, counted 11,442 cars on the scene, so early Klan predictions that 20,000 to 30,000 people would be taking part may not have been far off the mark. Presuming that more than one person arrived in each vehicle, the *Issaquah Press* estimated the turnout at a high of 55,000 Washingtonians who'd been attracted by the KKK's invitation to "learn first hand the exact nature of the work of the Klan."

Ida Maude Goode Walimaki, descendent of a five-generation Issaquah family, was only 11 years old at the time of the rally, but she forever retained a sharp memory of the immense crowd. "Everybody was milling around," she recalled seven decades later. "Daddy and my brother, George, and I walked over in the evening, and there were people like you wouldn't *believe*. No uprising, or anything. Cub Scouts have their own rallies, and this didn't seem any more violent than those. It was like a church social or a Grange meeting—nothing bloodthirsty about it that I know of. And no one was ashamed of their Klan membership. Meetings had been held for a long time in the Grange Hall. No cloak and dagger."

Today, a shopping center and Park-and-Ride bus station occupy the site where Klansmen held this konklovation. Nothing on that flat parcel of earth would indicate that it once was lit up by the torches of the White Robed Knights. The Issaquah Historical Society Museum can muster only a single reference to the 1924 event, the most widely circulated Seattle-area histories don't mention it, and Seattle newspaper files have almost nothing to show for all the hoopla in Issaquah. Even the *Issaquah Press* is sketchy on exactly what happened that evening.

Yet it's worth remembering that this demonstration in Issaquah was no mere aberration in the Northwest. For most of the last century, in fact, newspapers here have editorialized against white supremacist movements. We may not like to think that some of our neighbors have harbored such exclusionary attitudes, but they have. The better we recognize this fact, then the better we might understand why incidents of racist and religious prejudice continue to occur. Perhaps it's just as important to ask how the 1924 event could have been forgotten, as how it could have happened at all. You might say that the Ku Klux Klan represents a page of Washington's "hidden history."

In the early 1920s, nighttime Ku Klux Klan spectacles occurred in many Pacific Northwest communities, but photographs of these activities are rare. In this scene near Colfax, Washington, Klansmen gather under a hillside where flammable material in trenches forms a cross. *WSU Libraries 79-088*

Books about the state's past, when they recount radical elements of any sort, generally concentrate on the Wobblies or other leftists. But what of the Knights of the Ku Klux Klan? During the 1920s, the Klan cast itself as a hyperpatriotic body essential to maintaining American values. It gained a substantial following among people who worried about the United States becoming too liberal, and that the government was diluting its duties at home by becoming increasingly involved in international affairs. These feelings were powerful enough in the Northwest to influence state elections. In the South, the Klan had concentrated its discriminatory efforts against African Americans, but in the Northwest—where blacks represented a very small part of the population until after World War II—the Klan spread its bigotry around elsewhere. The Puget Sound area already had exhibited anti-Asian sentiments. In public rallies, as well as in a Klan newspaper published in Seattle, the KKK expanded its scope of prejudice by rallying against "Koons, Kikes, and Katholics," with special attention directed toward Catholics. At one point, the Klan even sought (and almost wrote into law) legislation in Washington and Oregon that would have restricted children from attending private Catholic schools.

If the 1924 rally helped "put Issaquah on the map," that was fine with its organizers. But what they really wanted was to plant the infamous Knights of the Ku Klux Klan firmly and permanently in Washington's political geography.

"The Invisible Empire of the 1920s was neither predominately Southern, nor rural, nor white supremacist, nor violent," Kenneth T. Jackson declares in an excellent study, *The Ku Klux Klan in the City, 1915–1930.* "Following closely in the nativist tradition of the Know-Nothing party of the 1850s and the American Protective Association of the 1890s, albeit increasing their intolerance, the Ku Klux Klan presented itself as the defender of Americanism and the conservator of Christian ideals. It received a charter in 1916 as a 'patriotic, secret, social, benevolent order,' but found ample occasion to denounce Catholicism, integration, Judaism, immigration, and internationalism as threats to American values."

Jackson explains that the Klan, which recorded more than two million members in the United States between 1920 and 1926, "commanded almost as much support as organized labor and was described with considerable accuracy . . . as 'the most vigorous, active, and effective force in American life, outside business.'"

The original Ku Klux Klan, given life by Confederate veterans in 1866, had carried on a spree of violence against emancipated slaves following the Civil War, but it became less powerful as the signing at Appomattox Courthouse faded further into the national memory.

By the early 1920s, however, times were ripe for a Klan revival. The United States was changing rapidly and was unsure of its eventual direction. The cataclysmic First World War had ended, but America hadn't yet fully settled down into a period that Warren G. Harding called "normalcy."

The country was experiencing the ramifications of its beginnings as a world power. Women, who went into the workplace during the war to fill shoes of men sent halfway across the globe, weren't ready to pick up their aprons again and head off cheerfully to the stove. They'd been emancipated, and many now were agitating for equality. Male laborers, too, were asking for more rights and protections, which brought forth new union action and protests, such as Seattle's General Strike of February 6, 1919, when 60,000 workers walked off their jobs. Meanwhile, immigrants were pouring into the country and acquiring new Americanized names at Ellis Island before they joined in competition against Americans, who'd once thought their jobs secure. Nothing was permanent—not even the traditional family farm, as a new industrial society fed its smokestacks at the expense of America's previous agrarian economy and social order.

"All of these changes would have taken place eventually," opined an article in the June 1974 *Oregon Historical Quarterly* (*OHQ*). "All of them existed in embryo long before war was declared. But the war had accelerated their growth so powerfully that they fruited, as it were, out of season, coming on so rapidly that they brought with them a powerful sense of dislocation of the orderly processes. Reasonable men were perfectly aware it was not possible to turn back into the past. But even reasonable men, bewildered by the new thinking, confused by unaccustomed scenes, battered about by unfamiliar faces, were resentful that it was not."

Instability has always opened a wide door to prejudicial movements, and the early 1920s offered a broad portal indeed. Providential timing ushered the Klan back into American life.

One factor in the Klan's revival took a most sweeping form—the 1915 release of D.W. Griffith's film, *The Birth of a Nation*. This first feature-length motion picture in American history showed a trampled South beating back the post-Civil War assault of Northern carpetbaggers and crooked politicos with the help of hard-riding Ku Klux Klan horsemen. Audiences across the South (and elsewhere!) cheered the silent black-and-white spectacle. In one theater, male viewers filled a silver screen with bullets as they tried in futility to protect a white heroine from a black villain.

One viewer in particular found inspiration in Griffith's apologia for Reconstruction-era violence. The spuriously titled "Colonel" William Joseph Simmons of Atlanta was "a tall man with a vacant, senatorial face, a cornpone manner, an unquenchable thirst for bourbon, and a weakness for amenable young women," explains the *OHQ* article. "He had been a revivalist [with the Methodist Episcopal Church], a crossroads orator, and, on the authority of some of his detractors, an unsuccessful garter sales-man." But here was a man with ambition. Shortly after *The Birth of a Nation*'s release, Simmons declared himself Grand Imperial Wizard of a new and fraternal Klan. He was less interested in the political possibilities of the Klan than he was in the mummery of a fraternal order (secret handshakes, coded jargon, and all the rest). He was enchanted by the hoary symbols of the hooded order, especially the burning cross, about which he penned this idolatrous bit of doggerel:

> Behold, the Fiery Cross still brilliant!
>   Combined efforts to defame
> And all the calumny of history
>   Fail to quench its hallowed flame.
>
> It shall burn bright as the morning
>   For all decades yet to be
> Held by hearts and hands of manhood
>   It shall light from sea to sea.
>
> We rally around this ancient symbol
>   Precious heritage of the past
> And swear our all to home and country
>   And to each other to the last.
>
> In the Fiery Cross I glory
>   'Neath its glow my Oath was made
> It shall live in song and story
>   I swear its light shall never fade.

Imperial Wizard Simmons helped spur Klan growth (perhaps even unintentionally), thanks to a particular prejudice he embodied, one that was barely related to the new missions of his order—he hated cities. Al-most all cities, including maybe even Atlanta, though he had voluntarily settled there after leaving his home state of Alabama. In 1920, Simmons declared, "the great city as at present constructed corrodes the very soul of our American life." Overgrown cities, especially, "are in themselves a menace," accorded the Wizard.

Until this time, the Klan had been thought of primarily as a rural phe-nomenon capitalizing on the distrust that small-town residents had for urban folk who did most of America's governing. City populations com-monly were thought to be too sophisticated and even-tempered, and thus lacking the superstitious and ignorant characteristics that could turn a burning wooden cross into a totem of power and magnificence. But as Jackson points out in *The Ku Klux Klan in the City*, increasing KKK prejudice against urban areas finally led that organization to infiltrate into cities with reform in mind. This change of direction was greatly assisted by a pair of Simmons-supported promoters from Atlanta—former newspaperman Edward Young Clarke and a divorcée with some money socked away, one Elizabeth Tyler. Savvy to national attitudes, Clarke and Tyler saw political and moneymaking potential in a movement that championed "100 percent Americanism" over the influences of "hyphenated people" (i.e., anybody who recently had adopted the United States as their home). They also recognized that large metropolitan populations had the numbers that could help enhance Klan power. So off to urban cores went the Klan.

First, it was Southern towns that witnessed "kleagles" (recruiters) walking the sidewalks. Atlanta, Knoxville, Memphis—all soon boasted Kluxer contingents, each working the political machine, generally within the Republican Party. The movement next spread quickly to Chicago, Detroit, Indianapolis, and then it ventured west.

"Numbers of King Kleagles were trained and sent forth," the *OHQ* recounted, "each assigned a territory, and each equipped with a kit which contained a list of prime prospects: Protestant clergymen, police officers, local officials, politicians, and local citizens who had, in the past, been associated with similar hate movements or who might be readily persuaded that personal advantage might flow from this one." Each new Klansman paid a $10 "gratuity" to enlist with the White Robed Knights, $4 of which found its way to the recruiter's pocket.

At the same time as the Klan hoped to change things in the cities, of course, urban environments changed the KKK. By the time it had crossed the Mississippi River on its way to Denver, Los Angeles, Portland, and Seattle, the Klan was no longer the secretive, snollygostering, horse-riding order birthed in Old Dixie. Its Southern Protestant roots were obvious in the Klan declaration that "America is Protestant and so it must remain," but the Klan cast itself as a political animal, too. It supported the 18th Amendment prohibiting U.S. liquor sales and maintained vehemently that "demon rum" was the root of crime and sexual debasement in America. It also insisted that the United States should remain isolationist and not join with advocates of international cooperation, such as the nascent League of Nations.

As Klansmen might have seen it, they were the exemplars of what it meant to be true Americans. "Masters in the use of such glittering phrases as 'the tenets of the Christian religion,' 'pure womanhood,' or 'just laws,' the professional recruiters preyed upon the fear that the country was endangered from organized elements within," writes Jackson. "Painting the KKK as the organized good of the community, the kleagles promised to combat these pernicious influences and to return the nation to older values."

Ostensibly, the "new" Klan also favored a separation of church and state, yet it decreed that the Bible should figure into classroom studies. It even sought to prove a relationship between burglary rates in selected cities and the number of years that Bible study in those places had been an aspect of the public school curriculum.

Its precepts bore a distinct flavor of fundamentalist religion. As one Klan paper in Seattle would later pronounce:

A Klansman is one who has the love of God shed abroad in his heart by the Holy Ghost given unto him—one who loves the Lord his God with all his heart, mind, soul, and strength. He rejoices evermore, prays without ceasing, and in everything gives thanks… HE KEEPS ALL OF GOD'S COMMANDMENTS, FROM THE LEAST TO THE GREATEST. He follows not the custom of the world, for vice does not lose its nature through becoming fashionable. He fares not sumptuously every day. He cannot lay up treasures upon the earth, nor can he adorn himself with gold or costly apparel. He cannot join in any diversion that has the least tendency to vice.

The KKK pushed its distinctive platform on anybody who would listen—an agenda the Klan portrayed as no more outlandish than that of the major political parties. They stirred up anti-Semitism and anti-Catholicism in Denver, and even moved their people into key positions within that city's government. In Anaheim, California, too, four Klansmen won seats on the five-member city council in 1924.

Oregon was quite receptive to the Klan. In fact, that state had long been segregationist. One of the reasons Oregon had strived to achieve statehood relatively early (1859) was due to the ramifications from a famous 1857 U.S. Supreme Court decision. In *Dred Scott v. Sandford*, the high court declared it illegal for a territorial legislature or the U.S. Congress to prohibit slavery in any federal territory—only a state was allowed to do so. Oregon didn't just plan to prohibit slavery, however, it wanted to prohibit all *blacks*—free or slave—from living there. If Oregon were a state, the reasoning went, legislators could rule against Negro incursion. For this ulterior purpose (and granted, for some other more respectable reasons as well), the 1859 vote for statehood was approved by a comfortable two-to-one margin.

These prejudicial sentiments were still omnipresent more than a half-decade later. As Portland historian Dick Pintarich explains in *Great Moments in Oregon History*, by 1922 it was estimated that active Klan membership in the Beaver State could be counted at 25,000 strong. One earlier authority put it this way: "Capitalizing on postwar tensions, the Klan claimed to have grown from nothing...to control of Oregon politics by 1922."

Indeed, Oregon's KKK had enough power to pass legislation that required children between the ages of 8 and 16 to attend only state schools, which the Klan predicted would cut lethally into education revenues that Catholic institutions had so long enjoyed. The Klan also almost single-handedly elected a dark-horse Democratic candidate, rancher Walter Pierce, as governor. The Klan soon regretted this latter effort, though, when Pierce became indifferent to KKK wishes after the inauguration. In June 1923, in fact, there was even a move among many Oregon Kluxers to recall Pierce. The effort was nixed only after KKK leaders realized it would cause divisiveness within the Klan and cost it any hold it might yet tenuously exercise on the state's highest office.

The Klan portrayed itself as a staunch defender of law and order, yet even Portland's King Kleagle admitted to the press in 1921: "There are some cases...in which we will have to take everything into our hands. Some crimes are not punishable under existing laws but the criminals must be punished." The Klan's barely closeted vigilantism may have been demonstrated best in the southern Oregon town of Medford, where, according to the *OHQ* account, hooded nightriders launched occasional raids during the early 1920s. "It was the particular amusement of this group of sterling citizens," the article related, "to kidnap an 'undesirable' (Kluxer definition), drive him to a remote area, fit him with a hangman's noose, throw the rope end over a convenient limb, and draw the poor devil up, leaving him to struggle and strangle until he had grasped the true inwardness of Klan justice. Upon which he was cut down and ordered to depart the country forthwith, in at least one case being hurried along by gun shots."

The first victim of this abuse was a black man. The second was white— a local piano salesman suspected of commiserating overly much with a certain young lady in town. After three almost-hangings, the salesman nearly died from a heart condition and had to be cut down. Almost immediately upon recovering, he went straight to the local district attorney to identify the attackers. However, Medford's mayor that year was bucking for Klan support in a coming U.S. Senate race and he managed to sweep the whole matter beneath a very thick rug.

When the editor of Pendleton's *East-Oregonian* obtained a copy of his town's Klan membership roster and began publishing parts of it, he was waylaid in the dark and beaten mercilessly. Even worse, hooded mobsters near the southern Oregon gold-mining town of Jacksonville reportedly lynched a black man, after he had allegedly stolen chickens and consorted with a white female. Also, "black women in northeast Portland were branded and warned to leave the city," Pintarich recalls. Despite these dire actions, Oregon's minute black population provided only a minor portion of the KKK's targets—blacks in Portland numbered less than 1 percent of that city's population. Instead, Klansmen mainly went after Asians and followers of the Pope.

Crosses burned on Portland's otherwise scenic Mount Tabor and Mount Scott, automobile "kavalkades" periodically choked the city's downtown streets, and return engagements of *The Birth of a Nation* were booked at the Blue Mouse Theater. In 1921 the Klan claimed to have initiated 150 Portland police officers into the Invisible Empire. Mayor George Baker, an old showman who aspired to political heights, might not have been a member of the Klan, but in December 1921 he announced that budgetary difficulties wouldn't weaken his police force because he'd engaged 100 Portland vigilantes to help keep down crime. These 100 men, of course, were chosen after consultation with the local Klan and most of them were card-carrying acolytes of the Imperial Wizard.

By the fall of 1923, 15,000 Portlanders counted themselves among the Klan's ranks, which was well over half of all KKK membership in Oregon. There was even a women's auxiliary, the Ladies of the Invisible Empire (LOTIES), as well as an affiliate body for foreign-born males called the Royal Riders of the Red Robe. (Yes, they donned red garments rather than white sheets for official ceremonies.)

Seattle was slower than Portland in embracing the Klan. Father Wilfred Schoenberg, a Jesuit and noted regional historian who has authored an unpublished book about Klan activities, attributes this in large part to the less intense tensions between Protestants and Catholics here than in Oregon. The KKK first had to enhance these prejudices just to get wedges into Washington's political and social systems.

King Kleagle Luther Ivan Powell, who'd made a tidy profit from Kluxing in California before hieing off to Portland and thence north to Seattle, did his best to make up for lost time. Arriving in Seattle in 1922, he organized a hundred-man order on the battleship USS *Tennessee*, anchored in Puget Sound. He launched a slender anti-Catholic weekly, *The Watcher on the Tower*, which adopted the motto, "The Klan, The Konstitution, and The Kross Shall Be Our Faith, Our Hope, Our Creed of Liberty." Filled with screeds against the Pope's minions and the increased incursion into the United States by "undesirable immigrants," as well as insulting parables about blacks and reports on Klan activities around the country, *The Watcher on the Tower* sought a role as counterpoint to William Randolph Hearst's vehemently anti-Klan *Seattle Post-Intelligencer*. Powell's office on the sixth floor of Seattle's Securities Building, at 3rd Avenue and Stewart Street, was central command for Washington and Idaho Klanism, as well as headquarters for the Junior Order of the Ku Klux Klan.

By late 1922, Exalted Cyclops John A. Jeffrey—a former Portland attorney seeking the unsown fields of Seattle to plant his gospel of skewed "Americanism"—proclaimed that the Emerald City contained 2,000 followers and was thus eligible for charter as Klan No. 4. (Klan No. 4's total membership between 1915 and 1944 was later estimated at 8,000.) Klansmen visited local churches and started talking about building "a combined auditorium, Klub Room, and Klan headquarters" to hold the expanding membership. In the absence of this grand facility, they often met at a Seattle restaurant called The Palm Cafe, which apparently took up space on Westlake Avenue now overgrown with Westlake Center. The Palm was so frequented by the white-hooded set that it soon began advertising itself as, "The Klansmen's Roost—Where Kozy Komfort and Komrade Kare Kill the Grouch with Viands Rare." (Klan poetry was often grating, but members were remarkably proficient in working *k*'s into all their printed statements.)

The Evergreen State may not have provided the Klan with particularly fertile fields of religious tension, but it was no stranger to racial sectarianism. The Chinese exclusion decree, passed at a Seattle congress in 1885, ruled that all Chinese should leave the Puget Sound area by November 1 of that year. No responsibility would be taken, said regional reps of that congress, for "acts of violence which may arrive from non-compliance." Unbelievably, this anti-Chinese agitation had been fomented originally just to unite workers in the state. The results were that vigilantes in Tacoma stormed the homes and business of those Chinese remaining after the deadline, and whites rioted in Seattle when a ship bound for San Francisco refused to be overloaded with Chinese. Martial law was declared to put down hostilities.

There had been racial and ethnic violence in Issaquah, too, dating back to when that Eastside community was called Squak Valley. It was there, just before Seattle's anti-Chinese assaults, that the first mass savagery against Asians in the Northwest was recorded. After protesting the employment of 37 Chinese hop pickers on the old Wold brothers' ranch (near what is now Issaquah Valley Elementary School), an unlikely alliance was struck between five non-Indian workers and two Indian ones in the valley. One night, the group lined up beside the Wolds' Chinese tent and emptied their guns into the fabric. By daybreak, three Asians lay dead, three others were wounded, and the remainder had fled the valley.

So why did the Seattle press eventually come down harder on the KKK than on those earlier persecution movements? Perhaps because many of those who fell under the Klan's prejudices were white Americans, people with money, people who supported the papers, folks who, though they might be called "hyphenated people"—Irish-Americans, Jewish-Americans, or Scandinavian-Americans—had come to Puget Sound long before the Klan raised its clenched fist here. Both the *Seattle Times* and the *P-I* opposed any Klan invasion of the Puget Sound area. The *P-I*, in particular, thought the Klan a menace. The blustering Hearst (who bought the *P-I* in 1921) had for years spoken and written volumes of disapproval regarding KKK activities. It made good copy, especially in his own expanding chain of newspapers. But news about fairly peaceful Klan events, such as the 1924 Issaquah rally, didn't even win an inch of copy in the fiery broadsheet.

Times editor and publisher Clarance B. Blethen could be just as vilifying as his counterparts across town. A year before the Issaquah rally, Blethen struck at the Klan in a front-page editorial:

The Ku Klux Klan is the most dangerous thing that has ever come into American life.

Washington wants none of it.

Seattle wants none of it.

Americans live here. They wish to live in peace, but they intend to choose their own neighbors.

Any attempt on the part of the Ku Klux Klan to move in without permission will be considered and treated as an invasion of our country and a violation of our homes.

And that is all there is to the matter!

Such fulminating, however, didn't stay Klan activities in Washington. A "Klan Directory" published in *The Watcher* in 1923 listed affiliate orders in Vancouver, Spokane, Walla Walla, Woodland, Castle Rock, Grays Harbor, Tacoma, Bremerton, Bellingham, Port Angeles, Everett, Dayton, Kelso, Olympia, South Bend, Colfax, and Wenatchee, as well as Seattle. Over the next year, other Klan chapters would open in Renton, Kent, and Issaquah.

In early 1923, planning had begun for Washington's first large-scale Klan convention to be held on Saturday, July 14, in Peoples Park at Renton Junction. Two thousand Seattle and Tacoma residents were expected to attend. King Kleagle Powell saw this event as the culmination of his efforts, but unfortunately for him, King County Sheriff Matt Starwich had other ideas. Starwich wouldn't prevent the rally from being held, but he insisted on "strict observance of the statute which prohibits concealing of the face by an assemblage of three or more persons, except for purposes of masquerade, fancy ball, or other entertainment."

Klansmen without their traditional hoods? Powell defied Starwich to enforce this rule. The sheriff countered by threatening to post deputies throughout the park to see that the law was observed. When Powell mentioned that one of Starwich's own officers was a KKK member, the sheriff found the man and dismissed him on the spot.

"Kluxers Back Down and Will Obey the Law," the *P-I* headlined two days later. Other public officials, it seems, had prevailed upon the King Kleagle and the Exalted Cyclops not to push their luck. Rather than the blowout event hoped for, a peaceful picnic was held beginning at 10 a.m. that Saturday, open only to card-carrying Klansmen. Fireworks began at 8 p.m. at Wilson Station, an interurban stop east of Orillia. "Although some from Renton attended the convention," David M. Buerge records in *Renton: Where the Water Took Wing*, "most residents were indifferent to it, and others had no tolerance for the Klan or other hate groups." Some 5,000 spectators were counted at the event. The King Kleagle insisted that 1,200 people were initiated into the Knights of the Ku Klux Klan that day—although other sources estimated the number at more like 500. Only one figure was spotted wearing a hood over his white robe, sitting atop a horse, and carrying "an illuminated cross." That was the man giving the new members their oath.

"Above a green sloping hill on which stand four large crosses, an endless line of white-robed Klansmen move in single file and closed ranks," *The Watcher* reported of the initiation ceremony. "Sharp words of command hurl themselves across the void, ranks open and move into position. The purple twilight deepens into the blue vault of night—one luminous star appears above the green hill, the giant crosses and the group of firs standing like sentinels above the ceremony. Fourteen electric globes on a double T glow into incandescent flame and the white horsemen ride down to their stations. The white lines extend and open till they form a square covering the space of five acres, Klansmen standing shoulder to shoulder. Suddenly a figure appears on the brow of the hill riding a brown horse. A young voice heralding the stars passes the word 'Every Klansman will salute the Imperial Cyclops.' Ten thousand hands are raised beyond the ring denoting the presence of Klansmen not taking part in the Ceremonial, thousands of hands over fifty acres of ground from cars packed in solid columns of tens, twenties, and hundreds. A patriotic hymn is being sung. Strong young voices cry out: 'Who are you, Sir Knight?' The response is lost amid the murmured appreciation of the multitude."

Never say that the Klan couldn't sling hyperbole with the best of 'em.

"The primary indicant of Seattle Klan deterioration," writes historian Jackson, "came in October of 1923, when King Kleagle Powell left the city [for Portland again] and *The Watcher on the Tower* ceased publication." Over the next year, the Klan's reformed reputation started to tarnish badly all over the country, as unsavory incidents were reported at length in the press.

Four men were shot in Massachusetts when "hostile crowds" clashed with Klansmen attending an outdoor initiation ceremony. When attempts were made to stop a Klan parade through Nilesa, Ohio, a riot broke out that left at least one person dead and many more injured. When the Klan attempted to organize in Glen Falls, New York, they were greeted by "a barrage of stones, clubs, and bottles of ammonia thrown by a mob of nearly 2,000 persons."

The California Klan split up when rival factions vied for leadership. Monetary bickering became common, too, among fragmenting Klan groups. Back in Atlanta, there was even something of a palace revolt brewing, begun after a Texas dentist tried to push the bibulous Grand Imperial Wizard, Simmons, into an allegedly higher but ineffectual position. In Tacoma, the husband of a missing woman told police, "he was head of the Ku Klux Klan in the Fern Hill district where he resided and that he intended calling out the Klan throughout the country to aid in the search for his missing wife." It turned out later that hubby had slayed the missus.

The town of Issaquah in 1924 hardly seemed worth the KKK's attention. Sure, it was a growing community, but still not much to write home about. There was a hip-roofed schoolhouse, a town hall, and a firehouse sporting a bell tower that rose above the orchards and farms. Prohibition provided some delight for local firefighters, as they often uncovered tubfuls of moonshine in gutted buildings. Hepler Motors, hoping to turn every local resident into a car owner, took horses, chickens, and even geese as trade-ins toward purchasing a new Model T Ford. Corn might grow 10 to 15 feet tall on Roy Pickering's farm. Coal was being mined from surrounding hillslopes. It took a whole day to reach Seattle, traveling by train around Lake Washington, but Issaquahans were known to go into the city for weekends of entertainment.

The Klan had organized in Issaquah only three months before the great konklovation on July 26. The local Klansmen's biggest previous showing probably was when they "burned a fiery cross in conjunction with the town's 4th of July celebration," in the words of Issaquah writer and history teacher Joe Peterson. The *Issaquah Press* reported that the Klan erected "a fiery cross and three large K's were burned on [a] summit northeast of town, and a number of sky rockets, bombs, and star showers set off." For the 26th, the Klan promised a "display of fireworks, being built specially."

That big event's ostensible purpose was to "naturalize" 250 candidates as members of the Ku Klux Klan. The local press did its part by treating the rally as a spectacle and ignored whatever message the hooded Klansmen hoped to impart. In the *Press*, the rally was described simply as orderly and peaceful. "The big crowd," it remarked, "was handled without the slightest incident." The paper commented not at all about Kluxer bigotry. No words recounted the KKK's violent history. The Eastside weekly seemed to look at these Klan goings-on in the same way it might look at a circus.

Nobody was saying so at the time, but it seems as if the Issaquah event was designed partly to help shore up Seattle Klan No. 4's crumbling foundation. In spite of the remarkable attendance, the evening apparently scored no major victory for the Klan. Either few casual attendees were persuaded to take another (more favorable) look at the KKK or, the local organization by now was so disorganized, it couldn't make use of whatever political capital it might have gained on that summer night.

Afterward, nothing was quite the same. On November 4, 1924, a Klan-supported initiative in Washington—like the one passed in Oregon two years before that would have prescribed compulsory "public" education for all of the state's children—was defeated handily at the polls. (The U.S. Supreme Court already had ruled that the Oregon school bill was unconstitutional.) Two weeks later, eight ranking officers of Seattle Klan No. 4 launched an open revolt against the Klan headquarters in Atlanta, protesting that "Atlanta is bleeding the Klans of the country" for dues. Hundreds of Puget Sound Kluxers met on November 17, 1924, to form a competing order called the International Klan of America, backing the "original" Atlanta Klan leadership. "Other local knights," Jackson relates in *The Ku Klux Klan in the City*, "simply turned their backs on the controversy and allowed the Klan to die a quick death in their city."

There still was enough interest in the Klan, though, that when an Imperial Wizard from Atlanta visited Seattle in 1927, the local chamber of commerce hosted a dinner in his honor. But for the most part, by 1925 the White Robed Knights had seen the last of their influence in Washington fade. There would be a small resurgence of Klanism in the mid-1930s, with Bolsheviks and Jews being the new targets, but the Northwest pretty much ignored this rebirth. Some former Klansmen joined 1930s neo-fascist groups, too, particularly the Silvershirt Legion of America.

The Klan's heyday in this area didn't last long, yet elements of its appeal in 1924 may well survive today, at least for some people who most need to create an identity by blaming and excluding others. Issaquah's Klan portrayed its members as good, wholesome nationalists—Americans through and through. It's not surprising, then, that Ida Walimaki's most vivid memory from Issaquah's mammoth KKK rally is of the fireworks: "One rocket, I remember, showed a beautiful American flag when it burst."

HEAD IN THE CLOUDS

EATTLE WAS ONCE A CITY where you could dub a restaurant "The Cloud Room," even though it floated a mere 11 stories above the streets. It's a corny name, and moisture-laden clouds probably seldom came down anywhere near this dining spot atop the old Camlin Hotel. But the name is ironic because the history of the Camlin Hotel never seemed anchored in reality anyway, and The Cloud Room only added to that impression. Surely, when the restaurant was christened, it was the heads of its developers that rested in the clouds, not the eatery.

When the Camlin's owners spent $50,000 in 1947 to convert what had been a penthouse suite into restaurant space, they wanted to boast about having the highest dining facility in the Pacific Northwest. Locals responded immediately. "It's been smooth sailing right from the start," Camlin manager John E. Graham told the *Seattle Post-Intelligencer* just after the restaurant and lounge opened. "We have been particularly well received, especially by those trying to show visitors our beautiful country."

The 360-degree outlook must have been something to behold in 1947, when the buildings surrounding the hotel's north downtown location stood much lower than today. Between sips of Sazerac, guests could gaze north to Lake Union, or west to downtown Seattle and the harbor beyond where the "mosquito ferry fleet" plied the Sound. The *Pacific Coast Record*, a restaurant trade journal, gushed over The Cloud Room as "the answer to all those who have bewailed the fact that there was no place in Seattle which took advantage of the wonderful views available from tall buildings." Until the Space Needle opened in 1962, the city offered no dining establishment closer to the stars.

For many Seattleites, a visit to this late-night noise box was their only contact with the Camlin Hotel. Many were enticed up to The Cloud Room by its name and its string of ceiling lamps easily espied from street level. Some remember visiting the lounge back when it was considered a bit seedy (and, therefore, oddly seductive) and was decorated with a sea of plush couches. They came to recognize The Cloud Room as an anachronism— a charming old-fashioned venue attractive for its quaintness and evocation of a more naïve, eccentric Seattle. The entire Camlin, on 9th Avenue between Olive Way and Pine Street, eventually carried that tang. Never the moneymaker that its builders hoped it would be, and overshadowed in its early years by the older and larger Olympic Hotel and later by better-marketed "boutique hotels" like the Alexis and the Sorrento, the Camlin became The Hotel That Time Forgot. Its early 21st-century conversion into a private vacation resort only confirmed the Camlin's status outside of the mainstream.

However, few of its rivals could claim a more unusual—or scandalous—history. Almost eight decades after the hotel opened, the story hidden behind its brick-and-terra-cotta facade has lost none of its appeal. It's a saga about two ambitious bankers, Adolph Linden and Edmund Campbell, who wound up doing time in the Walla Walla State Penitentiary. It's a tale involving KJR Radio, a yacht with a faulty bilge pump, a God-fearing man who walked with a limp, and a grandiose mansion in Lake Forest Park that was allowed to fall into peeling, creaking decrepitude. It's also the story of a halcyon moment in Seattle's past when the city was being built through pluck and plunder, and when some town fathers reached rather clumsily toward the clouds.

Elizabeth Linden remembers her father-in-law, Adolph Frederik Linden, as "a man of dreams and high hopes." No dream was too big for Adolph. A heavyset, bespectacled gent with dark hair who stood just over 6 feet tall, he was filled with that unstoppable entrepreneurial spirit that drives a person from one business enterprise to another. He always looked for the shining path that could lead to prominence and influence. At one point in the late 1920s, Adolph was the president of a Seattle bank, had just built the Camlin Hotel, was cutting himself in on Oklahoma oil ventures, and soon would launch into producing and selling phonograph records. Each new endeavor, each new risk, held the promise of success.

Linden was born on May 29, 1889, just a week before Seattle's great fire. Father Frederik, a Baptist minister, and mother Christina had shipped out of Sweden some years before. When Adolph took his first breath, the family was living in Des Moines, Iowa. But like many ministers of that period, Frederik saw the American West as a more fertile ground to spread his teaching. By the time Adolph was ready for high school, the Lindens were residing in Seattle. Reverend Linden assumed the pastor's post at the Swedish Baptist Church, 820 Pine Street—in the same block where the Camlin Hotel later would stand.

While attending high school in 1903, young Adolph worked at a lumber camp and a large delicatessen-cum-grocery store in the landmark Colman Building on 1st Avenue. Three years later, he got his first taste of the banking life as a manager for the Swedish American Bank, lugging hefty sacks of cash through the streets of Seattle. By 1910 Adolph had started on the staff of the Puget Sound Savings & Loan Association (PSS&L), then a nine-year-old institution.

In that same year, Linden married Esther Elizabeth Anderson. She was one of six children fathered by Aaron Frederick Anderson, also an expatriate Swede, who had set up shop as a shoe salesman in Michigan, and did well enough to escort one or more of his family members around the country by train each year. In 1908 Esther had embarked on a four-month excursion with her father that carried them finally to Puget Sound, where she met Reverend Linden's son, Adolph, during services at the Swedish Baptist Church. "I really don't know what she saw in Adolph," remarks Jim Linden, Adolph's grandson and an industrial engineer at the Boeing Corporation. "She was beautiful, and he was, well, kind of homely." Regardless, the two were wed in September 1910. He was 21 and she 15 months older. They set up house on Boylston Avenue. In the following year, Esther's family moved from Michigan to Puget Sound.

Esther's father, Aaron, had done well with footwear and he proved himself even more capable in the Washington lumber industry. He soon purchased large stands of timber in Snohomish, Whatcom, and Clallam counties, and his Discovery Bay Logging Company was once said to be among the Evergreen State's largest lumbering concerns. But Aaron Anderson, like his son-in-law, wasn't content with having his hand in just one business pot at a time. He owned three logging outfits, served as director of the National City Bank of Seattle and as vice president of the Federal

Consolidated Milk Company, and by 1916 was president of Puget Sound Savings & Loan.

Being the son-in-law of the boss didn't hurt Adolph Linden's career one whit. He and "A.F." (as confidants and family referred to Aaron Frederick Anderson) got along famously, both socially and in business. Adolph rose quickly through the ranks at PSS&L. By 1923, the year that A.F. passed away, Adolph Linden was vice president and treasurer of the company. Listed as vice president and secretary was one Edmund W. Campbell.

Though Campbell, like Linden, had been born in Iowa, it's unlikely that the two knew each other before their Seattle banking years. Edmund Campbell, a man of medium height with an ennobling gray coiffure, was 19 years older than Adolph. Campbell had lived in Los Angeles and it's unclear when he moved north to Puget Sound. (His death certificate indicates that he arrived in northwest Washington as early as 1889; yet his grandson, a Bellevue attorney who prefers not to be named, believes Campbell didn't move to Seattle until 1905.) Edmund Campbell apparently started out in the L.A. delivery service, using horse-drawn carts to haul goods in what was then a dusty village, still very Mexican in atmosphere and overshadowed by San Francisco. Campbell is said to have prospered in the delivery market, but he eventually lost the business due to a disease that decimated his horses. After that, Campbell bundled up his wife and one daughter, also named Esther, and hopped a northbound train. With a head for business, he went into banking.

At the time of Aaron Anderson's demise, it was Adolph Linden who took over as president of Puget Sound Savings & Loan. With this boost in title and salary, in 1924 Linden purchased (reportedly "on impulse," without first telling Esther) a Georgian-style manse in Lake Forest Park. The house had been erected 10 years before by Harry V. Wurdemann, a distinguished ophthalmic surgeon who'd moved to Seattle from Wisconsin in 1909. The two-story residence stood on about five acres of land at the entrance to the park, and just off what was then two-lane Victory Way (today's Bothell Way). The grounds were planted with rose bushes and apple trees, with a cherry orchard at the northeast corner from which the estate took its name, Cherry Acres. After Linden bought Dr. Wurdemann's house (family records say he paid $6,300 for it), he sold the orchard and then sank as much as $100,000 into improving the remaining acreage, the main house, and outbuildings.

He dug a fine wading pool in the side yard and encircled the property with a fence made partly of white wood latticework, partly of brick and iron. A gate on Victory Way opened into a driveway curving up to the white, pillared residence, then swept around to the rear and a *porte-cochere*. Unfortunately, that impressive entrance eventually had to be locked up, because travelers continually mistook the Linden home for a roadhouse, and would come knocking at all hours in search of lodging. (Could this have been where Adolph's idea to construct a hotel originated?) Linden decorated the inside of the house with Oriental rugs and turned what had been a pink, tapestry-lined music room into a library to hold his immense collection of books—including Abraham Lincoln's personal Bible, signed manuscripts by Mark Twain, an 1885 first-edition of Robert Louis Stevenson's *A Child's Garden of Verses*, and the original 19th-century manuscript of Henry Wadsworth Longfellow's *Footsteps of Angels*.

Even before Linden assumed the PSS&L presidency, he and Edmund Campbell had become partners in enterprises outside of their banking business. In the early 1920s, they bought into an Oklahoma oil concern, and in 1925 formed the Camlin Investment Company—"Camlin" being a contraction of their surnames. To get this investment firm off the ground, Puget Sound Savings & Loan advanced it a whopping $865,988. (If that "advance" smells a little off, keep it in mind—this and other monetary arrangements between the bank and its two top officers led to trouble down the road.) The first order of business for the Camlin Investment Company was to raise a ritzy hotel in downtown Seattle.

Now jumping ahead to Halloween, October 31, 1926—the day illusionist and escape artist Harry Houdini died in Detroit. This same day, an 18-year-old boy was "stabbed and beaten to death by an infuriated mob" in Italy after he tried to shoot Benito Mussolini. It was in the middle of Prohibition. Lydia E. Pinkham's Vegetable Compound was all the rage among the physically and emotionally infirm. In Seattle, everybody was talking about reports from Kelso, Washington, that steam had been seen rising from Mount St. Helens, but most folks scoffed at the idea of an eruption ever occurring in these modern times. The Bon Marché was advertising 65-cent silk neckties for men. Women's girdles could be had for $1.25 each. No matter where you went in town, it seemed someone was humming the latest hit song:

When the red, red robin
Comes bob, bob, bobbin' along, along,
There'll be no more sobbin'
When he starts throbbin' his own sweet song.

Camlin Hotel. *Webster & Stevens MOHAI 83.10*

People who knew Adolph Linden and Edmund Campbell probably figured these two men were entitled to sing their own sweet song of success. After all, October 31 marked the official opening of the Camlin Apartment Hotel. It came at a time when Seattle was positively swooning about its own rapid growth, and newspapers enthused over each new building.

The *Seattle Times* rhapsodized about the Campbell-Linden project, saying, "the exterior effect of the Camlin is such as [to] make it stand out from all parts of the city… Instinctively, the thought is born of the magnificent view of the Sound and the Olympics which is to be had from the lofty windows in the rear of this edifice. Nothing has been spared in the way of expense in its construction… The Camlin stands as a monument to Seattle's development, a mark which equals anything to be found anywhere on the Pacific Coast."

The tower's architect was Carl J. Linde of Portland, a one-time brewery designer from Wisconsin, who had worked under noted Oregon architect A.E. Doyle. Linde concentrated his efforts on the Camlin's main entrance and front facade facing 9th Avenue. Its basic style was Tudor-Revival, with lions' heads and other decorative gargoyles. Dark brick was sculpted into piers, with contrasting, light, terra cotta quoins and window trim. Lancet windows, cusped arches, and turrets of terra cotta provided more contrast on the 10th floor and along the parapet. The *Times* likened this newly minted property to "a gorgeously beautiful Italian castle." Interior appointments were equally lavish—a Tennessee marble floor and "Italian mural decorations" in the lobby, plus mahogany woodwork and deep carpetings. For "the lover of fine furnishings," the *Times* reported, "one of the most notable features of this hotel is the collection of original paintings and etchings which has been gathered here. Most of these were secured through the Anderson Art Gallery in Chicago and the Ackerman Gallery of London, and comprise of themselves a group worthy of an individual collection."

The Camlin wasn't put up primarily to serve as a hotel for travelers, but as quality long-term housing for affluent Seattleites. For this reason, its 93 original suites were much better equipped than normal hotel rooms. Only eight rooms on the Camlin's first floor—the "bachelor apartments"—were limited to a single chamber and bath. "All others had been completely equipped with dinette and kitchenettes," explained the *Times*. "No two apartments are similarly furnished, or decorated. In addition, each bathroom is an outside room. [Seventeen of these were supplied with modern "shower baths."] Uniformed waiters give service in private dinettes, with no additional cost." The penthouse, taking up the entire 11th floor, was touted as being choice quarters for any members of Seattle's social elite.

Like many commercial buildings produced during this era, only the 9th Avenue facade was decorated—the other sides of the tower were left plain, since it was optimistically assumed that newly built structures later would block these walls from public view. One such new high-rise was to have been a *second* Camlin Hotel, located to the north at the corner of 9th and Olive Way (today a parking lot). This adjoining hotel was to have stood 14 stories high with even more ornamentation than the first Camlin, though its Seattle architects, McClelland & Pinneh, tried to create a design in sympathy with Linde's existing edifice. The Camlin Investment Company paid $175,000 for the corner property, and construction was to have begun in the fall of 1926. But the second hotel never was built.

Linden and Campbell already might have been financially overextended at this point. Even before the Camlin was completed, the two men prepared to move Puget Sound Savings & Loan to a huge new center of operations on the east side of 4th Avenue, between Pike and Union streets. "We expect to erect on this site one of the finest financial buildings in the city," Campbell told the *P-I* in late 1925. When the institution's new Roman-style, terra cotta-faced headquarters opened in January 1927, that promise seemed fulfilled. The bank, also designed by McClelland & Pinneh, stood three stories tall with half a dozen massive pillars in front supporting a sculpted cornice. Inside, the main room floor was "furnished with silver gray sienna, with counters of imported marble, topped by bronze trimmings," the *Times* observed. "At the rear of the banking room are three huge colored art-glass windows, one each being devoted to shipping, commerce, and lumbering and elaborated by figures symbolic of these Northwestern activities. Diffused light has been arranged to give the effect of sunlight playing through the windows." The panes were designed by Hungarian-born artist Anton Rez, a son-in-law of early Seattle ship owner-turned-banker Joshua Green. Many of Rez's other glass works decorate West Coast churches.

The PSS&L had raised what could only be described as a monument to money. Yet its foundations were far shakier than most people realized. In late September 1926, only a month before the Camlin opened its doors, a member of the PSS&L board of directors discovered some questionable withdrawals from the bank's funds. These included: $865,988 used to grubstake the Camlin Investment Company and build the hotel; about $200,000 that had been "swallowed" up by Campbell and Linden's oil speculations; and another $27,850 loan to KJR, Seattle's first commercially licensed broadcast station. On September 30, these monetary "abstractions" were brought to the attention of the PSS&L board. Members were informed that about $1 million was missing from the bank's till, and that the diverting of funds may have commenced as early as 1924. Alarmed by such information, the board sought help from a man with a wonderfully Dickensian name, W.L. Nicely, the Washington state savings and loans supervisor. According to later court records:

This resulted in the meeting . . . of the officers and directors with the supervisor October 2, when it was decided, with [Nicely's] advice and concurrence, that instead of closing the institution, the interests of the shareholders would be better served by securing an agreement with Linden and Campbell to make restitution as far as possible by turning over to the association all of their personal and other holdings, including the Camlin Apartment Hotel, under a trust arrangement, and that, under the direction of the supervisor, an endeavor would be made to restore the impairment to the capital of the association, the same officers and directors to continue in office, and the completion of the Camlin Apartment Hotel, which was then under construction, to be carried out.

It took another year, until September 1927, before a trust agreement covering the withdrawals was drawn up and placed on file by Adolph and Esther Linden, along with Edmund and May Campbell. This agreement was valued at between $1,500,000 and $1,750,000. It included stock certificates and Esther Linden's share of her late father's estate (valued at $200,000 to $300,000), as well as the Linden family's Lake Forest Park mansion and Adolph's prized collection of books, together valued at more than $300,000.

None of this, however, was revealed to the public.

Such a confining, censorious arrangement must have been difficult for ambitious men to swallow. Although America in the 1920s and 1930s seemed to be rife with bank embezzlements (Seattle witnessed at least two other such cases during this period), neither Adolph Linden nor Edmund Campbell previously had been associated with shady dealings. Campbell always had been viewed as extremely "straight," a churchgoer, a self-made businessman, and a mild-mannered gentleman who wasn't known to smoke or partake of intoxicating beverages. Linden had prided himself on his ability to triumph with his wit and energy, and he wanted more than anything else to stand at the forefront of Seattle's growth. Both men insisted they hadn't been lining their pockets secretly with funds from PSS&L. The withdrawals were dutifully recorded in the bank's books, they claimed, to ensure that those monies would be fully repaid. But this excuse didn't satisfy the board of directors. Supervisor Nicely was invited, as "trustee," to take a more active role in running the bank.

In response, Linden and Campbell twisted the dial to a new frequency. They had for some time been interested in getting into the radio industry. In the spring of 1927, they started the Northwest Radio Service, the kernel of what they hoped would grow into a nationwide broadcasting empire. Over the next two years, Linden sank tens of thousands of dollars into building up radio holdings. He bought Vincent Craft's KJR Radio and soon expanded its activities, starting an all-live operation and retaining a large staff of announcers, singers, and musicians. Never one to go halfway, Linden also hired a dance band, symphony orchestra, and string quartet to entertain a swelling radio audience. Curiously, despite earlier objections from the bank's board and in the face of W.L. Nicely's continuing supervision of that institution's activities, Linden continued to withdraw funds from PSS&L to finance this new commercial enterprise. Between April 1927 and May 1928, Linden is said to have tapped the bank for "loans" amounting to more than $50,000.

In March 1928, Adolph Linden resigned as president of the Puget Sound Savings & Loan Association. Edmund Campbell took over his job, and soon after moved temporarily from his Capitol Hill home into the Camlin's palatial top-floor penthouse.

Meanwhile, Linden was sure he could make a go of radio, the remarkable new medium that, as the *New York Times* once put it, "let people see things with their own ears." The network's spread was phenomenal. By the summer of 1929, he owned KEX radio in Portland, KGA in Spokane, and KYA in San Francisco. He tied these in with six more outlets stretching as far east as Chicago. Later that same year, several East Coast stations were meant to join into what, by this juncture, Linden was calling the American Broadcasting Company (no relation to the ABC so well known today). Linden had pumped $117,000 into his ABC and already was thinking of other ventures to launch after the network had proved itself a consistent moneymaker. During ABC's rise, Linden and airplane manufacturer William Boeing were featured together in a *Christian Science Monitor* story lauding their efforts to "put Seattle on the map."

But then the castles in cloudy skies again began to dissolve. In August 1929, ABC suddenly was thrown into bankruptcy. Linden simply had too much outstanding credit and not enough money to satisfy his creditors' demands. With an unpaid bill of $90,000 due the Pacific Telephone and Telegraph Company, ABC's broadcast lines were pulled. The network's collapse took what remained of the Lindens' assets, save for their clothes, Esther's jewelry, and Adolph's big 1926 Lincoln LeBaron four-door sedan.

Consequently, it's no wonder they were heartened by news in October 1929 that the Twentieth Century Fox Company of New York was interested in taking over ABC—Adolph was giddy with excitement at this nick-of-time rescue. He loaded his wife and their 15-year-old son, James, into the Lincoln and set out for New York City, hoping to get in some sightseeing before the contract signing began.

They were on the road on October 29, 1929, when the American stock market catastrophically crashed. By the time that the Lindens finally spied the glittering towers of Manhattan, Fox had decided it couldn't risk buying the Seattle-based radio network. *Sorry, Mr. Linden. Sorry.*

The Lindens didn't return to Washington right away, since Adolph had depended on the ABC purchase to pay off his debts and give him a chance to move into some other enterprise. Without that money, he reasoned, he'd be just as well off remaining in Gotham. Adolph was able to secure a $3,500 loan from a friend in Chicago, and with additional cash raised from selling the car, he started a small restaurant in Manhattan called the Bunch of Grapes. It didn't amount to much as eateries go, and Adolph couldn't seem to make much, if any, profit from it. The Bunch of Grapes closed by the next winter and Adolph was back out on the street, hunting without satisfaction for work at a time of escalating unemployment. Esther labored for awhile as a floorwalker in Macy's Department Store at $23 a week—the first job she'd ever held—but by February 1931 she too was out of a job. James was attending Harlem High School as a sophomore. The family lived at the small Wellington Hotel on 7th Avenue and cooked meals in a little electric toaster. The fur coat Esther Linden had brought with her from Seattle had been put up as collateral for the apartment rent.

Shortly after midnight on February 17, 1931, Adolph Linden stepped through the front door of the Wellington Hotel and onto the sidewalk for a head-clearing stroll. The only money he had left in his pocket was a dime—half of what he'd had the morning before. Two New York cops hailed him with a "telegraphic warrant" from Seattle for his arrest. Linden, whose wife recently had cut his hair in preparation for another round of job hunting, and who appeared little the worse for his recent poverty, looked the policemen up and down for a minute. Then he said, "All right, where do we go?"

Several hours later, Esther learned that her husband of 20 years was being held at New York's Seventh District jail. From behind bars, Linden claimed he was innocent. "My wife, my boy," he murmured, "this is bitter medicine for them." But Esther (almost always described in contemporary newspaper accounts as "the former Michigan heiress") seemed to be taking the latest turn of events better than most folks expected. Although the *Post-Intelligencer* told of her crying when admitting "she was hungry," Esther was adamant in defense of her husband's business dealings—even though settling Adolph's loans had cost her a fortune. "I gave all I had and I would have given more if I had it," she said. "Everything he had went, too. We went through it together, as we always go through everything together." And Esther spoke confidently to people back in Seattle of Adolph's innocence. "Of course, there are others there…who say he stole money and is a fugitive from justice," she told the *P-I*. "How can they say that? He has been here all the time and everyone knew where he was. He was never a fugitive from anything. I don't understand business, but I am sure everything he did was perfectly legal. He didn't defraud anyone."

The authorities disagreed. Under armed guard, Adolph was put aboard a westbound train, with Esther and young James riding in the rear of the same car, and returned to Seattle to stand trial. Friends raised $15,000 for his bail and the Lindens moved temporarily into the Claremont Hotel on 4th Avenue. In April a grand jury began investigating affairs of the Puget Sound Savings & Loan Association, which had closed on February 7, 1931. The Great Depression was now catching up with—and clobbering—all kinds of speculative ventures. By the first week in May, a grand jury had readied indictments against Linden, Campbell, W.L. Nicely, W.D. Comer (who took over as president of the bank after Campbell left in August 1929 to go into the securities business), and Carl G. Nelson, who'd served as secretary of PSS&L during Linden's tenure. It was said that, collectively, these men defrauded the bank of up to $2 million.

There were three trials, due to the fact that the first two trials ended with jurors unable to reach a unanimous verdict. The last trial began on September 28, 1931. Campbell and Linden were each charged with three counts of grand larceny by embezzlement. In addition, Campbell was accused of making off with $3,681.25 worth of rugs and furniture during the time he occupied the Camlin Hotel's penthouse. Linden and Campbell, along with the three other defendants, pleaded not guilty. After two inconclusive jury ballots, Judge William Steinhart instructed the jurors not to base their ruling on whether Linden and Campbell had shown felonious intent in diverting funds from the bank, but simply on whether they had deprived that institution of money. Given such orders, the jury could reach no verdict other than "guilty." W.L. Nicely, the former state supervisor, was charged with not taking "proper action" to halt further alleged embezzlement after he was notified in October 1926 of Linden's and Campbell's withdrawal of funds. W.D. Comer was charged with fraudulent transactions that "really caused strangulation" of Puget Sound Savings & Loan. Former secretary Carl G. Nelson was acquitted. On March 11, 1932, Adolph F. Linden and Edmund W. Campbell were sentenced to 5 to 15 years in the Walla Walla penitentiary. The convictions were upheld in December of that same year.

Shortly thereafter, Campbell looked down from the second story of his large Capitol Hill home, thought about what it would be like to spend years in a cold prison cell, and closed his eyes—he jumped in a desperate suicide attempt. There was no dignity left; he fell into a bush beside the house and only broke a leg.

On March 28, 1933, the gates of the old administration building at the Walla Walla penitentiary creaked open to admit a man over six feet tall with something of a paunch and small oval spectacles. He was taken away to be shaved, have his hair trimmed close to the scalp, and for photos—front and profile. Instructed to strip, he was sprayed down with insecticide, issued prison fatigues, and led away by a guard to a special cell where he'd spend the next two weeks to ensure that he didn't have any communicable disease. The guard then went back to his station, reporting the securing of prisoner #14851—Adolph Frederik Linden.

In the last days of W.D. Comer's presidency at Puget Sound Savings & Loan, the Camlin Hotel was sold to the Vance Lumber Company. It already owned the $600,000 Vance Hotel, opened at 7th Avenue and Stewart Street in 1927, and had been interested in the Camlin ever since Linden's banking troubles became known to the public. The lumber enterprise started operating the Camlin in 1931. At the time, about 25 percent of the guestrooms were occupied by persons who considered the Camlin their home. However, Vance wanted to eventually convert the Camlin from a residential property into one that exclusively catered to travelers. In 1942 Vance proposed converting the Camlin's penthouse—which never had been as profitable as originally hoped—into a cocktail lounge and restaurant, defying the advice of at least one financial consultant, who cautioned, "frankly, I cannot see how any cocktail bar could absorb the amount of rental necessary to make this an attractive option to you."

Museum Quality

When Washington's Maryhill Museum of Art opened to the public in 1940, *Time* magazine dubbed it "the loneliest museum in the world." More than six decades later that description still fits. Perched on a remote, wind-scoured bluff overlooking the broad Columbia River Gorge, surrounded by gardens and lawns where peacocks fan their tails toward the sun, Maryhill looks like a princely palace that some blundering builder put up in the wrong place.

Who in the Sam Hill was responsible for erecting this edifice and then filling it with everything from Rodin sculptures to European royal regalia?

Why, none other than Sam Hill himself.

An eccentric Seattle millionaire, Harvard-educated lawyer, road builder, and confidant to some of the most powerful figures of his day, Hill in 1907 purchased 7,000 acres of scrubland on the north side of the Columbia, about 100 miles east of Portland, Oregon, and just south from the Washington hamlet of Goldendale. "We have found the Garden of Eden," proclaimed the mustachioed Hill, insisting that this apparently desolate property actually lay at an agriculturally ideal juncture between rainy western Washington and the state's sunnier eastern half. Here he began developing a farming community for enterprising Quakers like himself, as well as building an imposing chateau. Aware that his father-in-law, Great Northern Railway tycoon James J. Hill, planned to lay tracks along the Columbia's north shore, connecting Portland with Spokane, Sam Hill believed that this otherwise isolated settlement would have all the commercial connections it needed to survive. And thrive.

He hadn't reckoned, though, on Quakers spurning his invitation

Thus, the first of the Camlin's major renovations came two decades after the building's awkward birth. The *Pacific Coast Record* reported that 50 new guestrooms were added, and most were given accoutrements that made them seem more like residential living spaces than simply sleeping quarters. "During the day these rooms are comfortable, luxurious rooms, with ample facilities for lounging, entertaining, or reading," explained George Vance, managing director of Vance Lumber. "Whisk off the covers of the day-beds, and you have comfortable, spring-filled twin beds, inviting a good night's rest."

to live in the town he'd already named Maryhill after his wife and schizophrenic daughter. Two groups of Quakers came to look over the site—and both groups walked away unimpressed. All that's left of the planned community are a couple of foundations and an inoperative concrete fountain that stands where the main public square was to have been located.

More enduring has been the three-story concrete mansion that Hill raised nearby on the high bluff overlooking the Columbia. Designed by the Washington, D.C., architectural firm Hornblower & Marshall and begun in 1914, it bears a striking resemblance to Marie Antoinette's beloved Petit Trianon at Versailles. It also looks much like another Hornblower & Marshall edifice that Hill had built as his primary residence on Seattle's ritzy East Highland Drive in 1909. However, this riverside "ranch house,"

as Hill always called it, wasn't conceived as a second home, but as a showplace. Ever since 1903, when his wife (unable to adapt to Pacific Northwest rhythms and climate) rejoined her parents in St. Paul, Minnesota, Hill had spent more and more time socializing. The Maryhill manse would be the perfect place to entertain, seating as many as 250 people at formal dinners.

But the failure of his Quaker colony cooled Hill's passion for the Maryhill project. He became involved instead in campaigns promoting a Columbia roadway (today's historic Columbia River Highway) and extending the state road systems in Oregon and Washington. An inveterate pacifist, Hill also threw himself (and his money) into helping heal Europe's bloody World War I wounds. He constructed what may have been the first monument honoring the war's dead—a full-scale concrete replica of

In 1947, The Cloud Room was opened with chef Victor Bruzzi, formerly at Seattle's Roosevelt Hotel and the St. Francis in San Francisco, presiding over the restaurant kitchen. In 1960, to take advantage of the Seattle world fair's opening in two years, Vance authorized $1 million worth of improvements. The Cloud Room was redecorated. Also, 32 cabana units were tacked onto the hotel's west side to increase the number of available rooms, and, in a peculiar way, to attract those Americans fond of staying in conventional roadside motels. The Camlin also added a ground-floor swimming pool and sundeck. If the hotel had seemed like an anachronism

England's neolithic Stonehenge at the original Maryhill townsite, three miles east of the mansion.

A trio of remarkable women, however, revived Hill's interest in Maryhill. The first was choreographer and dancer Loie Fuller, an American star of the famous French *Folies-Bergère*. She usually is credited for coming up with the idea of turning Hill's Columbia castle into a world-class art museum. She certainly was instrumental in convincing Hill to purchase some of the working sculpting models from which her friend, Auguste Rodin, created *The Thinker* and other memorable sculptures. More than 50 Rodins are now part of the permanent Maryhill Museum collection. The second and better-known influence on Hill was Queen Marie of Romania. Grateful to Hill for aiding her country during and after World War I, Marie agreed in 1926 to contribute many of her own possessions to Hill's museum, including a throne, a replica of her crown, and a gold gown that she'd worn to the coronation of her cousin, the ill-fated Czar Nicholas II.

Sadly, Hill, Fuller, and the Queen all had passed away by the time that the Maryhill Museum finally opened on May 13, 1940—which would have been Sam Hill's 83rd birthday—under the watchful eye of a third Hill friend, Alma de Bretteville Spreckels. Wife of a California sugar magnate and the founder of San Francisco's Palace of the Legion of Honor art museum, Spreckels had assumed responsibility for Maryhill after Hill's passing in 1931.

Maryhill might not have turned out the way old Sam Hill expected. His 7,000 acres, while still intact, are now leased to ranchers and farmers of all religious persuasions, not just Quakers. He never held a single party in his "ranch house." Yet that building has become exactly what Hill hoped it would be—a showplace. More than 80,000 visitors come to the museum every year, whether to view the Rodins, marvel at Maryhill's elaborate Russian Orthodox icons, or study an extensive array of Native American artifacts.

before, the addition of the cabanas and pool certainly heightened that impression. It was if the Camlin's owners thought their property was out in the suburbs, not smack in the middle of a burgeoning metropolis famous for its inclement weather. How many people would, after all, be thrilled to swim or sunbathe while workers in tall adjoining structures gawked down from office windows?

Between 1960 and another $2 million restoration in 1985, the Camlin served as home to the Italian Consulate, among other things. But the high point of its story during this period seems to have been the floating of a 40-foot yacht in the Camlin pool as a promotional gimmick. Rooms on the boat were rented, and "carpets were displayed" on it around the start of 1964, recalls Gary Wilson, who managed the hotel between 1960 and 1965. The boat attracted a great deal of media hoopla, but could've drawn even more when its bilge pump went on the fritz and the yacht started taking in chlorinated water. "I thought it was the greatest promo stunt we could've had," says Wilson, with a chuckle. "Imagine the headlines: BOAT SINKS IN DOWNTOWN SEATTLE."

The yacht was saved just in time, but Campbell, Linden, and the Puget Sound Savings & Loan fared less well. After closing in 1931, the bank was reorganized and reopened in a new location. Meanwhile, the imposing bank headquarters that Linden had built at 1414 4th Avenue in 1927 was occupied seven years later by Joshua Green's Peoples Bank and Trust Company. It was demolished in the 1970s to make way for Peoples Bank's new downtown headquarters tower, which has since been converted into a hotel. All that remains of Rez's original fine stained-glass creations is a single arched window mounted in a stairwell on the tower's bottom floor, accessible from hotel entrances on either 4th or 5th avenues.

Edmund Campbell was paroled from the Walla Walla penitentiary in April 1937, at the age of 67. He took employment as a credit manager, and became very active with the Rotary Club, his transgressions apparently forgiven, if not forgotten. When his wife, May, passed away in the late 1940s, he lost a good part of his spirit. He went to live with his daughter's family. His grandson remembers him as being "very well liked. We had a good relationship, too. He enjoyed sports, and used to take me to ballgames." No mention ever was made in the Campbell household about his prison time. It wasn't until the late 1970s, long after Edmund had died from leukemia in September 1954, that the grandson and his sister took their mother, the former Esther Campbell, up to The Cloud Room for dinner. At about that same time, the grandson learned why it was that his grandfather always walked with a limp.

As for Adolph Linden, he was turned down three times for parole. During his prison stint, however, he managed to find a fairly cushy job recording parole pleas for fellow inmates. He heard from wife Esther once a week by letter. One of those missives in 1934 carried the news that his father, the minister, died five days short of his 50th wedding anniversary. Adolph finally was released on March 19, 1938, and, in characteristic fashion, his first thought was to "make a start in a business undertaking … At this time, my most important need is some capital with which to get going," he told the *P-I*. By the 1940s, he was in the phonograph record-pressing game. "You've got to give him credit for trying so hard after he lost so much," says Adolph's daughter-in-law, Elizabeth Linden. "He really did want to succeed."

Like Campbell, Adolph Linden suffered emotionally after his wife—the woman who had stood by his side through so much—perished from a stroke in 1960, yet he would recover his wit and charm. He spent his final years pursuing his love of literature, music, art, and theater. He'd sit for hours with his son, James, talking about the past, and enjoyed entertaining his grandchildren, to whom he sneaked ice cream on weekends. On Christmas Eve 1969, Adolph Linden—once a bank president, once a radio entrepreneur, once a hotel owner—died in an apartment for the elderly partly subsidized by city funds. He was 80 years old. He's buried with his wife and her parents in Capitol Hill's Lake View Cemetery.

Linden's mansion at the corner of what's now Bothell Way NE and NE Ballinger Way in Lake Forest Park—the property that symbolized the apogee of that banker's prosperity—went on to serve for a time as a Dutch consulate's residence. But its glory later faded. By the mid 1980s, the house, once pristine white, was dirty and peeling. Its shutters and French doors were askew, and the surrounding wood-and-iron fence was rusted and broken. One of the eight pillars bordering the home's front porch had toppled, and the wading pool was clogged with fetid muck. Its sweeping driveway was almost invisible beneath a blanket of moss and grass. The house had been on the market for years, but nobody seemed willing to save it. Not until the economic boom of the 1990s was the property finally purchased and expensively restored, to become the focal point of a small, upper-end housing development.

If one stands and gazes at the mansion long enough, erasing today's close-neighboring houses and traffic noise, one can still imagine what it must have been like that day in the 1920s, when Adolph Linden wheeled up the driveway in a Lincoln LeBaron to tell his wife that he was going to build a hotel called the Camlin, and how it was going to put him at the forefront of Seattle's phenomenal growth.

BIG BERTHA

W HEN THEY REMARK AT ALL upon the political career of Bertha Knight
Landes, modern historians generally draw attention to her call for
strengthened law enforcement in Prohibition-era Seattle, her efforts
to improve city planning and management of the municipal power company, and her demand that professional standards replace cronyism in
hiring civic administrators. Annalists observe how "peaceful" and "quiet"
Landes' two-year mayoral stint was when compared to those of her more
colorful but often less ethical predecessors. And they go on at some length
about her conviction that a city should be run under the same standard
of efficiency, decency, and morality as in a home.

But Landes wasn't yet recognized for most of these things in the early
1920s. Back then, she was known more widely as the woman who'd tweaked
Seattle's patriarchal establishment in a bloodless and brief coup that won
her not only the mayor's powers, but those of the police chief as well.

The story is rather comical. It seems that in the summer of 1924,
Landes was serving a first term on the city council and recently had been
elected to its presidency. Edwin J. "Doc" Brown, a flamboyant former "pain-
less" dentist and Seattle's latest "tolerance mayor," had decided to attend
the Democratic National Convention in New York City. During his absence, council president Landes automatically became acting chief executive. (The deputy mayor's office didn't yet exist.) Newspapers played up
Landes' precedent-setting temporary assignment, but nobody really

expected her to do much while Brown was whooping it up at Madison Square Garden.

On June 23, 1924, however, Landes summoned Police Chief William B. Severyns into her office. She handed him a letter explaining how disturbed she was by repeated violations of local bootlegging and gambling laws, and by the youthful chief's recent intimation to the press that probably a hundred men on his force were too corrupt to perform their jobs properly. If that's true, her letter read, "then it must follow as a logical conclusion that one hundred men should be removed." Landes wanted Severyns to act within 24 hours. When he balked, complaining that Landes was merely trying to score political points at his expense, the acting mayor dismissed him in favor of Joseph Mason, his top lieutenant. Mason also refused to carry out her order, so Landes canned him as well. Then, exercising an obscure provision of the city charter, she declared Seattle was in a state of emergency and appointed herself as its new top cop.

A palsy of shock passed briefly over the town as people realized that, for the first time in Seattle's history, the positions of mayor, police chief, and city council president all belonged to the same person—*and she was a woman!* But Landes didn't break pace. She dispatched bluecoats to close the town's most reprehensible speakeasies and gambling joints. Other violators shut down voluntarily to avoid Her Honor's righteous wrath. A special detail was assigned to investigate beat officers and boot out any who'd benefited from graft or bribes.

Threatened vice-operators and Brown's incensed supporters blizzarded the mayor in Manhattan with telegrams, begging him to immediately begin his three-day train journey home. Meanwhile, Doc's staff supposedly plotted an early end to Landes' reformist reign. With Brown still a day out from Puget Sound, his secretary had a pair of the mayor's suitcases dropped off at one of his favorite breakfast haunts, and then instructed Brown's chauffeur to retrieve them before picking Landes up for work. Bertha naturally inquired about the luggage, but the equally duped driver could only say, "It appears that the mayor is back in town." This impression was reinforced by what Landes found in Brown's office—another suitcase lying open with a pair of the mayor's shoes inside, some current-edition New York newspapers, and a lighted cigar reclining beside Brown's prized autographed photo of the perennial presidential candidate, William Jennings Bryan. Convinced that Doc Brown had indeed returned, Landes cooled her plans to shake up more city agencies.

When he did arrive home, Brown quickly set about undoing Landes' accomplishments, but not before the national press applauded her audacious 10-day rule. "Men in the past have been wont to talk patronizingly of 'women's instinct' as opposed to 'man's reason,'" editorialized the *Los Angeles Times*. "Seattle seems to prove that an instinct for getting things done is far more useful in the world than an intellect that only talks about them."

Not all of the local media were pleased, however. As the *Seattle Argus* groused, Landes "proved conclusively that woman's sphere is in the home or at any rate that hers is not at the head of the city government."

Two years more, and the *Argus* would be eating these words.

As the first female mayor of a large American city, Bertha Landes helped pave the way for women in politics. Yet she was hardly a classic feminist. "In fact," explained one of her longtime friends, "she was decidedly opposed to the Woman Suffrage movement when it was launched, believing that a woman's place was in her home, with her children."

Landes' own upbringing had been quite traditional. She was born Bertha Ethel Knight at Ware, Massachusetts, on October 19, 1868. Her family's pious American roots wound all the way back to the 17th-century Massachusetts Bay Colony. The youngest among nine children, she watched at least two of her siblings find their way into circles of fame. Her brother Austin entered the Navy and eventually became commander in chief of the U.S. Asiatic Fleet. Sister Jessie married David Starr Jordan, an ichthyologist and president of Indiana University, who later headed Stanford University. As a 19th-century woman, it seemed unlikely that Bertha would attain recognition except through marriage. Still, she was too filled with intelligence and dynamism to wait quietly by until her perennial smile, alert dark eyes, and olive skin swooned some ambitious gent.

In 1888 Bertha moved in with the Jordans in Bloomington, Indiana, enrolling at her brother-in-law's university. After only three years, she'd earned a degree in history. She also had developed an abiding interest in politics. Progressivism was on the rise—a movement largely among middle-class, educated, urban Americans who believed in trust busting, public welfare reforms, and a graduated income tax, all intended to restrain the corrupting power of the nation's wealthy minority. President Theodore Roosevelt was Progressivism's poster child and he incorporated the movement's liberal precepts (at least temporarily) into the Republican agenda. David Starr Jordan was a great fan of Roosevelt's and helped inculcate Bertha with progressive ideals. As a result, she thereafter labeled herself a Republican, though, even before her mayoral election, the GOP already was turning more conservative and away from egalitarian activism.

Another thing that her college experience provided was an introduction to geology student Henry Landes. Despite the conventional wisdom of the era, which labeled highly educated women as "unfit" for matrimony, he appreciated her strength and individuality. The pair wedded in January 1894 and the next year moved to Seattle, a town that by then already had survived fire and fiscal disaster but seemed stubbornly on its way to success. Henry joined the faculty at the University of Washington, recently moved from downtown to a single building (Denny Hall) on the north shore of Union Bay. Bertha slipped comfortably into motherhood. She bore three children, the two oldest of whom died early, and then adopted a 9-year-old girl. The family built a two-story University District home at the corner of Northeast 45th Street and Brooklyn Avenue (a site now occupied by a hotel), where they fended away cows that periodically loped up from Green Lake farmlands. Here, they also engaged impoverished students in debate, over copious helpings of Bertha's Boston baked beans. (She later joked that her beans won a good thousand votes from appreciative UW alumni in the city.)

Careerwise, Henry rode a fast track, being named dean of the new College of Science and very nearly UW's president. Bertha had family duties to think about, but as the children grew, she indulged in other interests. "She had to keep busy," her adopted daughter, Viola, told an interviewer in 1965. "She wasn't aggressive, but if she wasn't engaged in planning something or other, she was bored to tears." The future mayor volunteered for work at the University Congregational Church and the Red Cross, and seemed ubiquitous in women's clubs.

Today, clubwork seems a quaint avocation. For middle-class women of Bertha Landes' time, however, it offered unique chances to discuss community and world issues, as well as a friendly forum in which to amass the self-confidence necessary to secure more influential roles in a male-dominated society. It was through her leadership of several clubs that Landes first attracted the favorable notice of local businessmen and government archons. In 1921, after she'd organized a major three-day exhibit of the latest home-related products, Mayor Hugh Caldwell gave her his personal stamp of approval by tapping her as the only woman member of an ad hoc commission charged with suggesting remedies for the city's intractable unemployment problems.

More important than what the commission accomplished (actually, very little) was the fact that it broadened Bertha Landes' name familiarity. By 1922, women's organizations—and even a few men who'd come to respect her management abilities—urged her to try for a city council seat, along with boardinghouse operator Kathryn Miracle.

The odds weighed heavily against Bertha. Washington's women had earned the right to vote in 1910 (a full decade before nationwide enfranchisement), but many of them continued to eschew the polls. Although a female schoolteacher had been elected to the Kirkland City Council in 1911, Seattle's Republican plutocracy believed that women in public office would be unacceptably bad for business. Candidate Landes had to present herself in such a way as to not threaten men (who might be offended by a woman's political ambition and anti-vice zealotry) or offend more traditional women (who believed their place was in the home, not on the stump). Yet she also had to prove she was decisive and knowledgeable enough to address the moral and welfare concerns of Seattle's distaff element (40 percent of the population). These contradictions caused many of her speeches to sound like she was apologizing for running. Thanks to the passionate campaign assistance of clubwomen, when the votes were tallied in May 1922, Bertha Landes had won a landslide victory and also pulled Kathryn Miracle onto the council by her coattails.

At just over five feet tall, Bertha Landes wasn't physically intimidating. Nor was she a fiery orator. Police Chief Severyns once joked, "compared with Mrs. Landes, 'Silent' Cal Coolidge is a circus spieler." However, she possessed what the *New York World* described as "calm tenacity." Marshalling this alongside her probity and felicitous demeanor, the new councilwoman unexpectedly was able to get things done. During four years on the council, she could take principal credit for establishing a city planning commission, supporting public utilities, and stiffening regulation of allegedly salacious dance halls.

If anything had blocked more systemic change, Landes believed, it was Mayor Brown. He preferred a laissez-faire approach to governance, especially when it came to taming prostitution, drinking, and Seattle's other vivid vices. While Landes realized "a seaport cannot be run like a Sunday school," as one pro-labor newspaper phrased it, she and Brown often butted heads over matters of "civic decency." On most occasions he prevailed; but she notched up her triumphs, including her legendary 1924 reform spree as acting mayor.

Landes finally pulled out her heavy guns against Doc Brown when she proposed eliminating the mayor's office altogether. As some other metropolises already had done, she pushed to substitute a professional city manager in Seattle, someone beholden to the council who would run the town like a big business. It was a bold proposition—too bold for many voters. But Bertha refused to abandon it, even if it meant she'd have to run for mayor herself in 1926 and defeat Brown in order to blunt his opposition to the plan.

"I filed for Mayor much against my own personal inclinations," Landes would repeatedly insist. When she did so, however, it was with some careful calculation. By her figuring, she could win Doc Brown's seat and at the same time convince voters to sign off on the city manager plan. Although this meant she'd never actually assume the mayor's mantle, as president of the city council she'd still have gained the power necessary to overhaul municipal government. Furthermore, Landes told members of the news media (most of whom eventually endorsed her candidacy) that if the city manager proposal lost, but she unseated Brown, she'd run the mayor's office "as nearly like a city manager as the laws will permit."

It was a hard-fought campaign. Doc's backers spread rumors that, as mayor, "bluenose Bertha" would curtail Seattleites' personal liberties. Bertha struck back with allegations that under Brown, "general police and criminal conditions here are intolerable." This seemed to be confirmed by the well-publicized example of local rumrunner Roy Olmstead, whose trial for violating the Prohibition Act was concurrent with the Landes-Brown race. Bertha didn't have to run as a "women's" candidate, the way she had for city council. Instead, she cast herself as an anti-politician, someone free from the ties of finance and favor that held Mayor Brown in check.

The city manager idea earned a resounding "no" from voters. But 57-year-old Landes triumphed, if by fewer than 6,000 votes. One of her first official acts was to fire William Severyns—the police chief Brown had reinstated after Bertha's 10-day coup.

"Big Bertha," as Seattle's criminal contingent came to call her with equal measures of derision and respect, began her days at 9 A.M., when a chauffeur

Mayor Bertha Knight Landes, circa 1927. *Webster & Stevens MOHAI 83.10.990*

picked her up at the Wilsonian Apartments on University Avenue where she and Henry Landes had moved to enjoy their maturity. Her busy day-time schedule usually continued on into a nighttime of speechmaking. She proved to be a chief exec with an uncommonly strong social conscience and popular ideals. "Play the game fairly," she once declared. "Meet life honestly—never whine and play the coward, but take life as it comes… Don't be a shirker but do be a worker. Above all, so conduct yourself that you can look your own soul in the face. You cannot be true to yourself without being true to everyone else."

Almost from the hour of her inauguration, there was speculation that she might be the woman who was "man" enough to become governor of Washington or even take control of the White House. Male observers periodically remarked how her mind worked more like a man's than a woman's. "Was this a complement, or was it not?" Landes once mused. "I never did decide one way or the other."

Bertha pursued her goals with a diligence and effectiveness often referred to as "civic housekeeping." She worked to reduce Lake Washington pollution and put up a new public hospital. She made wide-ranging improvements at City Light, expanded the park system, installed qualified professionals at the helm of Seattle's public works departments, and saved the street railway system from immediate financial collapse. She was way ahead of the curve in advocating a merger of the Seattle and King County governments. She settled petty disputes between local law-enforcement agencies in order to win their unified support in curbing bootlegging and reducing traffic accidents. (By 1930, Seattle had one car for every four residents and more than its share of roadway mishaps.) Aside from ruck-uses she caused by trying to lower the wages of older city workers, and enlisting "stool pigeons" to augment police protection, her administration was remarkably without scandal.

As the newspaper columnist Emmett Watson put it in *Once Upon a Time in Seattle*, Landes "had no agenda beyond being the best mayor Se-attle ever had."

Yet only two years after she entered city hall, Seattle voters booted her out in favor of Frank Edwards, a poseur Progressive and the shady proprietor of several second-rate movie houses. "Old boy" politics was partly to blame. Edwards had twice as much money as Bertha in his cam-paign war chest, much of it collected from business operations fearing Bertha's civic-minded intrusions into their affairs. Rather than debate Landes in public, Edwards ran a steadily negative media campaign, during which he convinced Seattleites—against all the facts—that their city had suffered under Landes. Edwards even used Bertha's storied legislative acu-men and snowdrift of newspaper endorsements against her, painting her as too mired in "the system" to recognize its failures. And, he wasn't above shaming Seattle for obeisance to "petticoat politics."

"Elect Frank Edwards," read his pointedly sexist campaign slogan, "the Man You'll Be Proud to Call Mayor." After Landes lost, the Portland *Or-egonian* ridiculed Seattle for wanting to be a "he-man's town," and sug-gested that, at Edwards' inauguration, a pair of masculine breeches might fittingly be flown from the city hall flagpole.

But Bertha had to bear some credit for the defeat. She'd offended civil service employees by encouraging departments to lay off workers based on their efficiency, rather than just seniority. She also failed in six years of elected service to reach out sufficiently to the working class—the impres-sion of being a well-to-do bluenose still remained. As Sandra Haarsager states in *Bertha Knight Landes of Seattle: Big City Mayor*, Her Honor also may have erred by currying favor with businessmen rather than continu-ing to capitalize on her identity as "the woman's candidate." At age 59, her career as an elected official was over. Landes relocated to the college town of Ann Arbor, Michigan, where she passed away in 1943—a dozen years after voters recalled Frank Edwards from office for refusing to enforce anti-vice laws.

Ironically, Bertha's success as a clean town manager may ultimately have doomed her as a lawmaker. For a city accustomed to at least half-venal mayors—men such as Hiram Gill and Doc Brown—she may simply have charted too even and sane a course. As *The Nation* noted after her 1928 defeat, "in American cities today good-housekeeping is not good politics, shameful as it is to admit it."

B. Marcus Priteca at his Coliseum Theater office, 1916. *MOHAI SHS19,111*

ENCORE PERFORMANCES

W HEN THE SEATTLE THEATER OPENED at 9th Avenue and Pine Street on
the evening of March 1, 1928, there was no gaudy inaugural gala, no
parade of famous faces through its glass doors. Although huge spot-
lights lanced skyward from the street corner and multicolor banners
whipped along the building's flanks, the premiere wasn't preceded by the
kind of anticipation-building hyperbole so often associated with theater
launchings in that era. "So far as the management was concerned," scoffed
a *Seattle Times* reporter, "the occasion was little more than throwing open
the entrances of their playhouse to the public, the same as they will be
opened for the ordinary course of business in the future."

Nonetheless, thousands of city residents queued up around the block
that night, eager to find a seat to watch John Barbour conduct the Seattle
Grand Orchestra, listen to soprano soloist Virginia Johnson, and laugh at
a brief film, *Feel My Pulse*, featuring "sprightly" Bebe Daniels as a woman
falling into the comic company of Prohibition rumrunners. They also came
to eyeball an extravaganza that wasn't on the playbill—the theater itself,
filled with marbled foyers and broad staircases, silk brocade hangings, and
a sparkling redundancy of crystal chandeliers. As the *Times* breathlessly
described it, the theater rivaled "the massive magnificence of the fabulous
'pleasure dome' of Kubla Khan and [was] for certain the equal of any the-
atrical pleasure dome of modern times."

Almost seven decades later, that show palace—now the Paramount
Theater—enjoyed a well-deserved renaissance of popularity, thanks to an

expensive and thoughtful mid-1990s refurbishment. Destined for some new if posthumous plaudits, too, is the local architect usually credited with the Paramount's grandiosity, B. Marcus Priteca, who pioneered the look of movie houses.

Classically-trained in Europe, but a spirited innovator in American terra-cotta and Art Deco styles, Priteca served as the chief architectural planner for early 20th-century vaudeville impresario Alexander Pantages. Perhaps 150 major North American theaters were conceived on Priteca's drawing board and he consulted on, or remodeled, hundreds more. Around Puget Sound, Priteca saw his vision realized not only in Seattle's Paramount block (which includes an adjoining commercial/residential tower), but also in the Coliseum Theater (redone in 1994 as a Banana Republic outlet), the Central District's Bikur Cholim Synagogue (now the Langston Hughes Cultural Center), West Seattle's playful Admiral Theater, the late Longacres horse-racing track in Renton, and Tacoma's behemoth Pantages Theater (now the Broadway Center for the Performing Arts).

Priteca once told a Seattle columnist, "I don't think I'm a good architect. I've never been satisfied with any job I've done. In fact, I would like to start all over again." His only real claims to fame, he said, were that he was the only "Priteca" in the nation, that he smoked "more cigars than any person in the United States" (exceeding 20 per day), and he was one of the few Jews in North America entitled to wear a Scottish kilt.

But he was just being his modest self. The fact is that, along with Elmer H. Fisher, John Graham Sr., Carl F. Gould, and Henry Bittman, Priteca ranks as one of the design giants of the Emerald City's first 100 years. And his impact was equally acknowledged nationwide. As a former president of the American Institute of Architects remarked, following Priteca's death at age 81 in October 1971, "his greatest influence was on his fellow architects to practice on a high professional plane. To those who knew him longest, he was Mr. Architect of Seattle."

"Benny" Priteca took his first breath on December 23, 1889, the same year that downtown Seattle (today's Pioneer Square) burned to its foundations, leaving Elmer Fisher and other architectural contemporaries with a blank slate to work their skyline magic. Many years would pass, however, before Priteca learned of that disaster. He grew up in Glasgow, Scotland, blessed to parents of east European Jewish stock. His baptism in architecture came at age 15, when he was apprenticed for five years to Robert McFarlane Cameron, a director at the Royal College of Arts in Edinburgh. In 1909 Priteca received the equivalent of a bachelor's degree from that college, along with a traveling scholarship that would help him find professional work anywhere in the world. But where, he wondered, should he go?

It was then that he "got into an office discussion about a city in the United States called 'Seetle,' where they were about to stage an Alaska-Yukon-Pacific Exposition," Priteca told the *Times* several decades later. "My boss architect [Cameron]…insisted that 'Seetle' was on the Yukon River. I knew this was wrong, but was unable to find Seattle on any international map." A foray to one of Edinburgh's steamship company offices supplied him with a better map, in addition to some appealing photos of adolescent Seattle. He decided to visit the Emerald City during a tour taking him to post-earthquake San Francisco, after which, he supposed, he'd end up at some architectural firm in Vancouver, B.C.

Priteca remembered his introduction to Seattle as inauspicious, at best. He was "promptly arrested by a bucket-helmeted Seattle policeman for smoking a cigaret [sic] on a public street"—at that time, a statewide offense. But he was enthralled by the prodigious elegance of the Alaska-Yukon-Pacific Exposition, a sort of coming-out party for the city that recently had benefited as a jumping-off point to the Klondike and Alaska gold fields. Priteca decided that a place with such pretensions could nourish his own aspirations to greatness. He quickly secured drafting positions here, one of which was in the office of architect Edwin W. Houghton, an Englishman responsible for several local playhouses (among them the surviving Moore Theater at 2nd Avenue and Virginia Street) and who may have bestirred Priteca's interest in that architectural genre. Priteca's chance meeting with showman Pantages in 1911, though, is what put him on the road to independent fame.

Alexander (born Pericles) Pantages was an illiterate but opportunistic Greek, who had labored aboard steamships and worked on the first Panama Canal in the 1880s, before landing at Seattle in 1898. He was bound for the Yukon gold fields, so he didn't stay long. But, according to historical writer Ellis Lucia, he snapped up a copy of the *Seattle Post-Intelligencer* before hopping on a northbound vessel. This he had under his arm when he landed at Skagway, flat broke after a bad run of cards. To his surprise, news-starved prospectors there offered to buy the out-of-date paper at tremendously inflated prices. Pantages decided, instead, to schedule a public reading of the *P-I* and charge listeners one dollar a head. Three hundred

Wronged Writer

Few people today have ever heard of Bertrand Collins, frequently cited as this city's first native-born novelist. Yet in his publishing heyday, the late 1920s and early 1930s, his name spilled easily, if not always fondly, from the lips of Seattleites. Many residents back then greatly enjoyed Collins' thinly veiled portraits of their social-climbing neighbors in *Rome Express*, his first and best book. But just as many loathed him, too—some even threatened to horsewhip the silver-spoon-licking son of a former mayor who dared describe aborning Seattle in unflattering terms, as a town "of straggling wooden wharves, dirt streets, wooden sidewalks, droning sawmills and slag fires."

Collins grew indignant over such rebuffs. He knew his birthplace better than most of his detractors. His father was John Collins, an Irish émigré who had prospered from whiskey trading back east and logging on Puget Sound, before settling down at Elliott Bay in the mid 1860s. Collins *père* was quick to recognize Seattle's potential. He bought a one-third interest in the Occidental Hotel, a 30-room establishment at the corner of what's now 1st Avenue and Yesler Way, and eventually expanded it in ostentatious style. When the Great Fire of 1889 reduced this "leading hotel in the Northwest" to ashes, the undaunted Collins simply built a third incarnation, which he later renamed the Seattle Hotel (it stood until the 1960s, when replaced by a triangular parking garage). In addition to being a successful hotelier, the elder Collins was elected to Seattle's first city council, served as mayor for a one-year term (1873–74), and later was elected to the state senate in Olympia. With his second wife, he reared four children, the third of whom was Edward Bertrand Collins, born in 1890.

Son "Bertie," as all his friends knew him, grew up on then-fashionable First Hill and was a childhood playmate of Dorothy Stimson Bullitt, who one day would build up King Broadcasting Company. He went on to

and fifty sourdoughs showed up. The host forsook his mining ambitions on the spot. As Pantages remarked to an interviewer much later, "I found out there was more money to be made in giving the miners what they wanted than by competing with them in the gold diggings."

boarding schools in Massachusetts and graduated from Harvard University in 1914. During World War I, Collins enlisted in the U.S. Navy, and was attached to the London office of the American naval operations command in Europe.

Only after the war did Collins turn seriously to writing. His 1928 novel, *Rome Express*, recounted a romance between a girl from "Chinook, Washington" (read Seattle) and an Italian diplomat. The book's independent young heroine, "Greta Pendrick," with her "fine-cut olive profile, absinthe-green eyes, [and] straight blue-black hair," was based on local real-estate heiress Guendolen Carkeek, who had in fact married an Italian counsel. Carkeek had moved to Rome, traveled to Estonia right after World War I, and then returned to Rome when her husband became ill; he later died while she was away in Paris. (Unlike the novel's Pendrick, though, who went on to wed a titled Swede, Carkeek later married an exiled Russian aristocrat, Theodore Plestcheeff.) Although the

story doesn't rival Henry James' work for European sophistication, it received enough plaudits that Collins was able to sell two more novels—*The Silver Swan* (1930) and *Moon in the West* (1933).

Unfortunately for Collins, many Seattleites never shook off the sour taste left by his literary premiere. Bertie finally was forced to ignore the opinions coming from his "self-conscious" hometown, and in 1934 announced bitterly, "in my next novel, as yet unfinished, I am leaving Seattle out of it." If Collins attempted to fulfill this revenge, however, it went unnoticed—his fourth book, perhaps titled *The White Knight*, appears to never have seen print.

World War II found him in the U.S. Merchant Marine, and subsequently he authored an engaging series for the *Seattle Times* about wartime life during the Pacific campaigns. When he passed away in 1964 at age 74, Bertie Collins was as well known for the Oriental art he collected in his senectitude as for the few books he'd penned in the prime of his life.

Pantages drifted to Dawson City, a rough burg where drinking, gambling, and whoring were the tamest diversions. There he hooked up with a successful redheaded singer and dancer from Spokane, one Kathleen Eloise Rockwell, better known to history as "Klondike Kate." Kate loaned Pantages money to open a pocket-edition performance hall, which allegedly grossed $8,000 a week. Then she followed him to Seattle—an arts-hungry but still unsophisticated place despite visits from the likes of Sarah Bernhardt and Lillian Russell—where he bought a 10-cent variety house, the Crystal Theater, at 2nd Avenue and Seneca Street. Kate also fell in love with the dapper Greek—a mistake, as it turned out, for in 1905 while she was on a singing tour, Pantages jilted her to wed a California violinist. The Yukon Queen "went all to pieces," Lucia wrote in the lively biography, *Klondike Kate: The Life and Legend of Kitty Rockwell, the Queen of the Yukon*, and then tried to sue her quondam paramour for $25,000, which she claimed as her rightful share of Pantages' wealth. The case dragged on for years and soured the showman's reputation with many Seattleites who had loved the vivacious Kate. When the case eventually was dismissed, Pantages still held onto the millions of dollars he needed to create America's foremost amusement empire—a dominion that in 1926, at the apogee of his power, gave him ownership of 30 cathedrals of entertainment and control of 42 others, in both the United States and Canada.

Benny Priteca's connection with the impresario began in 1911, when on the strength of a handshake he agreed to design a showpiece Pantages Theater on the northeast corner of University Street and 3rd Avenue. Like many of the buildings Priteca would develop over the years, this six-story Classical Renaissance edifice (renamed the Palomar in 1936 and torn down in 1964) combined an ornate performance hall with an office block, in which the architect maintained his own business suite for half a century.

Pantages and Priteca seemed an unlikely pair. The former could be obdurate and Machiavellian, and he led a fast-paced existence. By contrast, the abbreviated and bespectacled Priteca attracted adjectives such as "cherubic" and "gentlemanly." (One of his obituaries would sum him up as "a sweet guy.")

Yet they worked profitably together for almost two decades, until Pantages sold his chain in 1929 just before the Great Depression hit. At least 30 of Pantages' theaters came from Priteca's deft pen, erections that in their very appearance reflected the fantastical nature of what was presented inside. After the Seattle Pantages, Priteca in 1915 created a rococo showplace on San Francisco's Market Street (today's underappreciated Orpheum Theater) with a Moorish facade inspired by a 12th-century cathedral in Leon, Spain. He followed that up by designing the mammoth 1,300-seat Pantages in Vancouver, B.C., a French Renaissance masterpiece opened in 1917 (since razed). The marginally more restrained Tacoma

Pantages was completed in 1918. One of Priteca's most flamboyant creations for the entrepreneurial Greek also marked one of their last collaborations—the still-extant Hollywood Pantages (1930) in Los Angeles, a veritable Whitman's Sampler of Art Deco detail that Priteca hoped would "best exemplify America of the moment." The motion-picture industry loved the 2,812-seat theater so much that the Academy Awards were staged there during the 1950s.

Priteca's expert Art Deco renderings demonstrated his breadth of skills, and most of his work also reflected his European training in using florid classical motifs. To satisfy grand tastes within miserly budgets, he made extensive use of glazed terra-cotta—basically, enriched molded clay block or brick. It was far lighter and cheaper than stonework, and terra-cotta could be modeled easily into an infinite variety of shapes before firing. It allowed designers to embellish buildings with gargoyles, cartouches, French nymphs, and even ribbons of walrus heads. Priteca became so adept with this material that many of his molds for neoclassical ornamentation became catalogue items, and eventually were used to decorate new structures up and down the West Coast.

Probably the finest local example of Priteca's terra-cotta artistry is Seattle's Coliseum Theater at 5th Avenue and Pike Street. Italian Renaissance in flavor, this gleaming pile originally was opened in 1916 by Joe Gottstein, an ambitious 23-year-old real-estate developer who would go on to build Longacres. According to the 1931 *Journal of the Royal Institute of Architects*, the Coliseum Theater was the first of the world's movie palaces, raised at a time when "flickers" were still a rough-edged novelty. Gottstein had correctly predicted that the public would flock to films if they were shown in classy, comfortable settings. Priteca's answer to Gottstein's vision was the 2,400-seat Coliseum, with its white face, beautifully dentiled cornice, and garnishes of urns, fruit, and bullock's heads. The sympathetic 1994 restoration of the Coliseum, supervised by the Seattle architectural firm NBBJ, polished up the exterior and removed the jeering neon grin of a marquee that in the 1950s had replaced an original entrance dome. Unfortunately, Priteca's interior—originally featuring fountains on either side of an orchestra pit, a Turkish-style men's smoking room, and an auditorium ceiling in which lights blinked in the Big Dipper's shape—long ago was altered.

Looking west down Pike Street on February 2, 1916. The new Coliseum Theater stands to the right at the corner of Pike Street and 5th Avenue. *UW Libraries, UW 22326Z*

Another Priteca-touched creation—the Paramount on Pine Street—weathered the decades better than the Coliseum, despite having suffered for many years as a raucous venue for rock-n-roll concerts. Its high-rise brick-and-terra-cotta facade, monumentalized with tall arched windows and a seven-story neon sign, has remained intact. The NBBJ's John Savo, who acted as project manager during its modern refurbishment, achieved success in bringing the Paramount's French Baroque innards back to life. Thanks to a mostly private venture spearheaded by former Microsoft executive Ida Cole, the theater's stage now has greater depth and width than before and equipment storage areas have been added. State-of-the-art lights were put in, and the original 1928 Wurlitzer organ was refitted with new electronic controls. Some original draperies are hanging again, too, after not seeing the light of day since the Marx Brothers played here and when local actress Frances Farmer served as an usher.

With the reopening of the Coliseum and Paramount theaters, John Savo says there has been renewed interest in Benny Priteca's local creations, both those that are essentially intact and some that have passed into memory, such as the 1927 brick-and-terra-cotta Orpheum Theater formerly located where the Westin Hotel now stands. According to Savo, "he was exceptional, both in that he did important work here and that his fame extended well outside of this area. Though his influence on other Seattle

Priteca Primer

Much of the architect's elegant work can still be appreciated in Seattle and Tacoma—

- **Admiral Theater**
  2343 California Avenue Southwest, Seattle
- **Bikur Cholim Synagogue** (Langston Hughes Cultural Center)
  104 17th Avenue South, Seattle
- **Coliseum Theater** (Banana Republic)
  Northeast corner of 5th Avenue and Pike Street, Seattle
- **Seattle Theater** (Paramount Theater)
  901 Pine Street, Seattle
- **Tacoma Pantages Theater** (Broadway Center for the Performing Arts)
  901 Broadway Plaza, Tacoma

architects may have been minimal—they tended to prefer less symmetrical and less ornamented construction—he did undoubtedly leave this city with some distinguished landmarks."

However, Savo believes Priteca might be receiving more than his due share of credit in the case of the Paramount. Contrary to most published accounts, the 1928 plans for this structure indicate it actually was the product of a Chicago firm, Rapp & Rapp, which also did Paramounts in New York City and Portland, Oregon. Priteca designed the adjoining commercial/apartment tower, however, and may have offered his ideas about the show palace's look, but he couldn't claim the Paramount in the same way he did the Coliseum, the Orpheum, or Longacres.

Priteca would have been the first to admit this, were he still around. That he isn't only makes the architecture he left behind that much more valuable.

Two years after incorporation in 1953, Bellevue received recognition as an All-America City by the National Municipal League and *Look* magazine. Upon the award's arrival on a rainy day in December 1955, the city closed the schools early and quickly organized a parade along Main Street. *MOHAI PI-27860*

DITTY'S CITY

T HINK OF OUR GREAT CITIES. What would Washington, D.C., have been
without Pierre L'Enfant? New York without Frederick Law Olmsted? Or
Bellevue without James Ditty?

Back in 1928, despite the jeers of armchair critics in the *Seattle Times*
editorial offices, Ditty devised a plan for a sweeping metropolis located
where Bellevue now stands. He saw nothing less than a *trés* cosmopolitan
urban center, with the *coup de grâce* being a fleet of silvery dirigibles to
ferry passengers from the Eastside to what would become a satellite city
to the west, Seattle. In fact, the dirigibles are practically the only element
of Ditty's audacious Eastside scheme that hasn't come to pass. Maybe we
should take him up on that too?

There's no way to know what Bellevue would look like today had it
not been for James Ditty—photoengraver-cum-visionary-turned-real-
estate mogul. Bellevue might yet be a small town, or even a nonexistent
one—an area still dominated by the calm, grassy roll of horse pastures.
And Kirkland could've been the nexus of Eastside business instead. If it
hadn't been for Ditty, there might be no Bellevue Square and office towers leaping skyward just west of Interstate 405. Without Ditty, the Eastside
today might not be Washington's fourth-largest population center, and
Seattle would stand smugly as the undisputed commercial king of Puget
Sound cities.

Ditty was one of the biggest believers in the town's potential, wield-
ing his influence with single mindedness. He was Bellevue's Kemper

Freeman Jr. of yesteryear. He was a dreamer on an expansive scale, unbridled by the pessimism that can be the failing of a more timid man. He was a West Coast planner extraordinaire. He was like the architect Edward H. Bennett, who in 1912 proposed constructing a Paris-like civic center in Portland, Oregon—complete with a fine arts complex and a towering city hall—only to see the plan fail because narrow-minded business and real-estate interests thought it ate up too much commercial land. Or, like L. Frank Baum, author of *The Wonderful Wizard of Oz*, who started wintering in San Diego, California, in 1904, and shortly thereafter announced to the press that he would construct a pleasure park for children and their parents—a miniature Land of Oz—on an island off the California coast. (Although never built, Baum's park was certainly the harbinger of future magic kingdoms in Southern California.) It may be difficult to credit Ditty with quite the same brand of romantic vision that Bennett and Baum enjoyed, but keep one crucial thing in mind—Ditty's dreams *actually came true*.

If Ditty also was thought of by some as a bit eccentric, what with his plaid caps and his almost-genetic proclivity toward contentiousness—well, sometimes geniuses come in unlikely packages.

In the words of his nephew, Kirk Mathewson, who followed his not-quite-famous uncle into the business of managing Eastside real estate, "Jim Ditty was, in so many senses, Bellevue's very first developer."

James Sanderson Ditty's history spills forth like a jigsaw puzzle in lots of little pieces that never seem to fit easily together. He was born in 1880 in the agricultural community of Hudson, Ohio, located just northeast of Akron. It was a place where abolitionist John Brown had spent part of his youth and manhood, but is too small even today to appear in most atlases. Ditty went through school no further than the eighth grade. At age 16, he began apprenticing as an engraver at the *Cleveland Plain Dealer*, and it was in the Cleveland area that he lived until he came to visit Seattle in 1904.

According to *The Bellevue Story* (1967) by Connie Jo Squires, Ditty was a photographer with the Newspaper Enterprise Association, which distributed shots to American periodicals. He was sent west in 1904 "to be close to the news releases" about the Russo-Japanese War (1904–5), a dispute over rival territorial claims in Asia that helped push Japan forward as a world power. He stayed in the Seattle area "for a short time," writes

Squires, "and then left for San Francisco, where he remained for two years. He was married soon after this and went to live in Los Angeles." Little seems known of Ditty's first wife, other than she bore him two children in the 1920s.

It wasn't until 1910 that Ditty took up permanent residence on the east side of Lake Washington. According to Lucile McDonald's *Bellevue: Its First 100 Years*, this was two years after an artists' colony, Beaux Arts, began germinating along the shore below Meydenbauer Bay. Yet Ditty generally has been described in the few press accounts of his life as one of the colony's founding fathers.

"We bought 50 acres and cut it up into lots," Ditty recalled for the *Seattle Times* in 1958. "We had 1,100 feet of waterfront with 10 acres in the center reserved for community artistic endeavor—sort of a do-it-yourself project. I later bought the 10 acres in 1925 for $3,000, intending to fence it in as a private park, with deer and quail."

Squires notes that shortly after Ditty moved permanently to Washington, he opened a photographic studio on 7th Avenue in downtown Seattle, in a building that also housed the old *Seattle Star* newspaper (a daily that went out of business in 1947). Ditty would run the Rapid Service Engraving Company until his retirement in 1937. It apparently was a lucrative enterprise. Photoengraving—the preparation of line drawings and photography for use by newspapers and other printing companies—was a fairly arcane art until much later in the century. Ditty is supposed to have been very good at his job.

Ditty met the woman who became his second wife, Helen Whaley, when her father was building Ditty's home in Beaux Arts. She was the daughter of an Eastside carpenter and the granddaughter of Isaac Bechtel, an early Bellevue resident and the area's first postmaster. After graduating from high school in 1918, she went to work for the *Star*, and in the hallways of that building, she grew to know Jim Ditty better. He began employing her in his studio in the early 1920s, and by 1932 he had decided to divorce wife #1. Ditty married Helen Whaley in 1933—she was 31 years old, and he 51.

At the time, Bellevue was still a Podunk sort of place. For years it had barely grown accustomed to having a name and was considered by census takers to be a part of Newcastle. The name "Bellevue" dated from 1886, when a new post office was established amidst the timber and needed its own moniker. Only after 1913 could some residents set aside candles and oil lamps for the glow of electric lighting. Lake Washington Boulevard finally reached Bellevue from the south by 1920, but it took some time before this had much affect on commerce. In 1922, according to *Bellevue: Its First 100 Years*, the community was "mostly a crossroads with a drugstore." Since 1916, a small whaling fleet had been operating out of Meydenbauer Bay. These ships were based each winter at the foot of 99th Avenue, and headed out each summer to hunt in Alaskan waters. In 1924, *Polk's Gazetteer and Business Directory* listed Bellevue's population as 878—"a town on Meydenbauer Bay six and a half miles east of [Seattle's] Pioneer Square, a banking and shipping point with four churches, telephones, railway express, and 16 daily boats to Leschi Park."

But Ditty was confident that Bellevue and the Eastside eventually would emerge out of Seattle's shadow. "Ditty predicted a day would arrive when 200,000 persons would live east of Lake Washington," recalls local historian Squires, and he wanted to prosper from this growth. In 1928 he "foolishly" (to quote his friends) purchased 38 acres of pastureland and strawberry fields located west of Lake Washington Boulevard. While he waited for the boom to come, he provided King County with access through his property for a new road to Kirkland (present-day Bellevue Way), built the old Lakeside Super Market, and rented out other parcels for horse grazing at $12 a year. "I sat on the fence," Ditty recalled in 1958, "waiting for Bellevue to grow up. Everybody gave me the horse laugh."

Especially comical to many critics was a model city plan that he drew up for Bellevue. Back then, it must've seemed as fantastical as Frank Baum's Oz.

"All aboard" yells the pilot, and the door shuts on a dirigible that will carry you from an airport just outside Beaux Arts into Seattle. Up, up you go, your craft's silver skin glinting in the sunlight, its propellers roaring behind the gondola. Sometimes it's hard to hear over the propeller noise as you float with other travelers—but then the view is always more interesting up here than the eavesdropping, anyway.

Far below, the sights of Mercer Island and Bellevue are becoming more difficult to make out. There's Bellevue's grand stone city hall, looking very much like an old Vanderbilt mansion that has been carted block-by-block across the continent from Manhattan. Next door is the amphitheater, where thespians trod the boards and civic concerts are regularly performed.

To the east climb the towers of Bellevue's business district, and beyond that, another, larger airport nestles against the busy railroad yards and prosperous, smoke-belching industrial plants. Looking west instead, you can make out the hotels and beach clubs that hug the lake shore. Now, quick, before Mercer Island disappears in the distance, look south. Can you still identify the airports at the north end, the huge tourist observation tower situated midway up the island, and the three bridges that connect Mercer Island to the mainland—one crossing from Beaux Arts, another from around May Creek, and the third strung westward to Seattle's Seward Park?

Pity those poor souls who have chosen, instead, to cross to the Emerald City on one of the 10-minute ferries from Medina and Mercer Island's northwest corner. They can't enjoy this kind of perspective on the Eastside. From up in this airship, the vessels that carry passengers over the lake appear puny, like things that bob in your bathtub water every time you shift a leg.

When Ditty began spreading this vision of Eastside development in 1928, while at the same time encouraging Bellevue to incorporate as a city, there already were ferries connecting Mercer Island with Seattle. But just about everything else in the above scenario—the airports, mammoth city hall, railroad terminus, and prosperous factories—were plucked from Ditty's fecund imagination. Dirigibles were being used for passenger and cargo transport, particularly in Europe, but they were hardly common sights. (Their heyday would arrive just before the German zeppelin *Hindenburg* burned while mooring at Lakehurst, New Jersey, in May 1937, killing 36 people and scaring just about every authority on the planet away from airship travel.) As far as bridges went, there had been one from Enatai to Mercer Island since 1923, but the Lacey V. Murrow Memorial Floating Bridge wouldn't be completed to Seattle until 1940.

What need was there for all of Ditty's imagined bridges, really? Ditty might've owned an automobile since 1924, but the Great Depression that clobbered the nation after 1929 kept a tight lid on the expansion of car sales (which continued until after World War II). And the notion of observation towers in the center of Bellevue and on Mercer Island? Well, the Space Needle wouldn't open until 1962; before that, viewing towers had seemed best reserved for the nation's amusement parks.

Seattle cartoonists poked broad fun at James Ditty's model city. *Seattle Times* illustrator Sam Groff made it familiar to everyone all over Puget Sound. "You may recall the 'Ditty City' that often appeared in Groff cartoons

"The Durned Thing Really Does Float!"

Not everyone was happy about a proposed bridge crossing the deep waters between Seattle and Lake Washington's eastern side. Although Mercer Island had been connected by a short driveable span to the Eastside mainland since 1924, a much longer steel link to the big city in the opposite direction made many islanders quail, fearing rising local crime rates and the denigration of their sylvan setting. Even the normally boosterish *Seattle Times* had its reservations about the project, warning that the proposed pontoon bridge—the first of its kind in the world, 6,561 feet long—might destroy the giant lake's scenic beauty, "would limit yachting," and couldn't be guaranteed to stay above water. By the time Seattle-ites and Eastsiders gathered together on opening day, July 2, 1940, however, most people seemed optimistic that the new Lake Washington Floating Bridge would benefit both Seattle and the Eastside. *Times* editor and publisher Clarance B. Blethen conceded finally that he was wrong to have opposed construction, adding: "What sinks me is, the durned thing really does float!"

As expected, the Eastside's population and economy have since grown substantially because of the Interstate 90 span (renamed the Lacey V. Murrow Bridge in 1967, to honor the state highways director who had pushed for its construction). A second roadway over the lake, the Evergreen Point Floating Bridge, was completed in 1963. These days, however, Bellevue has outgrown its suburban bedroom community-hood—it's now the state's fourth-largest city. Blethen was wrong when predicting that the bridge would hurt boating on Lake Washington, but he was right to doubt the dependability of the original floating span—it sank in 1990 and had to be rebuilt.

as a travel label on suitcases or on direction signs," Ditty would remark years later to a *Times* interviewer, with more humor than he had once found in Groff's and others' scoffings. As historian McDonald later explained, "Ditty didn't like being made fun of—he was dead serious about his view of the future."

Kirk Mathewson recalls his uncle as being "preoccupied with thoughts or ideas—he was full of them. And he'd want to share them. He would walk up to anyone and talk with them—it was quite embarrassing when I was a boy, I guess. He might just start talking to a mother with a couple of kids he'd encountered on a street corner. He'd have something on his mind, and he just had to run it by them, see what they thought."

Just as the public had shied away from Jim Ditty's model city plans, it also was leery of some of his other ideas. Early on he had gleefully described himself to the press as "a nonconformist," and that attitude was more noticeable as the years passed. In 1919, as a member of the Bellevue School Board, for instance, he voted to shut down the six-pupil, one-room Wilburton school located about a mile east of Bellevue. "They almost rode me out of town on the rail," Ditty remembered, describing the irate audience he faced at the closure hearings. Later, he had to put up with fellow Eastside entrepreneurs and land owners, most of whom balked at his plans to organize the "hodge-podge" of Bellevue-area communities into an incorporated, and inter-cooperative, whole. Many of the same people fought him as he sought to expand the definition of "downtown Bellevue" beyond Main Street. Politicians, wary of accepting the Eastside's expansionist future and reluctant to build more roads or develop commercial centers, were some of his favorite targets. "Ditty," the *Seattle Times* explained once, "is a thorn in the side of public officials, who often are the subject of Ditty-written and Ditty-purchased newspaper ads on the East Side." In the late 1950s, Ditty even endorsed annexing Bellevue to Seattle, so upset was he with local politicians. "Bellevue apparently is incompetent to manage its own affairs," Ditty proclaimed. "[Annexation is] the solution to our problems."

It must've been with sweet satisfaction, then, that James Ditty found his optimism about Bellevue's potential proved correct after World War II, when the area quickly began expanding. The 38 acres that Ditty had acquired "foolishly" two decades before turned out to lie smack dab in the middle of the expansion zone. Property for which he'd paid 1.5 cents per square foot in 1925 was suddenly worth $3 a square foot. In the late 1940s, he had begun selling off parcels of property, 10 acres of which went to entrepreneur Kemper Freeman Sr. (at a tremendous profit to Ditty), to become part of what is today Bellevue Square.

"His one criteria," says Mathewson, "was that it should go for commercial use. He could've sold the land off for houses easily, but he wanted to develop it as a commercial area. That took time, because people were skeptical. So he'd sell a piece, take that cash, build another building with it, and then just sit on the building until it leased up. He had some that were vacant for a couple of years. But he believed he was doing the right thing for the city."

The photoengraver-turned-real-estate baron erected the Bel Lane Shopping Center, and then in 1952—just a year before Bellevue finally incorporated as a city—he built a tower in his own honor—the J.S. Ditty Building (which stood on Bellevue Way NE until it was torn down in 2000). At the time of his death on June 2, 1962, when he was 81 years old, Jim Ditty was "landlord to more than 40 Bellevue professional men and business firms," the *Times* recounted.

Kirk Mathewson, now president of Ditty Properties, an Eastside real-estate firm, was only 20 years old when his Uncle Jim died. But he heard many stories about the man, mostly from his Aunt Helen, Ditty's second wife, with whom Mathewson worked for 12 years in the real-estate business, until she passed away in August 1981.

He describes Ditty as an avid reader, interested mostly in biographies; a baseball fan, who often tuned in to radio broadcasts of games played by the old Seattle Rainiers; and an adventurer, who once built a camper from an old La Salle and drove to Mexico, bringing back black-and-white film footage of bullfights. "He was also a great practical joker," Mathewson says. "I can remember once going to dinner with him, when I was young. He'd gone to the waitress beforehand and told her that, when he ordered turtle eggs, she was to bring him strawberries with sugar on them. I couldn't believe he was going to get real turtle eggs, and it was only when his dessert was finally delivered that I knew I'd been had.

"He was always inventing something. There was always a new contraption in his garage, like something that would make it easier to carry golf clubs. He was a big golfer," continues Mathewson. (Ditty once told the *Seattle Times*, "Golf comes first—to heck with business.")

"I remember Hayden Lake, Idaho, where he and my Aunt Helen had a summer house. He would always golf barefoot and in Bermuda shorts. He had a dark tan. Always. They'd go over to Hawaii a lot in those days; once they spent 12 winters in a row over there. My uncle was a health nut, and in those days, a tan was one of the symbols of good health.

"He was *very* health conscious. He used to go on vegetarian diets. He'd exercise, lift weights. He had a couple of barbells at home and a chin-up bar in his hallway."

Thanks to all this activity, Ditty was still "disgracefully healthy" at age 78, a "126-pound, youthful-dressing grandfather," according to one newspaper account. It was only four months before his death that Ditty started to show serious signs of illness.

"I remember he'd challenge himself," Mathewson concludes. "He'd do things like, on his 70th birthday he'd play 70 holes of golf or do 70 chin-ups. It was a way of proving himself. It was only later that everybody else started worrying about their health, too. My uncle, I guess, was right all along."

That Ditty also was right about many of his Eastside visions was accepted only slowly by critics, and sometimes with difficulty. Even the *Times* admitted it in 1953—a decade late, of course—when carrying the headline, "They Don't Laugh at Founder of 'Ditty City' Any More."

"The Japanese Must Go"

By 1941, Japanese-Americans made up Seattle's largest ethnic minority. For most, this was their home, their country, so they were just as appalled as any of their Caucasian neighbors by the Japanese bombing of Pearl Harbor on December 7 of that year. Yet their ancestry immediately made them "an enemy race." The FBI quickly clamped down on 9,600 Japanese-Americans in King County (and 100,000 others living elsewhere along the West Coast), arresting community leaders, teachers, and Buddhist priests whom they considered potential spies.

In February 1942, President Franklin Roosevelt—in the worst-yet violation of constitutional rights in American history—signed Executive Order 9066, which in the name of "military necessity" forced Seattle's Japanese into a Puyallup "assembly center." From there, most were evacuated to the Minidoka Relocation Center near Hunt, Idaho. As the months passed, the government's extreme policies were relaxed, and in January 1943 the Armed Forces even began admitting Nisei (second-generation Japanese-Americans) into military service. Other concentration camp residents were encouraged to move to the Midwest or East Coast, but by the war's end in 1945, they were allowed to return to the West Coast. Many, though, had little to return to— not long after the relocation began, for instance, Seattle demolished its distinct Japan Town, though an International District housing both Chinese and Filipinos survived.

June 1942—boarded up storefronts on Jackson Street following the Japanese-American expulsion order. *MOHAI PI-28069*

THE INQUISITION

T ENSION AND ANGER filled the hearing chamber as the next defendant, a
University of Washington English professor named Joseph Butterworth,
slowly approached the witness stand. He appeared "nervous and rankled,"
according to one newspaper report—with good reason.

Already on that day, July 23, 1948, half a dozen students, two lawyers, and a university veterans' counselor had been booted from the Seattle proceedings either for cheering on the defense attorneys, objecting
to testimony, or in other ways upsetting the session's progress. State Representative Albert F. Canwell of Spokane, who chaired the hearings, had
grown so irate over the incessant interjections of one defense advocate that
he declared, "If he persists in trying to disrupt these hearings he will be
removed, regardless of…the wish of his clients to represent them… Before this committee he has no standing as an attorney or as a citizen or as
a man." Sure enough, when that jurist next rose with a legal argument,
members of the State Patrol heaved him from the room, together with his
law partner.

This was especially worrisome for Butterworth: One of the ejected
attorneys had been hired to present the professor's case against charges
that he had "engaged in subversive activities." Instead, as Butterworth testified before Canwell and other members of the Washington Legislature's
new Joint Fact-Finding Committee on Un-American Activities (better
remembered as the Canwell Committee), he was left to rely on advice dis-
pensed by a barrister hastily recruited from the hearings audience.

William J. Houston, the committee's chief investigator, got directly to the point. "Mr. Butterworth," he asked, "are you, or have you ever been a member of the Communist Party?"

The professor hesitated. Then, with a slight stutter in his voice, he gave a response soon echoed by numerous other people in many other hearings conducted around the country when faced with the same query. "Because of conscience, and because I—this body has no right to force me to testify against myself," Butterworth stated. "I refuse to answer the question."

Three decades earlier—following World War I—there had been concern that the social and economic theories advanced by Karl Marx and Vladimir Lenin might take root outside of the young Soviet Union. There even were allegations that members of the Industrial Workers of the World or "Wobblies," who'd helped incite Seattle's General Strike of 1919, were closet "Reds." But not until after World War II did worries about Communism's spread seem justified. The fear and frustration that inspired Communist "witch-hunts" like Canwell's can only be fully comprehended by someone who was an adult in the early Cold War years of the late 1940s and 1950s.

That was an era fraught with threats—both actual and potential. Joseph Stalin was expanding Soviet domination in Eastern Europe. Communist uprisings in Turkey and Greece, China's reinvention as a Communist state, and the United States' unexpectedly early loss of its monopoly on nuclear weaponry convinced many Americans that, if they didn't watch out, Russians soon would rule the globe.

Recognizing the power that might accrue to anyone capable of channeling this paranoia for their own purposes, conservative politicians and economists in America—who'd been marginalized during the unprecedented 14 years that Franklin Roosevelt occupied the White House—took up the assault against the so-called Communist menace. They blustered about "creeping socialism" and alleged that America's "intellectual elite" (a favorite target of the far right, even today) was conspiring with the Russians to undermine our free enterprise system. Such notables as Albert Einstein, actor Fredric March, and historian Arthur Schlesinger Jr. were called "fellow travelers," and President Harry Truman and Dwight Eisenhower (then president of Columbia University) were denounced for being soft on Communism.

During the 1946 off-year elections, Republicans campaigned hard and heavy on the "Red scare" issue that they'd helped to create, even going so far as to raise doubts about the patriotism and loyalty of their opponents. When the dust cleared, the GOP had won majority control of Congress for the first time since the Hoover administration. Conservatives also had captured Washington's legislature after being out of power there since 1932.

Public hearings designed ostensibly to expose Reds and their sympathizers could only have been expected after such a rout. And Republicans—supported by some conservative Democrats—didn't disappoint. U.S. Senator Joseph R. McCarthy eventually would become America's best-recognized pursuer of "card-carrying Communists." But two years before his reckless charges made the national headlines, Seattleites got a bitter taste of what was to come.

Not long after taking office in 1947, Washington's new legislative majority approved a loyalty oath for state employees (which continued to be administered until finally struck down by the U.S. Supreme Court in 1963), and then created the Un-American Activities committee. This panel was given wide-ranging authority to investigate organizations and individuals suspected of trying to "undermine the stability of our American institutions." Its full report was expected by the 1949 session.

Leading the committee was freshman lawmaker Albert F. Canwell, a 41-year-old former freelance photographer and reporter, and onetime Spokane County deputy sheriff. Described by the *Seattle Times* as "slender, mild-mannered, [and] deliberate-talking," the 5-foot-7-inch Canwell had been a passionate collector of information on Communist plotters long before he entered the statehouse. Fellow members of the committee shared his views. Like Canwell, another four were conservative Republicans. Of the two Democrats on the committee, one also sat proudly on the state Senate's conservative coalition, and the other—a self-avowed liberal—died before the first hearing could be held.

The panel didn't have to look far to find Communists or other people who had supported Communist causes at one time or another. Washington boasted a long, proud tradition of radicalism, recognized by Postmaster General James A. Farley in his famous mid-1930s toast: "To the 47 states and the soviet of Washington." The Great Depression had convinced many workers here that their only hope for economic survival was to join labor unions, which conservatives presumed to be harbors for anarchists intent on seizing control of the government and economy. Other folks were attracted to such organizations as the United Front, the Technocrats, and, yes, the Communist Party, all of which promised to cure the world's many ills. During these times, ties to "Red" causes were considered downright fashionable, especially as American Communists sided with Democrats and other liberals and progressives to oppose European Fascism.

Investigators working for the Canwell Committee initially scrutinized the Washington Pension Union, a left-wing holdover from the Depression, in preparation for the panel's opening hearings in January 1948. They would later go after directors of the Seattle Repertory Playhouse, the city's first professional theater company (no relation to today's Seattle Repertory Theater), which in the aftermath of the Canwell probe was evicted from its UW-owned performance space and had to disband.

Even before the legislature convened in 1947, however, conservatives talked about pursuing what they believed was a much larger nest of subversives at the University of Washington. "It is common knowledge in many quarters," the *Seattle Post-Intelligencer* opined in December 1946, "that the Communists have infiltrated the University of Washington campus and that their supporters have found important places on the faculty." Addressing a real-estate board in March 1947, Senator Thomas H. Bienz, a Canwell panelist, contended that there were "probably not less than 150 on the University of Washington faculty who are Communists or sympathizers of the Communist Party." Rather than deny or contemptuously rebut these allegations, UW President Raymond Allen tried to explain away the presence of Communists on campus as an almost inevitable consequence of the region's broad-mindedness. In an introduction to a 1949 book accredited to the UW Board of Regents, *Communism and Academic Freedom: The Record of the Tenure Cases at the University of Washington*, Allen stated:

Throughout the history of this area liberal thought and freedom of action have been highly prized. But it is commonly accepted, I believe, except by those devoted to Communism itself, that Communism is parasitic on real liberalism, that Communism thrives best where there is a background of honest liberalism, and that Communism, generally speaking, has taken advantage of tolerance of liberal thought and action to further its ends. It is not strange, then, that problems of Communism and education have been more acute in the Pacific Northwest, perhaps, than in other parts of the United States.

Meanwhile, the UW Board of Regents had promised to recommend the dismissal of anyone "found by the Canwell Committee to be engaged in subversive activities." With the university's approval, the Canwell panel

Campaign poster for Albert W. Canwell's unsuccessful election bid in November 1952. *WSU Libraries 85-050*

served more than 30 subpoenas to members of the UW community in the summer of 1948. The inquiry began in July at Seattle's Field Artillery Armory (now the Seattle Center House). While pickets marched outside with large hand-painted signs, and armed guards kept sharp eyes out for provocateurs, Representative Canwell gaveled each day's proceedings to order from behind a long elevated table. Witnesses had to sit at a smaller table to one side, directly opposite a press box and in full view of a seating area regularly overcrowded with curious spectators. One observer likened the scene to a military court-martial.

But Canwell, insisting that "this is a legislative hearing, not a trial," didn't abide by the conventional rules of cross-examination and admissible evidence. Attorneys hired by faculty members accused of being current or past members of the Communist Party were severely restricted in the hearings. "They may freely advise their clients whether or not to answer; they may not argue before this hearing," the chairman explained. "We are not going to debate any of the issues regarding the constitutionality of this committee, or its method of procedure." The Constitution be damned, Canwell would have his way.

Under such conditions, some faculty members, like Joseph Butterworth, refused to testify altogether. Not a few others contended that Canwell's disregard for due process might do more to destroy democracy than the Communists ever could.

Committee investigators brought forward numerous witnesses—many from out of state—whose hearsay and innuendo were accepted as hard evidence against the educators. In this environment, freedom of thought and association were no longer considered as basic principles of democracy. Affiliation with left-wing organizations became confirmation of crypto-disloyalty to the United States. Gainsaying was dismissed as the inevitable behavior of guilty men.

"Accused persons, denied the means of testing the recollection, veracity, or personal prejudice of witnesses, had to listen in silence to whatever slander might be spoken," wrote UW philosophy professor Melvin

Loathsome Lothario

Roscoe Lee Hayton had nothing against divorce, but he couldn't bear the prospect of property settlements. So, rather than pay, he killed two—and possibly all three—of his wives, women he'd met through matrimonial agencies.

The 62-year-old carpenter first attracted the attention of Seattle police after his third spouse, Ellen, a plumply pretty 46-year-old, vanished in January 1948. Ellen's sister contended that, despite evidence of Mr. and Mrs. Hayton's wishes to separate, there was no reason to believe that Ellen Hayton would've left without notifying her family. Doubts mounted when detectives discovered that Roscoe not only had been withholding most of a $20,000 property settlement he'd promised to his wife, but that he'd lied to them about having that money in the first place. Hayton finally confessed to strangling Ellen after he'd put his arms around her one morning in a conciliatory gesture—and she slapped him. He led detectives to her shallow grave, just outside of Seattle. He also took them to Panther Lake, east of Bremerton, where three years before he had shot wife number two, Sarah Alice Lane Hayton, in the head, rather than endure what he said were her habits of squandering and stealing his hard-earned dollars.

With those confessions on the record and Hayton already eligible for life imprisonment, the police didn't dig too deeply into the fate of Mrs. Hayton number one, a mail-order bride from Kansas, even though there were strong doubts that she had died of natural causes.

Rader in *False Witness*, his memoir of these hearings. "Similarly, the public, which had the right not to be deceived, was denied the benefit of objective fact-finding procedures. The committee appeared less concerned with any legitimate legislative aim than with 'trial' of its victims by screaming headlines in the press."

If Rader sounded disgusted with all of this, it's understandable. He was among the professors under subpoena, incriminated by a former Communist from New York City, George Hewitt. The latter testified that Rader in the summer of 1938 had attended a secret school in upstate New York open only to high-ranking Communist academics—a charge that the professor hotly contested. "I have always been a liberal," Rader confessed. "I have never been a member of the Communist Party."

In the end, six witnesses were tried for contempt because they had refused to cooperate fully with the Canwell Committee, of which five were convicted. In addition, the university administration dismissed three faculty members accused of Communist connections, and placed another three on "probation." Melvin Rader was neither convicted nor cleared during the hearings. More than a year passed before Rader—using evidence collected by *Seattle Times* reporter Ed Guthman—proved to UW President Allen that he actually was at a Cascades mountain resort when Hewitt claimed he was in New York learning "the ethics of Soviet America for the destruction of our great country." Ed Guthman's series of stories exonerating Rader won the *Times* a Pulitzer Prize in 1950.

Anti-Communist passions increased nationally over the next few years, prompted significantly by Wisconsin's obscure Republican junior U.S. senator, Joseph McCarthy, who fueled the flames of demagoguery to increase his personal stature. Called by President Truman, "the greatest asset that the Kremlin has," McCarthy cost many government officials and others their jobs, before his attacks on the Army won rebukes from the Senate, and his "evidence" of widespread Red infiltrations were debunked by famed TV journalist Edward R. Murrow.

Meanwhile, Seattle was treated to two more series of Red interrogations—one in 1953, another a year after. But McCarthy's downfall had made the public and the media somewhat more skeptical of grand conspiracy theories involving Moscow. Even Al Canwell could no longer escape scrutiny.

In 1955, the state legislature determined that the FBI should receive all of the Canwell Committee's files—records that supposedly contained "40,000 subjects dealing with Communists, their front organizations and activities, and related materials." But officials who went looking for the files couldn't find them. Canwell—who'd lost his House seat in 1948 and never again would hold elective office despite five subsequent campaigns—later admitted that he'd destroyed the records. "Much of the reports went through the fireplace of my home," he told state House members. When asked whether he had the right to act as "sole judge of what was to be done with the records," Canwell answered: "Precisely, yes, sir. I was discharging a high responsibility, and there are people in this Legislature who should appreciate that I destroyed these records."

Amazingly, Canwell wasn't prosecuted for this act of extirpation. He returned to Spokane, where he kept chasing after Communists as head of a private "intelligence service" gathering information on prospective subversives and sharing it with government agencies. Reds had become his obsession. "Some people play golf; I do this," he told the *Seattle Times* in 1984. Although plagued during his last years by deafness and physical decline, Canwell kept defending himself until his death in April 2002, at age 95.

The University of Washington almost had as much difficulty shedding its own memories of Redbaiting and witch-hunts. The result of the Canwell hearings, Roger Sale wrote in *Seattle, Past and Present*, "was a bitterness that lasted until the whole generation of faculty involved had retired." Not until 1994—long after Raymond Allen had left the university, and eight years after he died—did another UW president, William Gerberding, finally apologize for the "disgrace" of 1948: "It was, in the dictionary sense, not in the perverted sense, un-American."

Waiting for "The Big One"

The worst earthquake in this city's history—magnitude 7.1—struck on April 13, 1949. The deep-rooted temblor (centered between Olympia and Tacoma) lasted only about 30 seconds, yet it damaged local schools, caused power outages, and killed eight people in western Washington. In Pioneer Square, it toppled decorative towers (including one on the landmark Pioneer Building) and brought ornate cornices crashing down to the sidewalk. In that quake's wake, the Square's aging turrets and other architectural embellishments that might someday pose hazards were removed. (A series of walrus heads decorating the façade of the nearby Arctic Building lost their original tusks, as well, before they could skewer pedestrians below. Plastic tusks were later installed.)

Together with subsequent shakers—especially a 6.5-magnitude one in 1965 (which killed five people and caused millions of dollars in damage)—the 1949 quake convinced the city to beef up its building codes and public safety plans. It also has left many Seattle-ites worried that more disastrous rumblings are on the way.

Fallen brick and crushed cars on 2nd Avenue outside the Busy Bee Cafe, located at the rear of the Seattle Hotel between James Street and Yesler Way. During the April 13, 1949, earth-quake, the cafe owner barred the doors to keep panicking patrons from rushing outside. Seconds later, the building's cornice crashed down on the sidewalk and parked automobiles. *MOHAI PI-22350*

Theodore Roethke, 1955. *Seattle Post-Intelligencer Collection, MOHAI 86.5.41028*

TURNING POINT

THEODORE ROETHKE—a hefty, eccentric, college instructor, and "the greatest American poet of his generation," according to one of his biographers, Jay Parini—took up a pen in earnest to make a reputation for himself in 1942, when he was 34. He wasn't yet famous by the early 1950s, still hadn't received a Pulitzer Prize, and hadn't won a National Book Award or traveled as a Fulbright lecturer in Europe. But all that would come about in the last decade of his life, a manic time of great success and literary exploration that began in the summer of 1953 in a cottage perched on the east bank of Lake Washington.

He was born on May 25, 1908, in Saginaw, Michigan. His mother was a local seamstress, his father a greenhouse-keeper from Germany who died of cancer when his son was only 14. Theodore went on to earn a degree from the University of Michigan and did graduate study at Harvard. He taught English at Pennsylvania's Lafayette College as well as at Pennsylvania State College, before putting in three years at Bennington College in Vermont. He was hired in 1947 by the University of Washington, where he remained until his death in 1963.

Roethke recalled once that he "became a teacher against the wishes of a family who wanted me to enter the law." A career simply writing verse hadn't seemed possible, certainly not when he was an undergraduate. (Roethke's wife, Beatrice, asked him many years afterward, "Did you want to be a great poet then?" He answered: "I wanted to be a great something.")

Even in his final decade, he refused to give up the lectern for a more lucrative living by just reading poems to appreciative audiences. "But I'm a teacher," was his boilerplate response to such offers.

Yet, it was in the province of poetry that Roethke found his greatest satisfaction. "Poetry for Roethke was more than a profession," remarked wordsmith Donald Hall, "it was reason for living and breathing." His earliest published works appeared during the 1930s in *The Harp*, *Commonweal*, and *The New Republic*. His first book of poems, *Open House*, was released in 1941.

By 1953 Roethke was in his sixth year with the UW English Department. He'd already published *The Lost Son* (1948), perhaps his best-known collection, which was full of imagery drawing upon his Saginaw childhood. He also was on the verge of seeing his book of selected poems, *The Waking: Poems, 1933–1953*, released by Doubleday & Company. In January of that year, he married Beatrice Heath O'Connell, a teacher herself and one of Roethke's former Bennington students. Following an extended visit to Europe (Roethke's first), the couple arrived in New York City in August 1953, then drove to Seattle, finishing the journey in early September.

During his bachelor years, Roethke had lived at #802 in the Malloy Apartments, 4337 15th Avenue NE, in the University District. But during the summer of 1953, the newly married couple rented "a house not far from where Beatrice was to teach in the Bellevue district of Seattle, on the east shore of Lake Washington," recalls Allan Seager in his fine book, *The Glass House: The Life of Theodore Roethke*.

Seager described the new abode at 1219 96th Street SE as "a stained shingled cottage, set about two hundred feet above the shore of the lake, the steep slope down to the water covered with wild jungly brush, ferns, and rhododendrons. They paid $75 a month rent for a big living room, kitchen, bath, and one small bedroom with an attic above." But what sounds like a romantic hideaway certainly had its downside. The only readily available water came from the lake, so the Roethkes had to get drinking water from a nearby gas station. They also had to put up with the previous inhabitants of the property—fleas.

In October 1953, Roethke wrote to fellow poet Stanley Kunitz about his new digs:

We're living in a rented cottage-like place on Lake Washington in Bellevue, where Beatrice teaches art & French in the high school. (She's v. good, I'm sure, and works like hell.) But with only one car we're loused up. I get up to take her to school, then come back, sleep a while & go to classes myself.

> Currently, we're plagued by…fleas. They're in the damned grass or wood, outside. The bites make big (1/2 inch) red welts. Sounds comic; but ain't.

Roethke had all too many opportunities to encounter these meddlesome insects. As Seager explains, "he had a kind of bower down the slope, a wooden platform where he worked in fine weather. What did he see in that calm, looking out over the water, scratching and swearing, hearing a wife in the kitchen of the house above?"

Surprisingly, the 800-square-foot summerhouse still stands, although several changes have been made to it since Roethke's era. (When I last visited the place, a former back porch had been enclosed to extend the living room; a large deck had been added off the back; the attic was converted into a master bedroom; and the house was painted salmon pink, rather than some stained color. A shed next to the home, which surely existed when the poet and his wife occupied the property, was listing badly and threatening to collapse. Plumbing had been added during the 1960s, although a pump that might've drawn water from Lake Washington for the Roethkes still sat on a nearby dock until just a decade ago. The steep slope from which Roethke once watched the lake and its seasonal inhabitants was so overgrown that any evidence of the poet's old writing perch might be impossible to locate.)

Bruce Gruber moved into the house after he left the Navy in 1980, and lived there for much of the next two decades. He described the place as "drafty, old, and tired." He confirmed that fleas still infiltrated the surrounding rhododendron and madrona overgrowth, saying, "they drive the dogs *wild* in the summer."

It was more than fleas, though, that distracted Roethke's attention. The Northwest's wet climate also seemed to take its toll on the man. Closing a letter he wrote to a friend in March 1954, the Bellevue bard complained, "such a stupid letter!—even worse than usual. But it's partly the weather, I think—the sun hardly ever gets out in these parts." Roethke later suffered painful arthritis and tried to get a job in California during winter terms, so he could feel some sun on his balding pate.

Also during this time, Beatrice Roethke discovered her husband's recurring, if not debilitating, mental troubles that plagued him periodically for many years, confining him for brief spells in sanatoria. This affliction would be his periodic companion until death. The UW already

The Heist

magine the surprise among proprietors at the Pioneer Safe Deposit Vaults when they opened for business on Tuesday, February 23, 1954—only to discover that thieves had broken into their strongboxes over the long Washington's Birthday weekend and made off with valuables worth between $200,000 and $500,000.

It was an audacious robbery, executed while most of Seattle's finest were being entertained at the 60th annual Policeman's Ball. Entering through a back door of the vault shop at 701 1st Avenue, three burglars expertly sealed the door's cracks so that nobody could hear them or see their lights. They then cut through a steel door from the vault office and set to work with picks and sledgehammers at an eight-inch-thick brick wall. Finally, they applied acetylene torches to open up another steel wall before reaching the 1,640 safe-deposit boxes. An informant later claimed that one of the cracksmen was a dope addict, who kept singing, "Hi ho, hi ho, it's off to work we go!" as his partners filched cash, jewels, gold, and negotiable bonds. The crooks only left behind their tools.

The case was never solved—and the only portion of the treasure ever recovered was a single bond, found in Nevada.

had taken measures to defend the poet's reputation for being temperamental. Midway through Roethke's tenure at the university, a state representative in Olympia asked UW president Frederick Theime: "Say, who's this professor you've got up there that's some kind of nut?"

Parini in *Theodore Roethke, an American Romantic*, notes that the poet, while instructing a class in the techniques of observation, once jumped up on his desk, "whereupon he did an Irish jig for several minutes before leaping to a window, through which he crawled. This particular class was held in a building three stories high, but Roethke seemed unperturbed. He moved giddily from window to window along the narrow exterior ledge, making faces at his students through the windowpanes. While the class sat there aghast, their professor shimmied out onto a flagpole, from which he was, in due course, removed by the fire department."

According to biographer Seager, "Ted had always been secretive" about his personality disorders. "He had not told Beatrice anything about them and she had not heard about them from anyone. Quite possibly, until his marriage, he thought that each episode would be the last, that he would

Experiencing Hendrix

Every year, 50,000 or more people visit Greenwood Memorial Park Cemetery in Renton, just to stand and gaze at rock musician Jimi Hendrix's grave. Some of these pilgrims heard his innovative guitar techniques live. Most realized only after his drug-related death in 1970 how significantly he had shaped the late 1960s musical experience. Even more than Nirvana's Kurt Cobain, Hendrix put the Emerald City on the rock map.

Born in Seattle in 1942, Hendrix worked as a pickup guitarist, playing with such acts as Ike and Tina Turner and Little Richard, until he was "discovered" in the mid 1960s. With his group, The Jimi Hendrix Experience, and the album *Are You Experienced?*, the guitarist electrified audiences, combining blues with acid rock. "He was the most incredible natural musician up to that time," wrote jazz guitarist Larry Coryell in liner notes to *Essential Jimi Hendrix, Volume 2.* Interestingly, it was Hendrix's music that was the original inspiration for ex-Microsoft mogul Paul Allen's $100 million Experience Music Project, which opened at the Seattle Center in 2000.

be able to keep himself under control. When he appeared one day late in the fall of 1953 at her school with a box full of assorted objects he had bought—she remembers glasses and a pair of scales—she thought it strange but the truth did not dawn on her. She did not yet know that a buying spree signaled a manic phase. He started keeping her up all night, talking incessantly, and it was then that her patience and everything she felt for Ted was tried. It was not bad talk; there were only moments of incoherence but in the end she realized that he was ill."

Beatrice persuaded her husband to seek medical assistance, and his doctor confined him to a hospital, giving him a series of barbiturate treatments for two weeks. He recovered by Christmas 1953, but "Beatrice had experienced the samples of what the marriage was going to be."

In spite of his illness, Roethke's Eastside experience was not altogether distasteful. According to Seager: "It was at the Bellevue house that [Roethke and Beatrice] gave their first dinner party. Beatrice had a *Joy of Cooking* and she made a dish of veal and mushrooms with sour cream, some sort of fish mousse, and a green salad… [T]he dinner went off very well."

Roethke and Beatrice enjoyed the opportunity to have people over—to talk to them in their home about literature and social trends and what have you. Yet in 1953, Bellevue was still considered a long way from mainstream Seattle life.

"Ted said they couldn't ask people to come all that way just for cock-tails—they would have to give them dinner as well," Seager noted. "So they started competing against themselves, and every dinner had to be better than the last. She would submit several menus, Ted sometimes saying, 'We can't have that—we had it last time,' until he found one that suited him. But the dinners were successful, partly because Beatrice was a good cook," (although Roethke never graded her meals higher than a B), "partly because she balanced the guests like many a hostess before her."

In early 1954 toward the end of their time in Bellevue, Roethke appeared at school one day to pick up Beatrice. He wore a coyote grin. "I got it, honey," he said. By that, he meant, of course, a Pulitzer prize for *The Waking*.

By 1955 the Roethkes resided at painter Morris Graves' house in Edmonds (once described by the English poet W.H. Auden as, "the most beautiful [home] in America"). The couple's last permanent address, beginning in 1957, was a large, 10-room house at 3802 East John Street in Seattle. They never again lived on the Eastside.

Words for the Wind appeared on American bookracks by 1958, winning Roethke not only the National Book Award and several other prestigious literary honors, but also reviews worthy of a major American poet. "Roethke," wrote *Poetry* magazine, "seems here to have accomplished (or, at the very worst, to be on the verge of) a language which many of the best poets of his age and younger, among them Lowell and Berryman, have been dreaming about and working toward." He'd go on to travel, and again spend time recovering from his mental disorders. Through it all he composed *I Am! Says the Lamb* (1961), *Sequence, Sometimes Metaphysical* (1963), and *Party at the Zoo* (1963).

In August 1963, while pruning and polishing a collection titled *The Far Field*—and while he and Beatrice were summering in a small house on Bainbridge Island, west of Seattle—Theodore Roethke, then 55 years old, took a dive in a private swimming pool. He was found several moments later floating face down in the shallow end. The poet was pronounced dead of coronary occlusion—only weeks after he'd bragged to a friend, "you know how I've stood all I've gone through?" He thumped his chest, "got a strong ticker." Roethke was buried beside his parents in Saginaw's Oakland Cemetery.

Decades later, Theodore Huebner Roethke remains a household name, at least in literary circles. But how many people remember the household he and his wife once kept on the Eastside, at the very beginning of his most productive and prosperous years?

Artist's rendition of the Space Needle. *UW Libraries, UW 10114*

WHY IS THIS MAN SMILING?

AVID STERN WAS LATE—OF COURSE. Who more likely to be late for an appointment than the man who, in the mid 1960s, developed the Happy Face? All those who believe—I say, *believe*—in the cultural and social merit of the Happy Face must lay feet lightly upon the gas pedal of life. They would forgive Stern his tardiness. The Happy Face says take it easy. The Happy Face says be at peace. The Happy Face says: *Yes, there are wars being fought all around us. Yes, there are children starving on our back steps. Yes, there are moral and political dilemmas at every turn. But hey, have a nice day.*

If the Happy Face had a neck, wouldn't you just want to *strangle* the thing?

Strangely, when I interviewed Stern, he neither looked nor sounded like someone who'd foist such a symbol of wanton naïveté upon the world. Soft-spoken, with tousled, graying red hair and an easy smile, David Friedman Stern, born in Seattle in 1937, seemed about as avuncular as a man could be and still get a date for Saturday night. Dropping his six-foot-plus frame into a fat gray chair, he told me about his years in the Seattle advertising business, the way he began his agency in 1963 with only a gaggle of car dealers and restaurants as clients. He recalled his involvement over the decades in local and national politics, how as a teenager he worked on Democrat Adlai Stevenson's failed 1952 presidential campaign and later handled Republican Slade Gorton's 1980 upset victory over powerhouse

U.S. Senator Warren G. Magnuson. (In 1993 Stern decided to employ that experience in a campaign of his own, running for Seattle mayor against Democratic incumbent Norm Rice, but lost by a nearly 2-to-1 margin. It was a memorable bit of irony that voters thought Stern came across as...well, too grumpy.)

And, in fact, there's been disagreement concerning the precise paternity of the Happy Face, a.k.a. the Smiley Face. Like other ubiquitous graffiti, notably Kilroy—the mischievous, bald-noggined visage that decorated bathrooms and barrooms during World War II over the slogan, "Kilroy Was Here"—the Happy Face is often said to have emerged from myriad creative consciences simultaneously. It was a noseless, browless, vapid-smiling wonder that exploded onto the scene out of a communal need for some comic relief to the seemingly endless bad-news cycle of the Vietnam-Nixon era. Yet Stern doesn't shy away from taking credit for the Happy Face's creation. Not for a minute. Which makes him to blame for inspiring the proliferation of Happy Face headlamp covers for trucks, Happy Face sanitation straps for motel toilets, Happy Face masks on Halloween, and a gazillion other products emblazoned with that round yellow mark of mirth—including buttons, glasses, coffee mugs, condoms, boxer shorts, neckties, t-shirts, wristwatches, golf balls, pillows, clocks, license-plate frames, handbags, bed sheets, lamps, night lights, umbrellas, and record albums (*Happy Polkas by Myron Floren*). Even Alfred E. Newman, *Mad* magazine's ever-popular mascot, was remade as the Happy Face on a 1972 cover, and in 1999—long after everyone thought interest in this perennially perky totem had passed—the U.S. Postal Service issued a 33-cent stamp chock-a-block with Happy Faces. All of which must cause Stern's accountant to cringe, as—believe it or not—this adman never made effort one to secure the rights to the symbol with which he'll be forever associated.

"Over the years," Stern has acknowledged, "I have been characterized in publications as 'the guy who was smart enough to invent the Happy Face and stupid enough not to trademark it.'"

The Happy Face was the wedlock-borne result of a union between the theater mask of Comedy and the three-pronged peace sign. It is allegedly the third-most-recognizable symbol in the world. (Sources are unclear about the top two contenders for this title—maybe the red octagonal STOP sign, and the circle with a bar through it that screams silently *don't, don't, don't*). Yet it forms the foot of a broad devolutionary curve that has led inexorably to waitresses named Chloe chirping "Have a happy day" as you pocket the change from your power lunch.

Why, David Stern, did you do this to us?

"I think the first time I found [the Happy Face] embarrassing, was when my doctor gave me a copy of it that appeared on a key-chain advertisement for a laxative."

Stern has slumped way down in his overstuffed chair, his tie now a tight wave riding his belly. He's philosophizing in his lighthearted way, while gazing across his office at a mounted display of press clips having to do with his sickle-grinned creation.

Although insisting that the Happy Face "is just as good now as it used to be," Stern concedes that it has lost general favor. I mean, when was the last time you saw one of those little Day-Glo yellow faces staring at you from a friend's lapel or an office bulletin board? They're most commonly used nowadays (in movies such as *Forrest Gump*) to drum up nostalgia for a moment in history associated with activist involvement, tie-dyed bell bottoms, casual sex, and too many flowers worn in too much hair.

"I think it's a lot harder to wear those buttons nowadays," muses Stern. "People have become less demonstrative about their feelings; you don't even see [political] buttons much nowadays. It used to be different."

"Used to be" can, in this instance, be dated to about 1966, a period of escalating protests against the undeclared war in Vietnam and the marked widening of traditional divisions between a hopeful youth and America's more conservative, more cynical establishment. That was the same year that President Lyndon Johnson abandoned his "peace offensive" and propelled U.S. bombing into the center of Hanoi; by the end of 1966, 385,000 American combatants were in Vietnam, and combat deaths had doubled from the previous year, to more than 5,000. Simultaneously, civil-rights protests were rocking the United States. Forty-three cities were hit with segregation-related riots in 1966, leading to some 3,000 arrests and 11 deaths. Not surprisingly, passions ran as high at the University of Washington as they did at other colleges across the nation.

Stern had a particular interest in the University District. His firm recently had been asked to take on the advertising account for the University Federal Savings and Loan Association, a single-branch institution based in the neighborhood. "We needed a totally new campaign for University

Savings," Stern remembers, "something that would set us apart from the big players." Something, also, that might revitalize business interest in the area and draw back customers who'd been frightened away by the protests and a proliferation of drug-taking "street people."

Looking for inspiration and a broader understanding of the S&L's environs, Stern and a radio newsman friend of his went out one night to roam the thoroughfares, alleys, and youth hangouts of the U District. "I was astounded," Stern says. "I'd read about the trouble, but it was far worse when you actually went out there. There was a pall over the whole area. It wasn't even just an appearance; it was an aroma, like the marijuana smoke in the air." The adman decided that a campaign for University Savings should emphasize the institution's interest in helping to resolve the problems of its surrounding neighborhood.

As coincidences will happen, it was at this same time that Stern and his wife, Margaret, went to see Dick Van Dyke in the Broadway musical *Bye Bye Birdie*. Stern left the performance humming that optimistic song "Put On a Happy Face":

> Gray skies are gonna clear up,
> Put on a happy face;
> Brush off the clouds and cheer up,
> Put on a happy face.

Later that night, Stern—unable to purge those lyrics from his mind—arose from bed to rough out a sketch of the Happy Face. The next morning he handed the drawing to staff artist George Tanagi, "and asked him to give it a little 'facelift' and a bigger grin and put it on a lapel button, black eyes and mouth on a deep yellow background. I pinned the button on my shirt and for the next four or five days, walked the U District," Stern explained in a brief memoir on Seattle's HistoryLink Web site. "My 'market test' went well. Nearly everyone with whom I came in contact asked me where I got the little button."

The first pressing of 10,000 Happy Face buttons quickly disappeared from University Savings counters. "People took handfuls of them," says Stern, "and we didn't stop them." Men and women came into the bank looking for buttons, and often walked out after opening new accounts. Stern tells stories about college reunion organizers asking for hundreds of buttons to pass along during festivities and of hospital patients who were enlivened by the very sight of them. Most Americans never knew of, or don't recall, the print advertisements that were built around those buttons ("Open a Savings Account and Put On a Happy Face") or even the fact that the University Federal Savings and Loan commissioned their development. From a sales viewpoint, they were of only short-term use.

And yet…and yet…David Stern may defend the enduring value of the Happy Face until the day someone pins one to his burial suit. "I think it achieved the goal we had in mind," he observes. "It didn't stop people taking drugs, and it didn't stop people fighting against the war. But it cheered people up, and that was important, too."

What if, as illustrator-cum-social critic David Macauley conjectured in his 1979 book, *Motel of the Mysteries*, the Happy Face should someday be interpreted by archaeologists probing detritus of the late 20th century as an important cynosure for American culture? Chances are that David Stern will be in his grave just putting on a…

Well, you know.

Elvis Sightings

"Back when we were in school, if you wanted attention, you put up your hand. That is what the Space Needle will do for the [1962 World's] Fair and Seattle." The speaker was Joe Gandy, a used-car salesman who, as president of the Century 21 Exposition, not only got this city—and its Space Needle—on the cover of *Life* magazine, but brought Seattle the sort of recognition it hadn't enjoyed since the Klondike gold rush.

Some heavy-duty persuasion was necessary to convince the Bureau of International Expositions (BIE) in Paris to bless then obscure Seattle as a world's fair host. ("Some officials of the BIE," wrote Don Duncan in his excellent fair history, *Meet Me at the Center*, "thought 'See-tul' was on the outskirts of Washington, D.C., and that its bad weather 'obscured the Washington Monument.'") State and federal officials were equally reticent to fund what they saw as a risky endeavor. But by the time President John F. Kennedy signaled the new fair's opening on April 21, 1962—using the same golden telegraph key that his predecessor William Howard Taft had depressed to open the 1909 Alaska-Yukon-Pacific Exposition more than five decades before—it was obvious that Seattle had learned how to throw a planet-wide party. In fact, the Century 21 blowout was one of the last world's fairs to actually turn a profit.

The extravaganza was a late bluster of innocence and optimism in a troubled century, a fantasy of what the future might hold, complete with simulated rides into outer space and houses with disposable everything. U.S. Attorney General Robert Kennedy, actors John Wayne and Danny Kaye, Prince Philip of England, and that photogenic canine Lassie were among the fair's 9.6 million visitors. Teenagers crowded around Elvis Presley as he arrived at the exhibition grounds to shoot a not very memorable film called *It Happened at the World's Fair*, while their fathers might be spotted at Gracie Hansen's phenomenally publicized strip show. Architecturally, the event was like *The Jetsons* come to life, with its sleek monorail link to downtown and, of course, the Space Needle (conceived by fair organizer Eddie Carlson on a napkin and brought to reality by architects Victor Steinbrueck and John Ridley). Culturally, however,

it proved more realistic. The Seattle Repertory Theater and the Seattle Opera Company can both trace their roots back to the fair, and the Seattle Symphony found its first fitting residence (the old Opera House) on its grounds.

The world's fair site is now Seattle Center, north of downtown, and home to Paul Allen's Experience Music Project and a pair of popular annual festivals— Bumbershoot (held every Labor Day weekend) and the Northwest Folklife Festival (every Memorial Day weekend). But what drew the most attention in 1962, and has continued to attract admirers ever since, is the 605-foot Space Needle, Seattle's equivalent to San Francisco's Golden Gate Bridge, St. Louis' Gateway Arch, and Paris' Eiffel Tower (a relic of the 1889 world's fair).

Saving Grace

Even before World War I, Seattle's commercial core began shifting north from Pioneer Square, leaving the original downtown to speakeasies, bawdyhouses, opium dens, and bleary-eyed pensioners. Eighty percent of the commercial rental space went vacant and the entire district was falling into despair, taking on a derogatory cognomen, "Skid Row"—a corruption of the nickname "Skid Road" given to Yesler Way, down which felled timber once was dragged to Henry Yesler's pioneer sawmill. In 1966, Mayor Dorm Braman thought he was doing the city a favor by endorsing plans to replace Seattle's historic quarter with parking lots and office territaries.

Local architects and preservationists were incensed. "I swear, my friends," wrote newspaper columnist Emmett Watson, "progress is going to be the death of this city yet!"

Maybe so, but at the 11th hour, progress found a small corner in its heart for Pioneer Square. Preservation supporters started to buy and refurbish some of the area's exquisite brick-and-stone edifices. Banks arranged low-cost loans for renovators. Federal dollars and tax breaks gave the area a brightness it hadn't known in years, and a generation of more progressive politicians ensured that saving Pioneer Square was a high priority. In 1970, that neighborhood earned designation as the city's first historic district. Ninety-one acres now are under government protection.

No less threatened during America's 20th-century urban renewal era was Pike Place Market.

Schemes for "improving" the more-functional-than-fancy public market had been advanced almost since the day it opened in 1907. Perhaps the first large-scale redevelopment proposal came in 1913, when the New York architectural firm Howells & Stokes offered sketches of a significantly enlarged market, linked to a grand waterfront complex of railways and marine terminals. Instead, the market expanded modestly, adding a four-story building on the hillside between Pike Street and Western Avenue. Still, this didn't silence critics who thought the Pike Place Market was too cramped and unimpressive for an aspiring metropolis.

Consequently, in 1924 Mayor Edwin J. "Doc" Brown proposed

constructing a brand-new market. He trotted out sketches by renowned Seattle architect John Graham Sr. of a gargantuan edifice 10 stories high and three blocks long that extended westward from Pike Place all the way down to the waterfront. In *The Pike Place Market: People, Politics, and Produce*, Alice Shorett and Murray Morgan explained, this "fantasy in concrete was to include a cold storage plant, space for hundreds of farmers, a civic auditorium seating thousands, a floor with space available for 'infant industries,' and facilities for a municipal radio station." Brown said the project would cost only about $800,000, but added: "Why be cheap? Why not spend two million and get a real market, with a roof garden and observatory?" He continued to flog this exotic proposal until he was voted out of office in 1926.

After World War II, Pike Place Market witnessed a serious drop-off in the number of farmer-vendors. The Alaskan Way Viaduct cut the commercial complex off from the waterfront in 1953, and nearby 1st Avenue's transformation into a honky-tonk strip was scaring people away from the neighborhood as a whole. In 1950 the *Seattle Post-Intelligencer* proposed alleviating downtown's worsening parking problems by replacing the market with a seven-story garage. Others wanted the site to bristle with a new hotel and office towers. Quickly, a preservation campaign was mounted, spearheaded in part by famed local painter Mark Tobey (whose heralded 1964 sketchbook, *The World of a Market*, helped draw attention to the complex's enduring value) and Victor Steinbrueck, the University of Washington professor of architecture who helped design the Space Needle. The cards seemed stacked against them. Again proving himself blind to the value of history, Mayor Braman dismissed Seattle's market as "a decadent, somnolent fire-trap." Yet a 1971 ballot initiative won overwhelming voter support, creating a seven-acre historic district that gave preservationists the time they needed to drum up the millions of dollars necessary to restore the public market.

Today, Pioneer Square and Pike Place Market are two of Seattle's liveliest attractions. No one talks anymore about replacing them with parking structures. Thank goodness.

In September 1944, a crowd gathers at Victory Square on University Street between 4th and 5th avenues. This location served as the hub of home-front activities during World War II, including war bond rallies, parades, and other patriotic events. *MOHAI PI-28279*

$\int \epsilon \text{ATTL}\epsilon$ TIMϵLINϵ

Circa 1786. Sealth, future chief of the Suquamish and Duwamish tribal groups, is born on Blake Island in western Puget Sound.

1792. After circumnavigating nearby Vancouver Island, the Royal Navy's Captain George Vancouver launches two separate explorations of the "inland sea" that Vancouver names Puget Sound after second lieutenant Peter Puget.

1803. President Thomas Jefferson sends explorers Meriwether Lewis and William Clark west to the mouth of the Columbia River, which they reach in 1805.

1846. Great Britain cedes lands south of the 49th parallel (including today's Washington state) to the United States.

1851. On November 13, seven months after leaving the Midwest, two dozen pioneers—adults and children—arrive at Alki Point aboard the *Exact*. Within four months, these settlers move east across deep Elliott Bay to the former site of a Duwamish Indian village.

1852. David "Doc" Maynard arrives at Elliott Bay and befriends Chief Sealth, whose name (slightly modified from the Salish original) he adopts for the new white settlement. Later that year, Henry Yesler builds Seattle's first steam-operated sawmill.

1855. Tensions between whites and Native Americans culminate in the "Battle of Seattle."

1860. The town's population stands at 250.

1861. U.S. Civil War begins. Washington's Territorial University (later the University of Washington) is founded.

1863. Seattle's first newspaper, the *Gazette*, rolls off the presses.

1864. Asa Mercer travels to New England, where he convinces 11 young women to return with him to become wives for lonely Seattle men.

1866. Chief Sealth dies at the Port Madison Reservation in Kitsap County.

1867. Samuel Maxwell, a former San Franciscan, founds the *Weekly Intelligencer*, a precursor to today's *Seattle Post-Intelligencer*.

1869. Washington's territorial legislature grants Seattle a city charter. The city council approves its first ordinance—to stop drunkenness and disorderly conduct. A second ordinance prevents hogs from running wild within the city.

1878. German immigrant and brewmeister Andrew Hemrich founds a small brewery in south Seattle, calling his beer "Rainier."

1879. The city's first big fire destroys wooden buildings along the waterfront, including Yesler's sawmill.

1884. Seattle's first horse-drawn streetcar begins service.

1886. Violence erupts when job-hungry Seattleites hold an anti-Chinese congress and demand that local Asians leave western Washington. Martial law is declared by government authorities to restore order.

1888. The town's first scheduled ferry service begins between downtown and West Seattle.

1889. Electric streetcars start operating in March. In early June, Seattle's Great Fire levels 30 city blocks. On November 11, Washington becomes the 42nd state in the Union.

1890. German immigrant Edward Nordhoff and his wife, Josephine, open the first Bon Marché store in Belltown.

1892. Kirkland begins as a steel-mill town (the "Pittsburgh of the West"). Reginald H. Thomson is appointed city engineer and begins a 20-year effort to flatten Seattle.

1893. The second-worst U.S. economic depression in history begins with the Panic of 1893. James J. Hill's Great Northern Railroad finally opens up transcontinental train service to Seattle.

1896. Alden J. Blethen becomes editor-publisher of the *Seattle Times*.

1897. The steamship *Portland* docks at Seattle with almost two tons of gold from Canada's Yukon, kicking off a rush for Klondike riches and prosperity for Seattle.

1898. Thousands of men bound for duty in the Spanish-American War are processed through a new U.S. Army base on Magnolia Bluff (today's Fort Lawton).

1900. Midwest lumberman Frederick Weyerhaeuser and partners acquire 900,000 acres of forestland in Washington and Oregon from railroad magnate James J. Hill. Seattle's population stands at 80,671.

1901. Opening of the Wallin & Nordstrom store, from which grew the present-day Nordstrom clothier chain.

1903. John C. Olmsted of the Massachusetts-based Olmsted Brothers landscaping firm begins developing a comprehensive parks plan.

1904. The 14-story Alaska Building is Seattle's first skyscraper.

1907. Ballard and West Seattle are annexed to Seattle, and the Pike Place Market opens in August.

1909. Seattle's first world's fair, the Alaska-Yukon-Pacific Exposition, begins on June 1 as Seattle's unofficial "coming-out party."

1914. The 42-story Smith Tower is completed—the tallest building in the United States outside of New York City.

1916. William Boeing tests his first airplane from a small hangar on Lake Union. In November, at least seven men die during "The Everett Massacre," a labor confrontation on the Everett docks.

Boeing B-52 Stratofortress over Mount Rainier, circa 1966. *UW Libraries, UW 10702*

1917. The United States enters World War I, and the Lake Washington Ship Canal opens.

1918. An influenza epidemic kills more than 1,300 Seattleites.

1919. Seattle hosts the nation's first general strike, when 60,000 workers walk off the job in protest against the growing power of capitalists.

1924. One of the Pacific Northwest's largest Ku Klux Klan rallies is held at Issaquah on July 26.

1926. Bertha K. Landes is elected mayor of Seattle, the first woman so honored in a major U.S. city.

1930. The last of Denny Hill is dumped into Elliott Bay as the city's regrading project comes to an end. Seattle's population stands at 365,583.

1931. The Great Depression causes unemployed men to build shantytowns, a.k.a., "Hoovervilles."

Hooverville at foot of South Atlantic Street near the Skinner and Eddy Shipyards, June 10, 1937. *UW Libraries, Lee 20102*

1936. Seattle sporting goods retailer Eddie Bauer introduces the first goosedown-insulated jacket, the Skyliner.

1938. Twenty-three mountain climbers stop long enough to open Recreational Equipment Incorporated (REI).

1940. Lacey V. Morrow Floating Bridge connects Seattle with the Eastside.

1941. The United States enters World War II.

1943. An acute labor shortage occurs as men leave to join the military services. Soon, more than half of all Boeing employees are women.

1947. The first recorded sighting of "flying saucers," reported near Mount Rainier by Seattleite Kenneth Arnold.

1949. Seattle's worst-ever recorded earthquake strikes in April, measuring 7.2 on the Richter scale.

1950. The Northgate Mall opening provokes the *Seattle Times* to declare Seattle as America's first "shopping city."

1954. The first Dick's Drive-In opens on Northeast 45th Street in Wallingford, offering a homegrown version of what's becoming the favorite American meal—burger, fries, and milkshake.

1957. In the King County area, nearly half of all workers are employed in aerospace manufacturing related to the Boeing company.

1960. The city's population stands at 557,087.

1962. Seattle's second world's fair, the Century 21 Exposition, opens for six months of successful operation.

1967. Civil-rights and anti-Vietnam War protests spread across the city. The Black Student Union takes control of the University of Washington's administration building.

1968. At age 13, future Microsoft mogul Bill Gates programs his first computer as a student at Lakeside High School. Seattle launches a Forward Thrust Program that includes a new domed sports stadium, street improvements, and new parks. Plans to construct a light-rail system, however, fail at the voting booth.

1970. Pioneer Square designated the city's first historic district.

1971. A ballot initiative calling for the creation of a 7-acre Pike Place Market historic district wins overwhelming voter support. Starbucks opens at its first location in the market, and Boeing lays off 8,000 people in one day after Congress kills plans for a supersonic transport (SST).

1974. Police go on the lookout for Ted Bundy, a handsome former UW psychology student suspected as responsible for the kidnapping, rape, and murder of young women in Washington, Utah, and Colorado.

1975. *Harper's* magazine declares Seattle the nation's most livable city, helping to set off a stampede of newcomers.

1976. The Kingdome—originally called the King County Multipurpose Domed Stadium—begins hosting sporting events beneath its 600-foot concrete dome (the world's largest).

1980. Mount St. Helens, erupting 100 miles away, sprinkles the city with ash.

1982. The body of the Green River Killer's first victim, Wendy Lee Coffield, is found floating in the Green River, south of Seattle.

1983. Thirteen witnesses to a holdup at the Wah Mee Club, an illegal gambling parlor in the International District, are shot to death—the worst robbery-related mass murder in U.S. history. The Washington Public Power Supply System (a.k.a., WPPSS, or "Whoops") defaults on $7 billion debt, ending hopes for cheap nuclear power in the state and causing a ripple effect through Seattle financial circles.

1989. Upset by a plague of huge, new skyscrapers, Seattleites approve a cap on the height and bulk of downtown buildings. Ted Bundy, the former All-American boy who confessed to more than two dozen killings (including 11 in Washington), is electrocuted at the Florida State Penitentiary.

1990. The Lacey V. Morrow Floating Bridge collapses into Lake Washington, but later is rebuilt. Seattle becomes known as the "Grunge Rock" music capital.

1995. *Time* magazine puts Bill Gates on the cover, proclaiming him "the world's richest man." Amazon.com sells its first book, *Fluid Concepts and Creative Analogies: Computer Models of Fundamental Mechanisms of Thought*, over the Web.

1996. More than 30 years after Forward Thrust made plans for light rail a priority, King County voters *finally* approve a plan for rapid rail and bus transit.

1999. November protests against the World Trade Organization (WTO) result in vandalism, arrests, tear gassings, and Mayor Paul Schell's declaration of a state of emergency. Total number of Starbucks outlets in the city: 2,300.

2000. Thousands of spectators on hand to see the Kingdome imploded to make way for constructing a new football stadium are chased away by the resulting dust. Boeing relocates its headquarters to Chicago. Seattle's population stands at 563,374.

FOR FURTHER READING

Adney, Tappan. *The Klondike Stampede*. New York: Harper, 1900.

Armbruster, Kurt E. *Orphan Road: The Railroad Comes to Seattle, 1853–1911*. Pullman: Washington State University Press, 1999.

Backhouse, Frances. *Women of the Klondike*. Vancouver, B.C.: Whitecap, 1995.

Bender, Barbara L. Drake. *Growing Up with Lake Forest Park: The Early Decades in North Seattle*. Seattle: Outdoor Empire, 1983.

Berner, Richard C. *Seattle, 1900–1920: From Boomtown, Urban Turbulence, to Restoration*. Seattle: Charles Press, 1991.

Berton, Pierre. *Klondike: The Last Great Gold Rush, 1896–1899*. Rev. ed. Toronto: McClelland and Stewart, 1972.

_____. *My Country: The Remarkable Past*. Toronto: McClelland and Stewart, 1976.

Binns, Archie. *Northwest Gateway: The Story of the Port of Seattle*. Portland: Binfords and Mort, 1941.

Blair, Karen J., ed. *Women in Pacific Northwest History: An Anthology*. Seattle: University of Washington Press, 1988.

Boller, Paul F., Jr. *Presidential Anecdotes*. New York: Penguin, 1982.

_____. *Presidential Campaigns*. New York: Oxford University Press, 1985.

_____. *Presidential Wives: An Anecdotal History*. New York: Oxford University Press, 1988.

Boswell, Sharon A., and Lorraine McConaghy. *Raise Hell and Sell Newspapers: Alden J. Blethen & The Seattle Times*. Pullman: Washington State University Press, 1996.

Brewster, David, and David M. Buerge, eds. *Washingtonians: A Biographical Portrait of the State*. Seattle: Sasquatch, 1989.

Britton, Nan. *The President's Daughter*. New York: Elizabeth Ann Guild, 1927.

Brodsky, Alyn. *Grover Cleveland: A Study in Character*. New York: Truman Talley/St. Martin's, 2000.

Buerge, David M. *Renton: Where the Water Took Wing*. Woodland Hills, California: Windsor, 1989.

Cameron, Frank B. *Bicycling in Seattle, 1879–1904*. Seattle: F.B. Cameron, 1982.

Clark, Norman H. *The Dry Years: Prohibition and Social Change in Washington*. Rev. ed. Seattle: University of Washington Press, 1988.

_____. *Mill Town: A Social History of Everett, Washington, from Its Earliest Beginnings on the Shores of Puget Sound to the Tragic and Infamous Event Known as the Everett Massacre*. Seattle: University of Washington Press, 1970.

Conant, Roger. *Mercer's Belles: The Journal of a Reporter*. Ed. by Lenna A. Deutsch. New ed. Pullman: Washington State University Press, 1992.

Crowley, Walt. *National Trust Guide: Seattle*. New York: John Wiley, 1998.

Dietz, Arthur Arnold. *Mad Rush for Gold in Frozen North*. Los Angeles: Times-Mirror, 1914.

Dorpat, Paul. *Seattle, Now & Then*. 3 Vols. Seattle: Tartu, 1984, 1988, 1989.

Duncan, Don. *Meet Me at the Center: The Story of Seattle Center from the Beginnings to the 1962 Seattle World's Fair to the 21st Century*. Seattle: Seattle Center Foundation, 1992.

Ferguson, Robert L. *The Pioneers of Lake View*. Bellevue: Thistle Press, 1995.

Frykman, George A. *Seattle's Historian and Promoter: The Life of Edmond Stephen Meany*. Pullman: Washington State University Press, 1998.

Gellatly, Judy. *Mercer Island: The First 100 Years*. Mercer Island: Centennial Committee, 1977.

Haarsager, Sandra. *Bertha Knight Landes of Seattle: Big City Mayor*. Norman: University of Oklahoma Press, 1994.

Hall, Lee. *Olmsted's America: An "Unpractical" Man and His Vision of Civilization*. Boston: Little, Brown, 1995.

Hobbs, Richard S. *The Cayton Legacy: An African American Family*. Pullman: Washington State University Press, 2002.

Holbrook, Stewart. *Far Corner: A Personal View of the Pacific Northwest*. New York: Macmillan, 1952.

Jackson, Kenneth T. *The Ku Klux Klan in the City, 1915–1930*. New York: Oxford University Press, 1967.

Kreisman, Lawrence. *Made to Last: Historic Preservation in Seattle and King County*. Seattle: University of Washington Press/Historic Seattle Preservation Foundation, 1999.

Lucia, Ellis. *Klondike Kate: The Life and Legend of Kitty Rockwell, the Queen of the Yukon*. New York: Ballantine, 1972.

McCormack, Win, and Dick Pintarich, eds. *Great Moments in Oregon History*. Portland: New Oregon, 1987.

McDonald, Lucile. *Bellevue: Its First 100 Years*. Fairfield, Washington: Ye Galleon, 1984.

Medill, Robert. *Klondike Diary: True Account of the Klondike Gold Rush of 1897–1898*. Portland: Beattie, 1949.

Meier, Gary and Gloria. *Those Naughty Ladies of the Old Northwest*. Bend, Oregon: Maverick Publications, 1990.

Morgan, Murray. *The Last Wilderness*. Seattle: University of Washington Press, 1976.

———. *Puget's Sound: A Narrative of Early Tacoma and the Southern Sound*. Seattle: University of Washington Press, 1979.

———. *Skid Road: An Informal Portrait of Seattle*. Rev. ed. New York: Viking, 1971.

Newell, Gordon, and Don Sherwood. *Totem Tales of Old Seattle: Legends and Anecdotes*. New York: Ballantine, 1974.

Ochsner, Jeffrey Karl, ed. *Shaping Seattle Architecture: A Historical Guide to the Architects*. Seattle: University of Washington Press/Seattle AIA, 1994.

Panati, Charles. *Panati's Parade of Fads, Follies, and Manias*. New York: HarperCollins, 1991.

Parini, Jay. *Theodore Roethke, an American Romantic*. Boston: University of Massachusetts Press, 1980.

Parkinson, John. *Incidents by the Way*. Los Angeles: Geo. Rice, 1935.

Petersen, Art, and D. Scott Williams. *Murder, Madness, and Mystery: An Historical Narrative of Mollie Walsh Bartlett, From the Days of the Klondike Gold Rush*. Williams, Oregon: Castle Peak, 1991.

Pierce, J. Kingston. *America's Historic Trails with Tom Bodett*. San Francisco: KQED Books, 1997.

Rader, Melvin. *False Witness.* Seattle: University of Washington Press, 1969.

Rand, Laurance B. *High Stakes: The Life and Times of Leigh S.J. Hunt.* New York: Peter Lang, 1989.

Rupp, James M. *Art in Seattle's Public Places: An Illustrated Guide.* Seattle: University of Washington Press, 1992.

Rybczynski, Witold. *A Clearing in the Distance: Frederick Law Olmsted and America in the Nineteenth Century.* New York: Scribner, 1999.

Sale, Roger. *Seattle, Past and Present.* Rev. ed. Seattle: University of Washington Press, 1978.

Seager, Allan. *The Glass House: The Life of Theodore Roethke.* Ann Arbor: University of Michigan Press, 1991.

Shorett, Alice, and Murray Morgan. *The Pike Place Market: People, Politics, and Produce.* Seattle: Pacific Search, 1982.

Simpson, Peter, ed. *City of Dreams: A Guide to Port Townsend.* Port Townsend: Bay Press, 1986.

Soden, Dale E. *The Reverend Mark Matthews: An Activist in the Progressive Era.* Seattle: University of Washington Press, 2001.

Speidel, Bill [William C.]. *Sons of the Profits; or, There's No Business Like Grow Business: The Seattle Story, 1851–1901.* Seattle: Nettle Creek, 1967.

_____. *The Wet Side of the Mountains.* Seattle: Nettle Creek, 1974

Squires, Connie Jo. *The Bellevue Story.* Bellevue: 1967.

Strong, Anna Louise. *I Change Worlds: The Remaking of an American.* Seattle: Seal Press, 1979.

Strong, Tracy B., and Helene Keyssar. *Right in Her Soul: The Life of Anna Louise Strong.* New York: Random House, 1983.

Taylor, Quintard. *The Forging of a Black Community: Seattle's Central District, from 1870 through the Civil Rights Era.* Seattle: University of Washington Press, 1994.

Thomson, Reginald H. *That Man Thomson.* Ed. by Grant H. Redford. Seattle: University of Washington Press, 1950.

Tobey, Mark. *The World of a Market.* Seattle: University of Washington Press, 1964.

University of Washington. Board of Regents. *Communism and Academic Freedom: The Record of the Tenure Cases at the University of Washington…* Seattle: University of Washington Press, 1949.

Warren, James R. *King County and Its Queen City, Seattle: An Illustrated History.* Woodland Hills, California: Windsor, 1981.

Watson, Emmett. *Once Upon a Time in Seattle.* Seattle: Lesser Seattle, 1992.

Will, Lawrence E. *Okeechobee Hurricane.* Rev. ed. Belle Glade, Florida: Glades Historical Society, 1990.

Williams, Jacqueline B. *The Hill with a Future: Seattle's Capitol Hill, 1900–1946.* Seattle: CPK Ink, 2001.

Woodbridge, Sally B., and Roger Montgomery. *A Guide to Architecture in Washington State: An Environmental Perspective.* Seattle: University of Washington Press, 1980.